89

Wheeler, Margaret

History Was Buried

DATE DUE		
MAR. 0 5 1992		
MAR. 1 9 1992		
MAR. 2 6 1992		

HISTORY
WAS BURIED

A Source Book of Archaeology

MARGARET WHEELER

GALAHAD BOOKS • NEW YORK CITY

© in Great Britain by Lady Wheeler under the titles of "A
Book of Archaeology" and "A Second Book of Archaeology".
Revised American edition © Hart Publishing Company,
Inc., 1967 under the title of "History Was Buried".
Library of Congress Catalog Card Number: 74-25489
ISBN 0-88365-285-4
Manufactured in the United States of America
Published by arrangement with Hart Publishing Company, Inc.

CONTENTS

The chapters in this book are arranged in chronological order, according to the date of the civilization of which they were a part.

LIST OF ILLUSTRATIONS

ACKNOWLEDGMENTS

Grateful acknowledgment is made to the following sources for permission to use pictures as listed below:

AIR FRANCE   Public Relations Department, 683 Fifth Avenue, New York, N.Y.

413

AMERICAN MUSEUM OF NATURAL HISTORY   Central Park West at 79th Street, New York, N.Y.

20 (7), 21 (3), 23, 24 (3), 27 (2), 28, 47, 50, 55, 70-71, 100, 104-105, 113 (top), 176, 181, 184-185, 186, 189. 190, 193, 194, 197, 223, 368-369, 371, 374, 376-377, 392, 396-397, 404-405, 408, 417

ASHMOLEAN MUSEUM   Oxford, England

131, 141

COUNT ALEXIS BOBRINSKOY   71 North End House, Fitz-James Avenue, London W.14, England

206

THE BRITISH MUSEUM   Great Russell Street, London WC1, England

114 (2), 117, 118 (2), 121 (2), 171, 224, 229, 230-231, 251, 333, 336, 342-343, 347, 360.

BRITISH OVERSEAS AIRWAYS CORP.   530 Fifth Avenue, New York, N.Y.

220-221, 391

PROFESSOR GEORGE G. CAMERON   The University of Michigan and The American Schools of Oriental Research, Ann Arbor, Michigan

208 (2), 221, 212

DANISH INFORMATION OFFICE   280 Park Avenue, New York, N.Y.

275, 276

FRENCH CULTURAL SERVICES   972 Fifth Avenue, New York, N.Y.

245 (2)

FRENCH GOVERNMENT TOURIST OFFICE   610 Fifth Avenue, New York, N.Y.

33, 36-37

ISRAEL INFORMATION SERVICES   11 East 70th Street, New York, N.Y.

303, 309

ITALIAN STATE TOURIST OFFICE   Palazzo D'Italia, Rockefeller Center, 626 Fifth Avenue, New York, N.Y.

315, 316-317, 321, 324-325

JERICHO EXCAVATION FUND   British School of Archaeology in Jerusalem, P.O. Box 283, Jerusalem, Jordan

61, 62, 65

METROPOLITAN MUSEUM OF ART   Fifth Avenue at 82nd Street, New York, N.Y.

80-81, 83, 84 (2), 86-87, 88, 89, 91, 92, 126-127, 132, 134, 136, 137, 139, 143, 144, 146, 148-149, 151, 152, 161, 165

MEXICAN NATIONAL TOURIST COUNCIL   2 East 55th Street, New York, N.Y.

179

MUSEO DE HISTORIA NATURAL   Quinta Normal, Santiago, Chile

385

NATIONAL MUSEUM   Le Bardo, Republic of Tunisia

261, 262 (2), 263, 264, 265, 266, 269, 270, 271

THE PALESTINE ARCHAEOLOGICAL MUSEUM   P.O. Box 40, Jerusalem, Via Amman, Hashemite Kingdom of Jordan

288-289, 291, 292, 295, 298-299, 300, 306

RUDER & FINN, INC.,   130 East 59th Street, New York, N.Y.

218-219

SIR JOHN SOANE'S MUSEUM   13 Lincoln's Inn Fields, London WC2, England

113 (bottom)

SOCIETY OF ANTIQUARIES OF LONDON Burlington House, London, England

SOVFOTO 25 West 43rd Street, New York, N.Y.

UNIVERSITY OF PENNSYLVANIA MUSEUM Thirty-third and Spruce Streets, Philadelphia, Pennsylvania

BARBARA WAGSTAFF, A.R.P.S. Heath Mount, Rake, Liss, Hants, England

FOREWORD

Why dig? So often is the question asked, and surely the answer must be that man is born with a curiosity that is insatiable—a curiosity that has led him from one experiment to another until now—300,000 years after primitive man's first question, "Why not chip a flint?"—twentieth-century man is able to ask, "Why not navigate beneath the Arctic ice?" "Why not go to the moon?"

If we pause for a moment we can almost hear our early ancestors discussing among themselves the possibilities of chipping a tool like the stone found that was so good for chopping, or of making a fire like the forest fire and keeping it within safe limits, or of making a wheel. Very slowly the questions have been asked and answered. And now, here we are, with electric fires, space rockets, and pneumatic drills.

But these material things are not the sum of man's curiosity. Soon he was searching for the answer to the tremendous question, "Who and what is God?" and, "Where is mankind going?"

It follows, then, that if a basic curiosity drives forward, the same force demands a backward search. From where have we come? By what paths have we arrived in the mid-twentieth century with all its paraphernalia? Historians and archaeologists have laboriously pieced together so much of the past that gradually the background has been brought into perspective, and the great tapestry of past human achievement unrolled before us.

So much, there is, we shall probably never know. What, for instance, were the great ceremonies performed at Stonehenge? Why was the man at Tollund cast into the bog with a halter round his neck? How was the civic organization of early Jericho controlled? These, and a myriad of other problems, must, most likely, remain a mystery; but what the archaeologists have been able to tell us is of tremendous importance.

They have traced the story of man's endeavor to raise himself from a primitive gatherer of wild foods into the complex town-dweller of today. They tell us that, for half a million years or more, man subsisted solely on the food that nature provided, without in any way adding to it by his own efforts; but that during all this long, dark period he was developing and perfecting his tools; and that, eventually, he was able to express himself through art, as shown by cave paintings like those at Lascaux in central France. Then, at last, he learned to cultivate grain and domesticate animals. He was now able to settle down in one place, and the time came when he built the first town.

What a revolution that was! By having a permanent home he had gained security, and leisure for things higher than the mere struggle for existence. At last, he had time to think between meals, and the mind was free to develop ideas and specialized crafts. This was the beginning of civilization.

Archaeologists have been able to indicate the lines of man's progress. "Here," they say, "is the earliest town as yet known in the world," and they point to Jericho, which can be dated by modern scientific methods to about 7,000 B.C. Elsewhere, again, they say, here man has learnt the art of making pottery", or "Here he has learnt to use metal", and "Here, he has invented writing." The written records of Mesopotamia and Egypt help archaeologists to interpret the story, but the great tomb finds at Ur and Thebes bring us into closer contact with Queen Shub-ad and Tut ankh·Amen than can any sketchy record of those times.

The following extracts are taken from books written by archaeologists who either found the remains of bygone peoples, or who have worked upon and studied those findings. Some of the extracts paint a picture of the men of the Old Stone Age, of men who lived when pottery or metal was first known, of kings and queens, art and writing. Sometimes, the traces are grim and tragic, such as the human remains dredged from the sacrificial well at Chichen Itza; sometimes the evidence points to masterly achievement, as shown by the tunnels and roads of the Incas; and sometimes to exquisite beauty created for the honor of the gods, as at the Parthenon in Athens. But all such traces are fascinating if we can pause for a moment to look backward, because they are the works, the ways, and an intimation of the thoughts and strivings of bygone

15

man. Although we can read the accounts and marvel, we must remember that it is only a shadow of what must have been.

I would like to thank many friends who have been kind enough to help me while I have been compiling these chapters: Dr. O. G. S. Crawford, C.B.E.; Professor M. E. L. Mallowan; Dr. Kathleen Kenyon, C.B.E., with her publisher, Benn Brothers Ltd., who have allowed me to include an extract from her book "Jericho: The Oldest Town In The World"; Dr. G. H. S. Bushnell of Cambridge University; Mr. R. L. S. Bruce-Mitford and Mr. A. Digby of the British Museum; Mr. John Hopkins of the library of the Society of Antiquaries; Mrs. Ann Orbach who made the translation from the Spanish for "The Boy from the Lead Mountain;" Dr. Glyn Daniel; Dr. Storm Rice; Count Bobrinskoy; and Miss G. Talbot of the library of the Institute of Archaeology.

MARGARET WHEELER

HISTORY
WAS BURIED

THE ANTIQUITY OF MAN

The Abbe Breuil, a French archaeologist, won world fame for his studies of Paleolithic man. He was the first person to draw attention to the remarkable cave art found in western Europe; for many years he had to fight the disbelief among scientists that these meticulous and realistic cave paintings are truly works of antiquity. Breuil himself copied thousands of cave paintings and engravings made by Paleolithic men towards the end of the great Ice Age in southern France and northern Spain.

In this extract from his book, "Beyond the Bounds of History," he discusses the development of man from primitive beginnings to the end of the Paleolithic era.

Excerpted from BEYOND THE BOUNDS OF HISTORY,
(P. R. Gaethorn, 1949) written by

THE ABBE HENRI BREUIL

HOWEVER long ago Man appeared on the Earth, he is the latest arrival amongst all the inhabitants; when he first made his presence evident, the oceans had already swarmed with living creatures for more than 500 million years. We find land animals and green plants in soil some ten million years younger. The vertebrates, the first of which were Fish, are about 300 million years old; amphibious Batracians come next at 285 million years; then the Reptiles at 270 million years—though their great development into gigantic creatures only took place later when the oldest known Mammal appeared, a type of little shrew (field mouse) 160 million years ago; and the forerunners of birds which evolved from Reptiles 120 million years ago. It is only about eighty million years ago that Mammals began to multiply and to branch out from the central group into those we know as carnivora, grazing animals, rodents, and tiny little lemurs, the forerunners of Apes: this was thirty million years ago.

As yet there were no Men, only small creatures heralding the Apes which were developing only in the Old World.

Pre-chellean Eolith

Acheulean Point

Harpoon

Aurignacian End Scraper or Plane

Chellean "Coup de Poing" or Hand Ax   **Chellean Side Scraper**   **Solutrean Carving To**

Stone Age Tools   The various phases of the Paleolithic or Old Stone Age in Western Europe are represented by these stone implements.

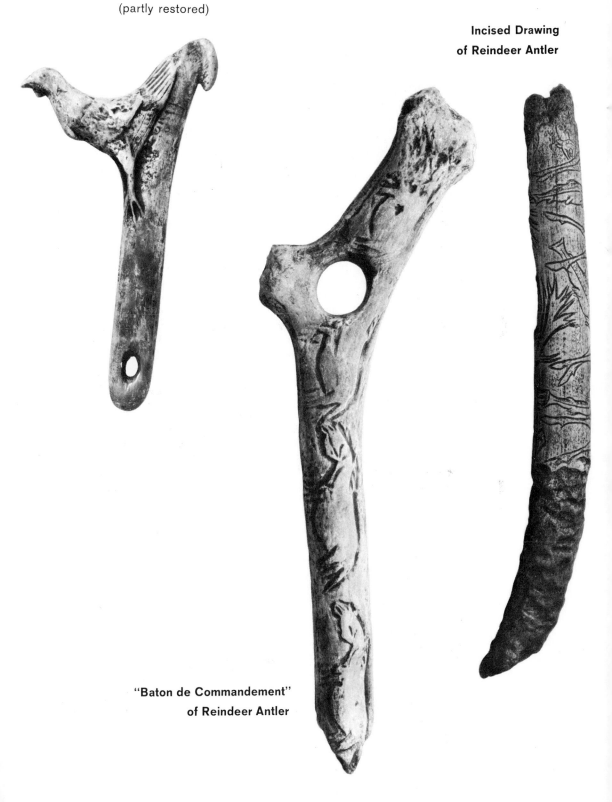

Dart Thrower of Reindeer Antler
(partly restored)

Incised Drawing
of Reindeer Antler

"Baton de Commandement"
of Reindeer Antler

Paleolithic Sculpture and Engraving   These examples of sculpture
and engraving are representative of the culture of the late Paleolithic or Old Stone Age in Europe.

Certain groups of these, 'Dryopithecus', accentuated various characteristics during several tens of million years before there are definite signs of Man, though these characteristics show us that they were the advance guard of Man. Some, chiefly in central and tropical Africa and in the Siwalik Hills of Northern India, developed an almost human set of teeth, a bigger brain and sometimes an upright attitude. These were not Men, however, though they resembled them, but Apes, doubtless not very different in behaviour from the Chimpanzees and Gorillas of to-day. We now begin to perceive the dawn or slow arrival of Man which lasted as far as we can judge for about two or three million years—attempts at a human type, most of which came to nothing and did not survive.

One day people noticed that all over the Old World—in Asia, Europe and Africa, but mostly in warm regions, from Pekin to Java and western Europe—there had been beings who had chipped stone into tools or weapons, using as well bones and deer-horns and perhaps wood (though that has perished), and who had captured Fire and maintained it, without perhaps knowing how to make it. Physically, though they were two-legged, they were not very different from the highest Apes, which I have already mentioned, but their brains were much bigger; they had feet upon which they could walk and human hands which, guided by an ingenious mind, began to make tools. For these reasons, they were Men, or at least, a kind of Man. They must have had some way of talking; they hunted and ate the flesh of their quarry, breaking the bones and skulls of their victims so as to eat the marrow and brains, and seemingly had a sort of worship of the skulls of their dead relatives. What they thought, even supposing that they did think in our own fashion, we do not know.

About this time the climate, for astronomical reasons, changed in regions not far away from the North and South Poles. There were heavy rains in the regions now tropical, and in the temperate zones and farther north, snowfalls led to the development of huge ice-fields. The ocean, deprived by this vast frozen area of much water which the sun had sucked up from it and which had not been returned, sank considerably, leaving uncovered and dry land-bridges which are to-day under the sea.

Tribes of Men, descendants of the preceding ones or of others we do not yet know, lived in the time of these great changes which obliged the animals, who liked a warm climate, to emigrate southwards. But, though life was hard, several tribes remained on the edge of the big ice-fields. In some of these their ancestral brutal appearance was exaggerated, as

The Stag Hunt   A cave painting in the Cueva de los Caballos, Albo-
cacer, Castellon, Spain.

Horse Carved in Mammoth Ivory

Head of Horse in Mammoth Ivory

Cast of Incised Drawing of Deer and Fish on Reindeer Antler

we see by remains found at Mauer (Baden, Germany). This happened during and between the first, second and third extensions of the ice in Northern Europe.

As the fourth Ice Age drew near, those races most brutal in appearance, such as that known as Neanderthal, prevailed in Europe and there they lived during the first half of this period, hunting mammoths, rhinoceros, great cave bear, wild horses, cattle, and reindeer. They took refuge in rock-shelters or caves. These Men lived from 187,000 to 70,000 B.C. Certain ways of burial, as well as the worship of skulls, are the only signs we have that their thought reached beyond the present life; Death, like Life, was therefore a problem to them.

It was only during the second half of the last Ice Age, after 70,000 B.C., that different groups of human beings like present-day Men appeared in Europe. They lived as hunters, like their predecessors, whom they no doubt killed off like animals. But the life of the individual, as the life of the race, grew complicated; there are signs of commerce, of the division of labour, of very advanced specialization in the working of stone, or bone—anything wooden has perished. Thanks to the graves and various somewhat involved rites in which red ochre—symbol of life—played a significant part, we know that they ornamented themselves with shells and pierced teeth made into necklaces or bracelets, or artistically arranged and sewn on to their fur garments and hoods. The cold in winter made this warm apparel absolutely necessary and, from a certain date, bone needles with eyes were made for the purpose of sewing these skin clothes together.

Javelins no doubt replaced primitive spears, and these were soon hurled by a throwing stick. These weapons in turn were later replaced by bows and arrows. Sharp stone points, cleverly made, were given to the arrows, or there were deer-horn, bone or ivory darts, sometimes decorated with figures or ornamental patterns, for these newcomers were also admirable artists. The oldest of their works were small female figures of ivory or stone; subsequently they fashioned animals.

Later still they made, in mass, freehand drawings on small objects, some on small flat stones or bone flakes or hunting amulets. But long before this art of 'miniatures' developed, they had learnt to trace animal silhouettes on the walls of caves—probably places where there were sacred ceremonies. These were mostly of the beasts they hunted, more rarely of imaginary or composite animals—semi-human creatures, their heads usually covered by an animal or grotesque mask. The use of hunting disguises led to the wearing of ceremonial masks which were supposed to have magic power. Thus, if these people wished to represent spiritual beings, or even God, He or even they were disguised as powers controlling the animal world.

We see all this in the engravings, bas-reliefs, and paintings which are sometimes remarkably perfect and of gigantic size; one bull in the cave of Lascaux is about eighteen feet long. The painting technique blossomed out at different stages and in cycles; there were two outstanding periods with intervals of lesser achievement between.

These invaders, therefore, evolved somewhere towards the East or South-East, whilst their predecessors carried on and intensified the physical characteristics and elementary civilization of early times. The newcomers quickly suppressed the degenerate remains of an older humanity, but of the origin of these invaders, who were certainly our direct ancestors, we know nothing. When we meet them in Europe they are already mature and of varied type, with a civilization which has passed its early stages, but which they ceaselessly improved. Waves of them followed each other during the last thirty thousand years before our era, each wave bringing fresh elements which mingled with the first, each sharing in the evolution of this steadily developing civilization.

The reign of these people—brilliant hunters, lovers of art and adventure, nomads and, in their own way, religious and thinkers—lasted as long as the Ice Age fauna remained in our Western world, that is to say until about 10,000 B.C.

But other branches of the same races, deep in what are now the Asiatic steppes and African deserts, having discovered pastoral life, laboriously collected flocks and herds; whilst yet others found out how to cultivate plants yielding food and textiles. These peoples had partially blended before they were driven from their original steppes by drought which brought them daily nearer famine. They started marching westwards towards the lands where forests and meadows had gained on the 'tundras' and 'barren grounds' of the last glacial era.

Pushing before them the weak Mediterranean and Baltic tribes who were better at gathering shell-fish than at hunting, they absorbed the more gifted races devoted to big game hunting. Setting out, perhaps 25,000 years ago from their original birthplace, they reached, step by step, our part of the world and were the first to start Agriculture. They built the first fortified cities and armed themselves to protect their harvests, both of flock and grain. This took place between 10,000 and 5,000 B.C., according to the regions.

Then, in the Near East, the dawn of written history broke, our Europe was established and the peoples whom we know

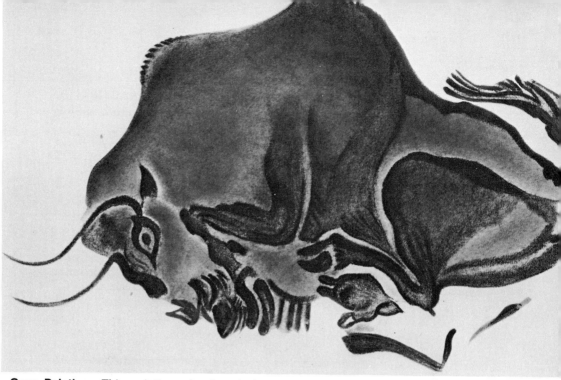

Cave Painting   This painting of a female bison is on a wall in a cave in Altamira, Spain.

Stone Engraving   Bison engraved on a flat stone from the rock shelter of Laugerie-Basse, Dordogne, France.

The Venus of Willendorf

settled there, forming the base of the present nations. Not one of them remembers the very distant past, the alternating advances and retreats of the glaciers during many thousands of years, or the migrations of warm or cold-loving animals, or the tribes which lived upon them.

Some half-symbolical legends, preserved by shepherds, were all that retained a few confused echoes of the most recent of these far-off days in which the first type of Man, armed with flints and surrounded by gigantic monsters, blazed the trail to the Empire of Humanity.

All that—the deserts, first fertile, then sterile; the seas which swelled upward for about three hundred feet and then sank to double that amount, leaving coasts, archipelagos or land-bridges, first high and dry and afterwards submerged—all that, no one remembers exactly, although, until the discovery of Agriculture at least 15,000 years ago in the East, it was the terrifying setting to life for almost a million years.

Less than two centuries ago the big fossil bones of elephants were still thought to be those of the semi-legendary heroes of proto-historic times. At Hoxne in Suffolk, in 1797, John Frere was the first to declare their animal nature and their association with pointed stone axes made by Man—a detail already observed in 1690 by Conyers in London, although he believed that they belonged to the days of Caesar. John Frere never stopped trying to rouse scientific societies from their torpor on the subject. But it was not until 1847 and onwards that the repeated announcements of his discoveries near Abbeville by Boucher de Perthes brought about a change in learned opinions. It was the tenacity of this literary and philosophical genius which, in 1858–9, induced the visit and control by English savants—Falconer, Prestwich and John Evans—who, with the celebrated geologist, Charles Lyell, certified the accuracy of his claims. A few months later scientific opinion altered, and Prehistory was born and developed by giant strides.

Not until less than 100 years ago did Humanity come to possess solid proof of its unbelievable age, of the numberless generations through which its physical and ethical types were established; the silent stages during which Fire was first harnessed; then stone-chipping learnt; and then, much later, the art of sculpture and the engraving and painting of living beings. What a marvellous romance, surpassing in its reality all the imaginative dreams of Jules Verne and H. G. Wells!

Is there any problem, any subject, freer from the gloom of present-day history, on which to exercise our imagination or that of our children? Anything farther removed from our economic and social worries? Anything more encouraging of hope in the distant future, than this History of Man in which the Age of Fire takes the place of our Age of Atomic Force?

In the beginning, when Man used Fire incautiously, he must many times have set his straw hut alight, or the dry grass of the steppes, or the forest, before he learnt to control it and use it judiciously. Paying dearly in this way, he discovered how to use Fire as his chief protection against wild beasts, making it serve kitchen and forge and the family hearth where he warmed his limbs. Is not this very much like what is now happening to us with the terrible atomic power, as yet hardly discovered?

In truth, though almost a million years old, Humanity is still in its infancy; after this short phase of three or four thousand years of written history it has still a long road to travel, doubtless longer than those forgotten childish years, the history of which prehistorians search for in the ancient sea-beaches, river terraces, and dark caves.

May Humanity at last see the victory of Peace, thanks to a parallel development on the spiritual side of Thought and Ethics. May the contemplation of this long, splendid and laborious Past be a comfort and refuge to my young readers, amidst the turmoil of the Present. May it create serenity by showing to each of us how humble is our position and bring the hope of a juster, truer human order, in which the conquests of the Soul and the Ideal will equal those of Physical Force and its application to Industry.

LASCAUX: A PAINTED CAVE

Our Stone Age ancestors eked out a frugal existence in meager rock shelters. Entirely dependent on hunting and food-gathering, they must have suffered severely during the long, cold winters when vegetation was scarce and terrifying wild beasts roamed freely.

To aid them in their struggle with nature, they often turned to magic. In the dark caves formed in the limestone cliffs near their shelters, they held magical ceremonies, and on the walls of these caves they painted pictures of animals, of battles, and of masked medicine men. These pictures, carefully executed, were probably imbued with magical significance that related to the hunt or to fertility rites.

Among the most famous and most striking of these early cave paintings are those at Lascaux in southwest France. The story of their discovery has become a classic in the history of archaeology.

Excerpted from LASCAUX AND CARNAC, *(Lutterworth Press, 1955) written by*

GLYN DANIEL

THE story of the discovery of Lascaux has often been told; indeed, like the *'Toros! Toros!'* story about Altamira, it is now one of the standard anecdotes of prehistory. Nevertheless, because it is true and relevant and exciting, it demands re-telling. On the morning of 12th September, 1940, when the Battle of Britain was being fought out and France itself was divided into an occupied and a so-called unoccupied zone by a line that ran from Bordeaux north-east to Burgundy, five young men from Montignac went out rabbit-shooting. They were Ravidat, Marsal, Queroy, Coencas and Estreguil. Ravidat, Marsal and Queroy were local boys; the other two were refugees from occupied France. Ravidat, aged seventeen at the time, was the oldest of the five and the leader of the party. They had with them two guns and a dog—a famous dog to whom archæologists should erect a statue—the little dog Robot.

The boys climbed about on the ridge of hill called Lascaux, which belonged, and still belongs, to the Comtesse de la Rochefoucauld, and which lies to the south of Montignac. Twenty years before their expedition a storm had blown down a tall fir tree, and the hole revealed by its torn roots did not fill in. A donkey fell in, broke his legs and died. On 12th September, 1940, the dog Robot disappeared down this hole. The young lads had no idea what had happened to him and shouted his name. Muffled barks came from within the hillside, and at last they stood around the tree-root hole where the donkey's bones lay whitening. Ravidat, the dog's owner, decided he would go down the pot-hole and rescue Robot. The five young men widened the hole with sticks and knives until it was large enough for Ravidat to slip through. He slithered down and fell on to the slippery floor of a cave twenty-five feet below the surface of the earth. The other lads followed him. They lit matches. There was Robot, and in the gloom around them on the walls of the cave were the magnificent paintings of the main hall of Lascaux which now make the small town of Montignac a place of world pilgrimage— horses, stags, bulls. Marsal, Ravidat and the others were the first to see this art for fifteen thousand years.

When they got back to Montignac, the five lads did not at first tell anyone else. For five days they kept their amazing discovery to themselves, and while they guarded this secret they explored the cave fully. Then they told their old schoolmaster, Léon Laval, who had taught them about Upper Palæolithic art and taken them to see the famous caves of Font de Gaume and Combarelles. Monsieur Laval thought they were pulling his leg, but changed his mind as soon as he got inside the cave. On 21st September the Abbé Breuil, who was staying at Brive, on the borders of occupied and unoccupied France, twenty miles from Lascaux, came over to see the new discoveries. He studied the paintings and drawings together with other prehistorians. Less than a year later the Abbé Breuil, Monsieur Peyrony and the Comte Begouen held a sort of informal inquest on their discoveries and decided that Lascaux was to be closed to the general public for the time being. In October 1940, a preliminary report by Breuil was presented to the *Académie des Inscriptions et des Belles Lettres* in Paris. In this report Breuil said that if Altamira was to be described as the capital of prehistoric cave art, then Lascaux was the '*Versailles de la Préhistoire*'.

After the war the Historical Monuments Commission of the French Government took charge of Lascaux. The *aménagements* are, as always—or almost always—in French antiquities, very well carried out indeed. Two massive doors protect the cave from the outside, and the cave itself is well and tastefully lit. Lascaux is just over a mile from the centre of Montignac, and is open to the public most of the year from 9.30 a.m. to 12 noon and, after a long midday gap, from 2 p.m. to 7 p.m. Two of the guides and guardians are the original discoverers, Ravidat and Marsal, although, alas! the real original discoverer, the little dog Robot, is no longer.

I first saw Lascaux in the spring of 1948 soon after it had been opened to the public, and have seen it almost every year since then. It is one of the prehistoric sites which never palls and which always, on revisiting, lives up to one's memory. Indeed, it always seems to me that the Lascaux in one's mind's eye is not so brightly coloured and the painting not so vigorous and breath-taking as the reality when one sees it again. A visit

Stone Age Painting   A bull on a wall of the Lascaux Caves.

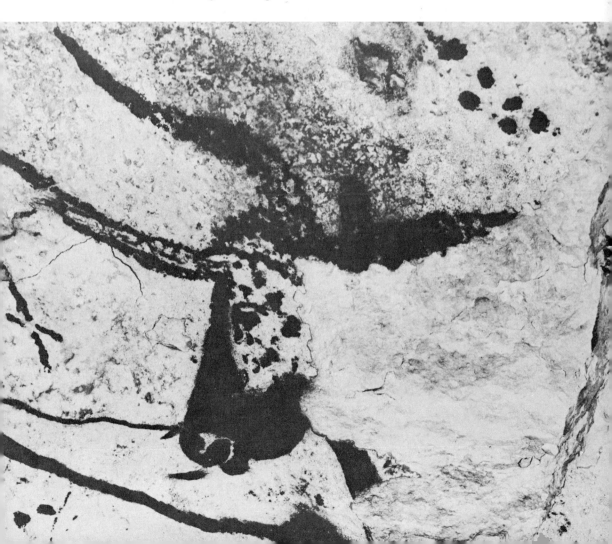

to Lascaux is not long; unlike Font de Gaume and Combarelles, there is no scrabbling through narrow passages and a long walk before the Palæolithic art is found. You pass through the second door, and within a minute from leaving the sunshine of the hillside, and the postcard stalls, you are in the main hall, or, as it is often called, the Hall of Bulls. This is a good name, because one of the main features of this first hall is the fresco of bulls. Four of these bulls are intact, and there are two others not complete—the largest of the bulls is as much as sixteen to seventeen feet long. They are all painted in black outline, probably with manganese, and the surfaces spotted with black. These fine black bulls are painted on top of older paintings in dark red ochre.

The first animal on the left as you enter the hall, and before you see the bulls, has caused a great deal of comment, and has been nicknamed the Unicorn. Its body is that of a rhinoceros, but its head (according to Miss Dorothea Bate) is that of the Pantholops, the Tibetan antelope. From the main Hall of the Bulls a passage leads off to the right, and another goes straight on. For convenience of reference we may call these the right-hand passage, leading to apse and nave, and the left-hand gallery; these are the names by which they are known in the books. The right-hand passage or lateral passage, as it is some-times called, leads into two wider areas of the cave called the apse and the nave; among the astonishing treasures of Palæo-lithic art to be found here are the frieze of stags' heads, and the splendid pair of male bison, tail to tail, painted in dark brown. On the left-hand wall of the nave below the forelegs of a painted cow are curious polychrome, nine-squared, chequered figures. No one has succeeded in explaining the meaning of these figures, unless they be, like one explanation of the 'tectiforms', marks of artists or tribes.

From the end of the apse there opens up a vertical pit or well, which is not open to the general public. At the bottom is painted one of the most remarkable things in the art of Lascaux, or, for that matter, in Upper Palaeolithic art. First of all there is a bison with head down; he has been transfixed with a spear and his innards are tumbling out. In front of the bison is a very oddly drawn man falling backwards. The man has a birdlike head. Near by is a bird on the end of a rod, and in front a spear-thrower, while further to the left is a rhinoceros. What does all this mean? Has the hunter himself been killed in the act of hunting the bison, and is the bird on a stick his totem? It is all a matter of guesswork. We have already commented on the absence of human beings from Palæolithic art, and the absence of scenes. That is what makes the Lascaux painting so unusual and interesting.

The left-hand or axial gallery has many wonderful works of Upper Palaeolithic art; the visitor should note particularly the frieze of little horses over which a cow seems to be jumping, the horse falling upside down at the end of the gallery, and the roof paintings of cattle and horses. You can visit Lascaux many times and still be surprised by the delightful masterpieces you had forgotten about. The best way to get the most out of Lascaux is to visit it in the morning, having driven over from Les Eyzies. Then, with the paintings and engravings fresh in your mind, climb up the hill to the little farmhouse which now advertises itself as the Café-Restaurant Bellevue. Here you can sit on the terrace looking out over the Vézère Valley, or, best of all, eat lunch. You will be given an inexpensive and exciting lunch—*foie gras, confit d'oie, omelette aux truffes, salade*, and then perhaps *beignets*, with white and red wine—everything, including the wine, but with the exception of the salt and sugar, the product of this charming hill farm.

And while you savour your lunch you can think over the problems which crowd into the average traveller's mind as he sees Lascaux. Is it genuine? We have spoken about the controversy relating to the authenticity of Upper Palæolithic art that raged from the discoveries at Altamira to the famous day at La Mouthe. By now most people accept Upper Palæolithic cave art, but when Lascaux was discovered, some said, could it be true? It was and is so much fresher and better than the other sites. That is due to the special circumstances of its position. It is well below the level of the ground and unaffected by frosts and changes of temperature. Many of the paintings, moreover, have been made on a thin calcitic film, which acted as a varnish on the wall and has made the paintings keep their colour more than have those of many other Palæolithic caves. Yes, Lascaux is a genuine example of Upper Palæolithic cave art. What, then, do these painted and engraved caves mean?

The entrance by which you now visit Lascaux is not the original entrance. This has yet to be found, and it may well be that, originally, at Lascaux, as at Font de Gaume and Combarelles and La Mouthe, a long passage led in from the open hillside to the dark, painted chambers within the hill. Why were these caves so painted with animals? Many explanations have been suggested at various times. These are not houses or tombs. They must be special places of assembly, not, surely, art galleries, but of special assembly for magico-religious purposes. Did you notice at Lascaux that some of the animals have arrows and spears drawn across their sides? This is quite a common feature of Upper Palæolithic art, and the most

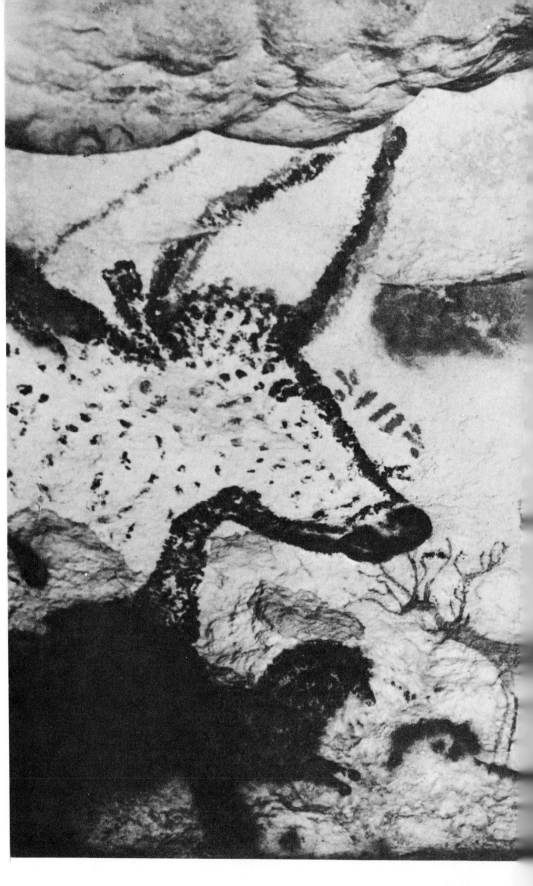

Lascaux Caves A painting of bulls, horses and deer on a wall of the Lascaux Caves.

cogent explanation we can give at present is that perhaps sympathetic magic was practised in these dark caves; that around and on the paintings and drawings rites were enacted that guaranteed or were hoped to guarantee, the success of the hunter. This is, of course, guesswork, as all explanations of prehistoric art and symbolism must be, but it seems to fit all the puzzling features of this art: its remoteness, the fact that paintings and drawings are often put on top of each other, the concentration of animals—and often of pregnant animals— and the arrows and spears drawn in the sides. These were probably fertility and hunting magics, and in other Palæolithic sites, though not in these we have been looking at in the Dordogne, there are clearly shown masked human figures. These masked figures—humans wandering around in animal masks—were the priests or medicine men, or artists as well, who controlled and assisted at whatever rites took place in these ritual caves.

But even if we do not agree with this explanation of the purpose of this art, we can admire its vigour and energy and natural charm. We have to wait a great time in the history of European art before we find again the same naturalistic treatment of animals we have here. Indeed, some would say that there is a Walt Disney feel about some of the animals— like the little horses in the axial gallery. Your lunch finished, go down the hill and see Lascaux again, and pause, taking in these fine bulls and horses. You are seeing these paintings under the best possible circumstances of lighting. We know that prehistoric man, who fifteen to twenty thousand years ago explored these caves and made these paintings, had lamps of limestone in which he burnt vegetable oil, but it would be a very different thing from our present viewing when the great Hall of the Bulls was full of masked figures lit up by these guttering lamps and by torches. It may well be that we in the present century are the first persons to see Upper Palæolithic art well lit as art, and not as magical symbolism.

Two final reflections as you drive down in your car or walk down to Montignac. Are the paintings at Lascaux fading, due to their present exposure to light and their inspection every day by hundreds of visitors? There is a persistent legend that this is so, but I am assured by Monsieur Blanc of Les Eyzies, who is Supervisor of Antiquities in the Dordogne, that it is a legend, and that no change in the appearance and quality of these paintings has taken place since that day in September 1940, when the five boys burst into the hillside and dropped into this prehistoric temple. And, finally, how many more such exciting stories are there to be told in the next fifty to a hundred years? It is only fifteen years since Lascaux was discovered. I cannot believe that the quiet Dordogne hillsides do not contain more prehistoric sanctuaries. But it may well take more than the accident of a dog falling down a hole to find them.

THE FROZEN MAMMOTH

For thousands of years Stone Age man shared the forests and rivers of Northern Europe and Siberia with great beasts that are now extinct: beasts such as the woolly rhinoceros, sabre-toothed tiger, great stag, cave bear, and mammoth. Terrifying as these animals must have appeared to our prehistoric ancestors, man with his wits, flint weapons, and magic was able to conquer them and survive them.

Much of our knowledge of these early mammoths comes from intact specimens that have been preserved in the northern ice of Siberia. From these specimens we learn that the great beasts ate grasses, pine tips, and buttercups; these plants have been collected, frozen, from their stomachs. We know, too, that they stood 12 to 13 feet high at the shoulder, that their tusks could be as much as 9 to 10 feet in length, and that their huge hides were covered with rusty brown hair.

The following extract quotes from the diary of Otto F. Hertz, a Russian zoologist who dug one of these formidable prehistoric animals from the ground.

Excerpted from THE MAMMOTH, *(Witherby, 1926) written by*

BASSETT DIGBY

IN the winter of 1900 a Cossack named Yavlovski, living at Sredne-Kolymsk, a small Arctic settlement of stockaded log cottages in north-east Siberia, obtained by barter a number of mammoth tusks which had been collected, here and there, along the shores of rivers in the wilderness by a Lamut tribesman.

'You see that one,' said the Lamut, pointing to a fine tusk on the heap. 'I chopped that one out of the mouth of one of those great hairy devils, up on the undercliff of the Beresovka.'

'Really?' said Yavlovski, dissimulating his excitement and proceeding to pump the Lamut, whose name was Tarabykin, for further information, then bidding him keep his mouth shut.

'There ought to be money in this,' rightly concluded Yavlovski. Not knowing enough of the world, however, to know how to set about capitalizing his knowledge, he sought the advice of one of the Russian police officials—Sredne-Kolymsk was a place of exile for political exiles—and this man, whose name was Horn, lent his aid in return for a share of the proceeds.

Horn sent a message through to Governor-General Skripitsin at Yakutsk, and he telegraphed to Petrograd. Thus it was that in the middle of April, 1901, the Imperial Academy of Sciences in the capital received tidings of a mammoth, apparently in a satisfactory state of preservation, frozen into the cliff of the River Beresovka, a right tributary of the River Kolyma, 200 miles north-east of Sredne-Kolymsk, and 800 miles west of Behring Strait.

A grant of £1,630 for the recovery of the carcass was promptly made by Count Witte, the Finance Minister. An expedition was fitted out under the leadership of Dr. Otto F. Hertz, a zoologist on the staff of the Academy's museum. He was accompanied by M. E. V. Pfizenmeyer, a zoological preparator of the same institution, and M. D. P. Sevastianov, a geological expert of Yurievsk University.

The expedition left Petrograd on 4th May. The story of how it found and excavated the great prehistoric monster of flesh and blood, which had been lying in cold storage for perhaps half-a-million years, is best told by Dr. Hertz's own diary, jotted down from day to day.

13th September-18th September
Upon reaching Mysova, on the Kolyma river, I was informed that the Cossack, Yavlovski, had gone but a few days previously to the region where the mammoth had been found, about eighty-five miles away, having understood that the Academy expedition would not reach Sredne-Kolymsk before winter. I was told that upon his return, in three or four days, I should be able to continue the journey.

Yavlovski arrived on 16th September, and though the tidings he brought were somewhat discouraging, there was still hope for success. He had intended to visit the mammoth region in the spring, but had been hindered by a serious illness from which he had only recently recovered. Were it not for this mishap he would have covered the find with stones and earth, and thus prevented it from injury by rain and beasts of prey. He tells us that rains during the summer had washed a mass of earth down the slope in which the mammoth lies, so that bones were torn from the hind part of the body, the entire back was exposed, and most of the head skin was devoured by bears and wolves. The trunk had already gone when the carcass was first found. Yavlovski reported that he had collected all the bones lying about, placed them on top of the animal, and covered them with earth and stones, so that no more damage would be likely to result before my arrival. As he saw no hair or wool on the exposed parts, he thought that either there had been none, or else that it had been washed away by the rains.

I am very sorry I could not see the Lamut, S. Tarabykin, who discovered the mammoth, but he was absent at this time. I can, therefore, give the details of the discovery only as related to me, as follows, by Yavlovski:

About the end of August 1900, while the Lamut, Tarabykin, was chasing a deer, he found a mammoth's tusk, weighing about 166 lb., a little above the present find, and, continuing the search, soon discovered the well-preserved head of a mammoth protruding from the ground. On this head, however, there was but one tusk. On account of the superstitious fear that the Lamuts have of whole mammoth bodies, the excava-

Stone Age Man Drawings These sketches of mammoths were found on the walls of a cave at Font de Gaume.

43

tion of which they believe produces sickness, Tarabykin returned to his shelter, about fifteen miles distant, and told of his discovery to the two Lamuts, M. Tapchin and V. Dietkov. These two men visited me twice at the place of discovery and, after close questioning, informed me that at the time of finding the animal the skin upon its head had already partly decayed, and that there was no trunk, or 'nose', as they described it. The Lamuts said that at the part where they chopped off the tusk, on the day following the discovery, there was left only a small piece of decayed skin. They believed that the head had been exposed for about a year before they found it, but insisted that they had never seen it before, as it was the first time they had visited the place, and that they had never previously seen a mammoth. The Lamut, Tapchin, was more than ninety years old.

Toward the middle of September 1900, all three Lamuts went to the Kolyma, where they sold the tusks to Yavlovski, telling him that the smaller tusk, weighing a little over 63 lb., belonged to a mammoth which was probably still in the ground in a good state of preservation, but which they dared not touch. The Cossack, Yavlovski, being more intelligent, understood the importance of this discovery, and agreed to meet them on 14th November and go with them to see the mammoth. He told the Lamuts that if what they related were true he would report to the Tsar, which might result in the fitting out of an expedition to transport the entire animal to St. Petersburg. This satisfied the Lamuts, but it is to be regretted that Yavlovski did not instruct them to cover the mammoth with earth.

Toward the end of October 1900, Yavlovski, accompanied by the Lamuts, visited the mammoth. He cut a piece of skin from the head, a similar piece from the left thigh, and secured a small portion of the stomach, with its contents, and brought these, together with the tusk, to Sredne-Kolymsk as proofs of the discovery. He gave them to the assistant police commissioner, N. L. Horn, who decided to convince himself of the importance of the find, and then to report the matter to the Governor of Yakutsk. The parts mentioned were forwarded to the Imperial Academy of Sciences at St. Petersburg, where they were due after our departure.

At the end of December, Horn and Yavlovski together examined the mammoth and reported the matter to the Governor of Yakutsk, who sent Horn's report to St. Petersburg.

24th September, 1901

It was so warm today that the soil became loose and easily

handled, and I was able to begin the work of excavation.

The mammoth lies a third of a mile from our tents and 115 ft. above the present level of the water, on the left bank of the River Beresovka. The body lies in a cliff that faces east and extends in a semicircle for a mile. . . .

According to the Lamut natives of the region, the head of the mammoth was exposed two years ago by the breaking away of a considerable mass of earth. The rest of the body was exposed only in mid-September 1900. . . .

I began to open up the mammoth mound. The skull was soon exposed. Unfortunately most of the head skin had been devoured by carnivorous animals during the past summer.

To my great surprise I found well-preserved food fragments between the teeth, which proves that our mammoth, after a short death struggle, died in this very position. The fact that what we found was food, and not substance carried into the mouth recently, was later proved by comparing it with the stomach contents.

Upon the left half of the bone between the jaws I could see marks of the axe which the Lamuts used in chopping off the tusk. I could thus determine definitely that the tusk which I had seen in Sredne-Kolymsk was from this particular mammoth, for I had carefully measured and studied the cuts upon it. The right tusk evidently had fallen out long ago, for I could find no traces of its forced severage from the head. The lower jaw, which was fast in the ground, lay upon a large piece of skin which appeared, from subsequent examination, to belong to the upper part of the chest.

I first gave orders carefully to remove the mound of earth about the mammoth, beginning with the soil which had been placed over the head. At a depth of 2 ft. 3 in., we found the left fore-leg, still covered with hair on all sides up to the humerus. The epidermis had apparently completely rotted, but on account of the moist earth the hair still clung to the skin. We may perhaps succeed in getting it, frozen, to St. Petersburg.

So far as a preliminary examination can determine, the hair on the upper part of the fore-leg consists of a yellowish brown matted under-coat, 10-12 in. long, with a thick upper bristle-like coat, the hairs of which have ragged ends, are rust-brown, and from 4-5 in. long. The left fore-leg is bent, so that it is evident that the mammoth tried to crawl out of the pit or crevasse into which probably he fell, but he appears to have been so badly injured by the fall that he could not free himself.

Further excavation exposed the right fore-leg, which had become turned almost horizontally under the abdomen by the beast's fall. Only a very insignificant portion of the upper bristly coat was preserved upon this leg, though the yellowish brown under-coat was preserved in several places. Upon the left hind-leg I also found portions of decayed flesh, in which the muscular bundles were easily discernible. The stench emitted by this extremity was unbearable. We had to stop work every minute or two. A thorough washing failed to remove the horrible smell from our hands, yet we were obliged to perform part of our task with bare hands.

25th September

After we removed the earth from under the left leg, the thick hair on the underside came to view, especially that on the foot joint. Some of the hair fell off with the earth, but the larger part will be saved by bandages. In the midst of the yellowish brown under wool, which resembles in colour the summer coat of a young camel, there are very thickly set hairs of the bristly coat, 4-5 in. long. The colour of this hair on the underside of the leg is roan, while that on the outer and inner side, up to the middle of the fore-leg, is dark brown—somewhat lighter at the ends. Five hoof-shaped blunt nails could also be seen at the end of the digits.

The wool of the left hind-leg, varying in colour from rust-brown to roan, was not so thick as upon the fore-leg, judging by the loosened remains of the hair, and the yellowish brown under-coat was here a little shorter. The length of the ragged end-hairs varies from $1\frac{1}{2}$-5 in. The roots of the hair had rotted away, along with the epidermis.

In the afternoon we dug away the mound of earth to a depth of 8 ft. on the right side of the mammoth. In the mound, lying between the upper layer of earth and the vertical ice-wall, we found roots and other parts of trees and boulders. Beneath this layer of soil, 8 ft. thick, I first struck ice, 7 in. thick; then a thin layer of earth; then another layer of ice, after which the right fore-leg of the mammoth came into view. The wool that had probably covered the upper side of this leg had entirely gone. Most likely it had been torn away by the sliding masses of ice and soil. The same was true of the wool on the other side of the animal.

The right fore-leg was so placed as to indicate that the mammoth, after falling, had supported himself on this leg while trying to step forward with the left one. We concluded that while in this standing position he became exhausted and died on this very spot, and that he had by no means been washed there by the water from elsewhere. The presence of a thick wool shows that the animal was well adapted to endure cold, and it is improbable that he died from hunger, for a large quantity of fragments of food was in his stomach. His head faces south.

26th September

I searched the vicinity for bones of other animals, and found horns of the northern deer lying about everywhere.

27th September

Hoping to find remains of the trunk, I ordered that the mound be opened up further south and south-eastward; but I made no discovery. This part was no doubt exposed before the rest, and had long ago either decayed or been devoured. I examined every shovelful of earth, but I found only indefinite fragments of very brittle hair.

After dinner I began clearing the ice away from the right side. Near the outside of the right fore-leg the ice was brownish, with bubbles. It was 9 in. thick and 10½ in. over the sole of the right fore-foot, which also faced the south, as did the left hind-leg. Beneath both legs there was a layer of ice 1½ in. thick which, after the final loosening of the animal, was found to extend beneath the whole body. From the right leg northward, in the direction of the high land, the ice ran thicker, being at

Woolly Mammoth   This drawing is an artist's reconstruction of the northern mammoth (Elephas primigenius) as he walked the forests of Northern Siberia over 15,000 years ago.

first 21 in.; while 33½ in. from the foot it was 28½ in. thick. Then came the earth layer. The ice layer, 27¾ in. at its thickest part, extended to the middle of the right side of the abdomen, where it became 4 in. thick.

A very interesting discovery was made at a distance of 5 in. from the upper edge of the sole of the right hind-foot—the very hairy end of the tail, which was thawed out and examined.

28th September

The snow has completely melted from the cliff. I have stopped further excavation, however, until my companions, who were left behind, arrive, and M. Sevastianov can make the geological survey. In order to be able to dismember the mammoth after severe cold weather has set in, I am inclined to build over the carcass a shed that can be heated. I must give orders, one day soon, for the timber to be cut and trimmed. Meanwhile, I have covered it with tarpaulin to protect it from being buried by a sudden heavy snowfall.

29th September

In clear weather I climbed to the top of the hill east of here and collected some fine specimens of mountain flora.

30th September

The cliff region extends along the loop made by the Beresovka and along the deep channel of this river half a mile farther south, where it gradually becomes lower. While the flood waters come down in spring, masses of soil are broken away from the cliff.

Further geological research will determine how the region was formed. Yet, though I am not a geologist, I regard it my duty to express my personal views on the matter. In my opinion, the entire cliff region rests upon a glacier, which was disintegrating and in which there were deep crevasses. The whole was later covered with a layer of soil, upon which doubtless there developed a rich flora that served as excellent food for mammoths and other animals. Whether this flora was identical with the present flora can be determined only when the food fragments found in the mouth and stomach of the mammoth have been examined and compared with the plants I collected on the cliff. The upper layer of earth at that time was not yet firm enough everywhere to support the weight of mammoths. Probably our specimen fell through into a crevasse, which would account for his position and for the fracture of such heavy bones as the pelvis and the right fore-leg. After falling, the mammoth no doubt tried to crawl out, the position of both fore-legs being peculiarly like that of an animal making such an effort, but the injuries were so serious that his strength failed, and he soon perished. . . .

1st October

We moved today from the tents into the new winter house that I have had built in the forest, in a spot sheltered from the north wind. By evening we had settled in nicely, and felt it very comfortable to sit down to supper in a well-warmed room.

2nd October

In several pits in the earth I found well-preserved parts of *Betula nana* (birch), which is absent from exposed places, though in sheltered spots one occasionally finds stems about as thick as a man's arm. The timber with which a shed will be put over the mammoth is already cut and trimmed. We can begin to put it up as soon as our fellow-travellers arrive. Although the mammoth is frozen it smells abominably.

3rd October

M. Pfizenmeyer arrived this afternoon with the rest of the transport equipment. To my surprise, M. Sevastianov was not with him, as he returned from Mysova to Sredne-Kolymsk with M. Horn.

4th October

Today, in our winter quarters, we began to thaw out the end of the tail which we found on the 26th. We soon had to stop, as all the hair threatened to fall off. This piece of tail is $8\frac{1}{2}$ in. long, and the hairs at the end, penetrating an icy earth mass, are 4 in. long. The hairs stand in clusters round the tip of the tail. When warmed, however, these separate from the skin, together with the epidermis. Only at the very end part is the hair still fast in the skin. The hairs on the basal end of the tail and a little farther down are dirty yellow-ochre, and those at the distal end are black. The thin ends of the hair are partly broken off. The hairs at the middle of the tail end are a very few centimetres longer than the others, and their colour is ochre at the base; then black; and at the tip whitish.

The shed over the mammoth is nearly finished. As we proposed to build this structure below the upper wall of the skull, we removed the latter. We were then able to take out the remnants of food from between the molars on the left side. These remnants appear masticated and apparently contain not parts of pine or larch needles, but only bits of various grasses. The imprint of the tooth crenations is well preserved upon the half-chewed food. There is also a small quantity of food upon the well-preserved tongue, but I can secure this only

when the lower jaw is removed.

The most devoted mother could not carry her child more carefully than I carried these fragments of antediluvial fauna to our winter hut. When the Lamuts discovered the mammoth they could not see the fragments of food, for the lower jaw was then still in the ground. This was confirmed by Tarabykin's companions, whom I questioned closely on this point.

9th October

Today I took the chief measurements of the mammoth. I also collected the plants which are partly under the snow.

11th October

We have finished the roof over the mammoth.

13th October

We made today the first experiments in heating the shed. The arrangements seem to be excellent. However, we have yet to build a wooden partition, so that the animal may not be exposed directly to the fire, however low it may be. Still it is necessary to keep a steady fire going, day and night, to prevent it freezing again.

14th October

As we found the shed too dark for our work, a second opening has been made, near the door. We have put sheets of ice in both openings as windows, and hung an elk's pelt over the doorway.

15th October

We have begun to clear away the soil from the occiput and back. In doing so we exposed several broken ribs; we dug up, too, some lumbar vertebrae which had been torn out by wild beasts or else forced out by the sliding earth.

Under the right middle part of the abdomen, which was still covered with soil, we found a yellowish brown under wool, $7\frac{4}{5}$-$11\frac{7}{16}$ in. long. It was so mixed up with mud that we saved only a small portion of it.

We also collected and deposited in a bag the under wool and bristles from the right cheek. The latter are $7\frac{4}{5}$ in. long, and broken off at the ends. The colour varies from black to pale blonde. The black hairs predominate and are lighter toward the ends.

Frozen Mammoth   In the winter of 1900, there was discovered the body of an ancient mammoth preserved for over 15,000 years in the snow and ice of Northern Siberia.

16th October

After removing the last layer of earth from the back, some food in the stomach was exposed. It was badly decayed. We could not continue our work on account of the solidly frozen condition of everything. After dinner we removed the right side of the abdomen in order to thaw the interior of the body.

17th October

Before noon we removed the left shoulder-blade and part of the ribs. Then we cleaned part of the stomach, which contained an immense quantity of remnants of food. The walls of the stomach first exposed were dark coffee-brown, almost black, and were badly decayed and torn.

We amputated the left front-leg, between the shoulder and fore-leg, this afternoon, in hopes of saving the wool which still clung to the leg and which might have fallen away during subsequent thawing. The amputation was necessitated also by the left side of the abdomen.

18th October

We skinned the left side and exposed several ribs, which were mostly very well preserved. The stomach with its contents is becoming more and more exposed, while the other organs are destroyed. Then we skinned the head, of which the following parts were preserved: the cheeks, the right eyelid with the deep eyelash-fold, part of the skin from the sinciput, three-quarters of the upper lip, and the very well-preserved underlip. This latter was also beset by scattered spines or bristles, which, however, adhered to the ground and were mixed up with other hair, so that it was impossible to pick them out. The skin from the head, which was already decayed in several places, we immediately treated with alum and salt.

In the afternoon we removed the left shoulder, leaving on it the tendon and muscular fibres.

The flesh from under the shoulder, fibrous and marbled with fat, is dark red and looks as fresh as well-frozen beef or horse-meat. It looked so appetizing that we wondered for some time whether we would not taste it. But no one would venture to take it into his mouth, and horseflesh was given the preference.

The dogs ate whatever mammoth meat we threw them.

The layer of fat beneath the skin is nine centimetres thick. It is white, odourless, spongy, and readily cut. The flesh between the ribs and skin, as well as the membrane under the ribs, could easily be pulled off in separate layers without special effort.

The skin on the left shoulder is $\frac{741}{1000}$ in. thick, and on the right side $\frac{741}{1000}$ in.

The big clusters of hair that lay in the frozen ground near the lower lip, and which belonged to the chin and chest, are 14 in. long, torn as they are. Estimating the broken-off ends to be one-third the entire length—based on the thickness of the hair at the break—it may be assumed that these hairs were about 19½ in. long. The bristly hairs which stuck in the ground immediately behind the lower lip are black; those pointing toward the fore-legs are ash-blonde. As it is impossible to pick out these hairs uninjured, I shall take the entire clod of earth and keep it frozen.

Of length similar to that of the above-mentioned hairs is the hair shed from the outer side of the left shoulder-blade, which I removed. Judging by the remnants of the separate hard bristle-like hairs which I noticed on the skin, they were of the same length, extending perhaps along the back. Beginning with the destroyed epidermis, up to the very ends, these hairs are ashy or pale blonde. The shoulder bore the longest hair found thus far, and is probably what has been erroneously called the mammoth 'mane'. The applicability of this term will be possible only when it is proved that no other parts of the mammoth were covered with such long hair.

The hairs upon the belly are reddish brown at the base, chestnut-blonde in the middle, and yellowish at the ends.

The hairs on the left cheek are 9 in. long, partly chestnut-brown to black, partly blonde. The under wool is not so thick as on the other parts of the skin, the hairs being yellowish, as everywhere else, and 13½ in. long. The bristle-like hairs of the spine retain their elasticity so long as they remain in the cold air, but in the warmer temperature of our house they hardened instantly and became very brittle. I keep everything, accordingly, in the natural outdoor temperature.

19th October

We bandaged the left fore-leg, packed it in hay, then wrapped it in sackcloth, so the wool will probably remain intact. In Sredne-Kolymsk we shall sew all these things up in hides, of which I have not enough here.

We have removed from the stomach about 27 lb. more of the remains of food. We then amputated the right fore-leg above the shoulder-blade, cut it open down to the fore-arm, and removed the shoulder-blade, which was broken in the middle, evidently injured when the mammoth fell. We should have liked to transport the leg intact, but it was too heavy for one dog-sledge. The flesh and fat are well preserved, and will be packed for shipment. No hair was found on the outer and anterior sides of the right fore-leg, and from the underside of this leg I succeeded in saving only what I found in beautiful layers of ice.

I collected bits of frozen blood. They looked like small pieces of potassium permanganate. When melted these bits turn into dirty, dark red spots, which are easily washed off. They feel like coarse dry sand. Similar blood occurs also between the stomach and the sternum, whereas blood that was taken from above the sternum and the shoulder-blades had a bright clay-yellow colour and felt like chalk. I placed these two kinds of blood in a bag, separated by a layer of cotton.

The stench is not nearly so bad as it was, perhaps because we have grown accustomed to it.

20th October

After packing the right leg today, we went on cleaning out the stomach. The parts of the stomach that were exposed to the air for any length of time tear even when most carefully touched, just as the membrane beneath the ribs did.

By afternoon we managed to expose the part of the body which we had not yet been able to reach, and which still lay in the frozen soil. This part was $3\frac{1}{2}$ in. lower than the left fore-leg, and 5 in. lower than the sole of the left foot. It proved to be the protruded male genital, $33\frac{1}{2}$ in. long above, and 41 in. long below, four inches above the urinary meatus. The diameter of the flattened-out penis is $7\frac{2}{5}$ in.

21st October

The more the hind-quarters are freed the more difficult the work grows. The left side of the broken pelvis was removed. The flesh beneath the pelvis is still frozen as hard as stone, like the flesh about the shoulder-blades. Near the stomach there is a lump of ice which we must remove little by little. The cross-bone or sacrum was intact.

22nd October

We cut off the left hind-leg this morning, and the right hind one this afternoon. The thigh bones, which were very troublesome to sever, on account of the frozen meat that surrounds them, were so strongly connected with the tibia that it was necessary to cut all these bones out together, to be dismembered tomorrow.

The colour of the hair of the right hind-femur varies from rust-brown to black. The best preserved of all the hair was that in the fold of the skin between the penis and the left hind-leg. The crumpled hair of the under wool is $11\frac{7}{10}$ to $13\frac{13}{20}$

in. long. The bristly hair is 12½ in. long. I extracted some pathological growths from the right shoulder, and some layers of hair, with careful notes of their position on the body.

23rd October

After removing some 270 lb. of flesh, we started the raising of the abdominal skin, which proved to be still quite bulky. We decided it would have to be cut up. After raising the piece of skin, which weighed about 470 lb., we discovered, to our joy, the entire tail of the mammoth. The joy that possessed

St. Petersburg Mammoth   The reconstructed skeleton of the St. Petersburg Mammoth.

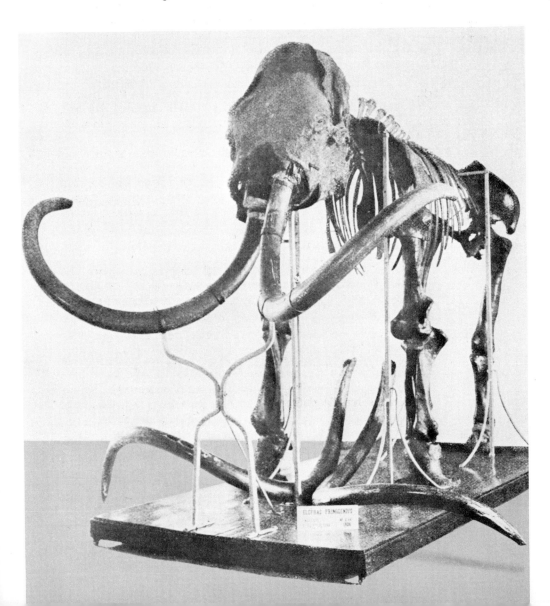

us at this new find was so great that, lowering the skin to the ground again, we gave three loud cheers. We could not decide to cut up the still intact piece of skin, as we wanted to be able to take back this interesting object intact to the Academy.

The tail is short, and appears to consist of from twenty-two to twenty-five caudal vertebrae. It is not as long as the drawing made under von Brandt's supervision, and more nearly resembles the tail drawn by Boltunov, though it is defective in other respects.

The hard, bristly hairs, which are broken off to about one-third their length, indicate that the end of the tail was covered with long hairs that became stuck in the layer of ice underneath the entire body. However, these hairs were pulled out of the ice with great care. They are $7\frac{4}{5}$ to $9\frac{3}{4}$ in. long, and, like the bristly hair on the anterior side of the left fore-leg, rusty brown, their somewhat darker colour being due to deterioration under the influence of damp. Some of the hairs are half a millimetre in diameter at the base of the tail. On the underside of the tail they stood closer at the very end. The length of the tail, measured on the underside, is only 14 in., its circumference at the base being $12\frac{1}{2}$ in.

The width of the anal opening is 11 in., and the length of the somewhat drawn-out skin extending between the base of the points and that of the tail is 4 ft. The base of the tail, together with the anus, were located 4 ft. 4 in. lower than the underside of the left hind-tibia.

The reason that Boltunov in his drawing figured excrescences on the fetlocks, which indicated the presence of rudimentary metacarpal and metatarsal bones, is explained by the fact that the mammoth he saw in all probability had just such a mass of hair at the bend of the leg as this mammoth found on the Beresovka.

24th October

Snow fell today. Very soon we shall have to get away. The problem is: which track is the more convenient—down the Beresovka to the Kolyma, or direct overland through the forest? I sent Yavlovski on ahead to examine the forest track.

25th-27th October

We are working unceasingly to get everything ready for our departure, which has been fixed for the 28th. We have prepared ten sledges, each laden with pieces of mammoth. When Yavlovski returned today (the 27th) with tidings that the track through the forest was feasible we were highly delighted.

28th October

As our horses were not enough to take away the whole expedition at once, I sent Yavlovski ahead with parts of the mammoth and some of the men.

7th November

We all met again at Mysova yesterday. As the transport seems to be going ahead smoothly, we went on in advance to Sredne-Kolymsk, where we arrived today.

The expedition then safely accomplished the long sledge journey overland to Yakutsk, up the frozen River Lena, and again overland to Irkutsk. Here, at last, it reached the Trans-Siberian Railway, by which it covered the last lap of its journey to Petrograd.

De Windt, who, with De Clinchamp and Harding, was travelling north down the Lena, on his plucky trek to the Behring Strait, met the party between Olekminsk and Yakutsk. The mammoth had now made itself more at ease, and was travelling on twenty sledges instead of the ten in which it left the Beresovka, records De Windt, who adds that Dr. Hertz had had a difficult journey, the passes being choked with snowdrifts and deer being scarce.

JERICHO: EARLIEST PORTRAITS

Jericho is the oldest town as yet known in the world.

Today, ancient Jericho is a vast mud mound standing 70 feet high. Dr. Kathleen Kenyon's expedition has excavated through all the varied layers of human occupation to the first town at the very bottom—a town which was built upon the natural rock some 8,000 years ago.

The early town-dwellers did not know how to make pottery and had no knowledge of metal, but they had genius enough to organize themselves into an urban community. The town was protected by a huge wall and by a ditch cut into the rock. We know the types of houses that these people lived in; how they put reed mats upon the burnished floors of their mud-brick homes and what stone tools and implements they used. No doubt they used wooden vessels also and skins for water storage, but all trace of these artifacts has vanished with the years. We knew little of their art until these wonderful discoveries made in 1953.

In the following extract, Dr. Kenyon describes the finding of seven human skulls. Features are modelled upon these skulls with clay. The features are beautifully done. Dr. Kenyon suggests that here are the world's first portrait heads.

Excerpted from an M. S. REPORT *written by*

KATHLEEN M. KENYON

THE next finds were far more exciting. In the area on the west side of the mound, a portion of a human skull had, in late 1953, for some time been visible in the side-wall of the excavation. But I have already explained that it is most important that the sides of cuttings be kept straight, in order that the stratification, the lines of the floors, walls and so on, can be clearly seen. Also, it looks most untidy to have the sides of the excavation pock-marked by bits dug into them. Excavators are therefore trained not to go burrowing into the walls of the trench or square to get out objects, however inviting they look.

So the skull remained where it was until digging had stopped. But the skull of an individual perhaps some seven thousand years old is something of a special case, so one morning, after I had finished my drawing of the side of the trench, I rather unwillingly gave permission for the site supervisor to get it out. I then went off to draw a section in another area. In the course of the day the site supervisor came over with a mysterious report that the skull seemed to be covered with a coating of clay. He was told to proceed as carefully as possible, but we were none of us prepared for the object he produced in the evening. Only the photograph of it can convey any comprehension of our astonishment. What we had seen in the side of the trench had been the top of a human skull. But the whole of the rest of the skull had a covering of plaster, moulded in the form of features, with eyes inset with shells.

What was more, two further similar plastered skulls were visible at the back of the hole from which the first had come. When these were removed, three more could be seen behind them, and eventually a seventh beyond. The whole time-table of the end of the dig was disrupted. The furniture had all been packed up, the kitchen cleared and the servants dismissed, the dark-room and repair room dismantled, and most of the material packed up. For nearly a week we lived in considerable discomfort, sitting on the floor and eating picnic meals while the photographer and repair assistant did wonders of improvisation. The excavation of the heads was a very difficult and tricky business. They lay in a tumbled heap, one skull crushed firmly on top of another, with stones and very hard earth all round. Each successive group was farther back from the face of the section and increasingly difficult to get at; the bone surfaces were exceedingly fragile, and the greatest gentleness had to be used.

It took five days to extract them all, and it was a triumph of patient work to do so. We heaved a sigh of relief when no more were visible behind. But the family group of seven heads was well worth our trouble. They were all most remarkable as realistic human portraits. One was very much more beautiful than the rest. The photograph of it, still in position in the ground, never fails to produce a gasp of astonishment when I show it on the screen at a lecture. The reason why it stands out from the rest is that it alone has the lower jaw in position. In the others, the plaster representing the lower jaw is actually modelled over the upper teeth, and the heads therefore have a somewhat squat, chubby appearance. Six of the seven have eyes composed of two segments of shell, with a vertical slit between, which simulates the pupil. The seventh has eyes of cowrie shell, and the horizontal opening of the shells gives him a somewhat sleepy appearance. The state of preservation of five was excellent, but the other two were less good, one having little more than the eyes surviving intact.

Each head has a strongly marked individual character, though the technique and method of manufacture were similar. The interior of the head was packed solidly with clay, and a clay filling put into the eye-sockets as setting for the shell eyes. The lower part of the skull was then enveloped in plaster from the level of the temples, the crown of the skull being left bare. In all the intact specimens, the base of the skull was completely covered, with a flat finish to the plaster, so there is no question that they could ever have formed part of complete figures. The features, nose, mouth, eyes and eyebrows, are modelled with extraordinary delicacy. The plaster

Jericho Portrait This is a picture of one of the Jericho skulls as it appeared when it was first discovered.

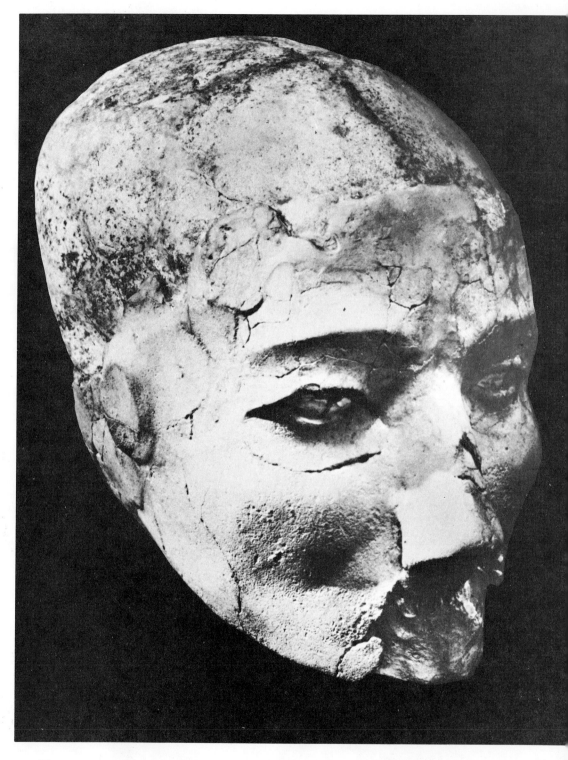

62   **Sculptured Portrait**   This remarkable skull with plaster-molded features is dated around 5,000 B.C.

of one head is coloured to represent a fine ruddy flesh-colour; others show some colouring, but not so pronounced.

Modern anthropology provides the only close parallel for such a use of human skulls. In New Guinea, and especially in the Sipek River Valley, skulls were similarly given features up to comparatively modern times, though the features take the form of masks rather than the complete encasing of the skull. In some cases these heads seem to be those of venerated ancestors, in others those of enemies, preserved as trophies. It would be possible to interpret the Jericho skulls in either sense. I have personally always been convinced that they are the heads of venerated ancestors, largely owing to the impression they give of being portraits, and to the loving care which the skilful modelling of the features suggests. There is now some archæological evidence to support this view.

The source from which the skulls were derived would allow of their interpretation either as those of venerated ancestors or of enemies. They were found in a discarded heap beneath the plastered floor of a house. That they were typical of this phase is proved by the discovery in 1956 of two more, some ten feet away from the others, but beneath the floor of the same house. They lay in the debris of an earlier house, presumably the one in which they had been treasured. Beneath the floor of the lower house, we came upon an extraordinary number of skeletons, about thirty in a comparatively small area. From many of these bodies the skull had been removed, often leaving a displaced lower jaw. In some cases, where the bodies were very tightly packed, the bones seem literally to have been ransacked to remove the skulls, at a stage when the bodies were sufficiently decayed to allow of the separation of the limbs from the trunk, but the ligaments were still sufficiently intact for the bones of the limbs to remain in articulation. Burial beneath the floors of the houses was certainly the normal custom, but this number of burials was quite exceptional. It suggests a disaster, a plague, or a massacre, and other circumstances to which I refer below to make a massacre a possibility, though the actual skeletons show no evidence of violent death. If this were the case, it would still leave the two possibilities. If the attackers were the victors, the heads might be trophies taken from the bodies of massacred defenders, while if the defenders drove off the attackers, though with casualties to themselves, the heads might be those of important individuals, whose memory was preserved in this manner.

But though, in this instance, the evidence is ambiguous as to the interpretation to be put upon the custom, further excavation has shown that the custom was not confined to this single

63

stage. As we have cleared layer after layer of superimposed houses in the various areas excavated, beneath almost every single floor we have found burials. In a large number of instances, the skull has been removed. The action of enemies can obviously not be invoked in all these cases. It does therefore seem probable that the removal of the skull was a general practice, and that they were kept as mementoes of dead members of the family. It is true that the instances I have described are the only ones of this phase in the history of Jericho in which we have found the detached skulls. They may have been removed to some central sanctuary lying outside the excavated area, or they might be in parts of the houses not excavated, for in no case does the complete plan of a house lie within any of our areas.

From this treatment of skulls, it may be deduced that the early inhabitants of Jericho had already developed a conception of a spiritual life as distinct from the bodily one. They must have felt that some power, perhaps protective, perhaps of wisdom, could survive death, and somehow they must have realized that the seat of these extra-corporeal powers was the head. They perhaps believed that the preservation of the skull secured the use of the powers to succeeding generations, perhaps that it placated the spirit, perhaps controlled it.

A further fascinating aspect of this find is the artistic and technical skill shown in the modelling of the plaster features. People who could do this modelling certainly did not lack the technical skill to make pottery; it can only be that they did not feel the need for it.

Head Dug Up at Jericho   The shells in the eyes are cowries, probably coming from the Red Sea.

A ROYAL TOMB AT UR

The city of Ur, the Biblical city of Abraham, is today a tumbled patch of desert near the Euphrates River in southern Iraq. At one time, 5,000 years ago and more, it was populous and wealthy. In its midst rose a high terraced platform known as a ziggurat whose topmost platform bore the city's principal temple. Farmers, traders, and craftsmen, all contributed to the busy and picturesque life of the city which was dominated by priestly rulers.

During the 1920's and 1930's, Sir Leonard Woolley, a British archaeologist, headed archaeological excavations in Ur. Digging deep below the present surface, in 1927 Woolley came upon tombs so dramatically rich that they must have contained either members of the royal family or ritual burials of similarly exalted persons. In the following extract Sir Leonard Woolley describes his macabre discoveries in one of these tombs dating from about 2600 B.C.

Excerpted from EXCAVATIONS AT UR, *(Ernest Benn, 1954) written by*

SIR LEONARD WOOLLEY

IN that season, 1927-8, digging in another part of the cemetery area, we came upon five bodies lying side by side in a sloping trench; except for the copper daggers at their waists and one or two small clay cups they had none of the normal furniture of a grave, and the mere fact of there being a number thus together was unusual. Then, below them, a layer of matting was found, and tracing this along we came to another group of bodies, those of ten women carefully arranged in two rows; they wore head-dresses of gold, lapis lazuli, and carnelian, and elaborate bead necklaces, but they too possessed no regular tomb furnishings. At the end of the row lay the remains of a wonderful harp, the wood of it decayed but its decoration intact, making its reconstruction only a matter of care; the upright wooden beam was capped with gold, and in it were fastened the gold-headed nails which secured the strings; the sounding-box was edged with a mosaic in red stone, lapis lazuli and white shell, and from the front of it projected the splendid head of a bull wrought in gold with eyes and beard of lapis lazuli; across the ruins of the harp lay the bones of the gold-crowned harpist.

By this time we had found the earth sides of the pit in which the women's bodies lay and could see that the bodies of the five men were on the ramp which led down to it. Following the pit along, we came upon more bones which at first puzzled us by being other than human, but the meaning of them soon became clear. A little way inside the entrance to the pit stood a wooden sledge chariot decorated with red, white, and blue mosaic along the edges of the framework and with golden heads of lions and bulls, silver lionesses' heads adorned the front, and the position of the vanished swingletree was shown by a band of blue and white inlay and two smaller heads of lionesses in silver. In front of the chariot lay the crushed skeletons of two asses with the bodies of the grooms by their heads, and on the top of the bones was the double ring once attached to the pole, through which the reins had passed; it was of silver, and standing on it was a gold 'mascot' in the form of a donkey, most beautifully and realistically modelled.

Close to the chariot were an inlaid gaming-board and a collection of tools and weapons, including a set of chisels and a saw made of gold, big bowls of grey soap-stone, copper vessels, a long tube of gold and lapis which was a drinking-tube for sucking up liquor from the bowls, more human bodies, and then the wreckage of a large wooden chest adorned with figured mosaic in lapis lazuli and shell which was found empty but had perhaps contained such perishable things as clothes. Behind this box were more offerings, masses of vessels in copper, silver, stone (including exquisite examples in volcanic glass, lapis lazuli, alabaster, and marble), and gold; one set of silver vessels seemed to be in the nature of a communion-service, for there was a shallow tray or platter, a jug with tall neck and long spout such as we know from carved stone reliefs to have been used in religious rites, and tall slender silver tumblers nested one inside another; a similar tumbler in gold, fluted and chased, with a fluted feeding-bowl, a chalice, and a plain oval bowl of gold lay piled together, and two magnificent lions' heads in silver, perhaps the ornaments of a throne, were amongst the treasures in the crowded pit. The perplexing thing was that with all this wealth of objects we had found no body so far distinguished from the rest as to be that of the person to whom all were dedicated; logically, our discovery, however great, was incomplete.

The objects were removed and we started to clear away the remains of the wooden box, a chest some six feet long and three feet across, when under it we found burnt bricks. They had fallen, but at one end some were still in place and formed the ring-vault of a stone chamber. The first and natural supposition was that here we had the tomb to which all the offerings belonged, but further search proved that the chamber was plundered, the roof had not fallen from decay but had been broken through and the wooden box had been placed over the hole as if deliberately to hide it. Then, digging round the outside of the chamber, we found just such another pit as that six feet above. At the foot of the ramp lay six soldiers, orderly in two ranks, with copper spears by their sides and copper helmets crushed flat on the broken skulls; just inside, having evidently been backed down the slope, were two wooden four-wheeled wagons each drawn by three oxen—one of the latter so well preserved that we were able to lift the skeleton

Hall of Justice   A wing of a prominent building in Ur, dated around 3,000 B. C. E.

entire; the wagons were plain, but the reins were decorated
with long beads of lapis and silver and passed through silver
rings surmounted with mascots in the form of bulls; the grooms
lay at the oxen's heads and the drivers in the bodies of the
cars; of the cars themselves only the impression of the decayed
wood remained in the soil, but so clear was this that a photograph showed the grain of the solid wooden wheel and the
grey-white circle which had been the leather tyre.

Against the end wall of the stone chamber lay the bodies
of nine women wearing the gala head-dress of lapis and
carnelian beads from which hung golden pendants in the form
of beech leaves, great lunate ear-rings of gold, silver 'combs'
like the palm of a hand with three fingers tipped with flowers
whose petals are inlaid with lapis, gold, and shell, and necklaces of lapis and gold; their heads were leaned against the

Ur. A diorama showing the city as it was around 2,000 B.C.

masonry, their bodies extended on to the floor of the pit, and the whole space between them and the wagons was crowded with other dead, women and men, while the passage which led along the side of the chamber to its arched door was lined with soldiers carrying daggers, and with women. Of the soldiers in the central space, one had a bundle of four spears with heads of gold, two had sets of four silver spears, and by another there was a remarkable relief in copper with a design of two lions trampling on the bodies of two fallen men which may have been the decoration of a shield.

On top of the bodies of the 'court ladies' against the chamber wall had been placed a wooden harp, of which there survived only the copper head of a bull and the shell plaques which had adorned the sounding-box; by the side wall of the pit, also set on the top of the bodies, was a second harp with a

71

wonderful bull's head in gold, its eyes, beard, and horn-tips of lapis, and a set of engraved shell plaques not less wonderful; there are four of them with grotesque scenes of animals playing the parts of men, and while the most striking feature about them is that sense of humour which is so rare in ancient art, the grace and balance of the design and the fineness of the drawing make of these plaques one of the most instructive documents that we possess for the appreciation of the art of early Sumer.

Inside the tomb the robbers had left enough to show that it had contained the bodies of several minor people as well as that of the chief person, whose name, if we can trust the inscription on a cylinder seal, was A-bar-gi; overlooked against the wall we found two model boats, one of copper now hopelessly decayed, the other of silver wonderfully well preserved; some two feet long, it has a high stern and prow, five seats, and amidships an arched support for the awning which would protect the passenger, and the leaf-bladed oars are still set in the thwarts; it is a testimony to the conservatism of the East that a boat of identical type is in use today on the marshes of the Lower Euphrates, some fifty miles from Ur.

The king's tomb-chamber lay at the far end of this open pit; continuing our search behind it we found a second stone chamber built up against it, either at the same time or, more probably, at a later period. This chamber, roofed like the king's with a vault of ring arches in burnt brick, was the tomb of the queen to whom belonged the upper pit with its chariot and other offerings: her name, Shub-ad, was given us by a fine cylinder seal of lapis lazuli which was found in the filling of the shaft a little above the roof of the chamber and had probably been thrown into the pit at the moment when the earth was being put back into it. The vault of the chamber had fallen in, but luckily this was due to the weight of earth above, not to the violence of tomb-robbers; the tomb itself was intact.

At one end, on the remains of a wooden bier, lay the body of the queen, a gold cup near her hand; the upper part of the body was entirely hidden by a mass of beads of gold, silver, lapis lazuli, carnelian, agate, and chalcedony, long strings of which, hanging from a collar, had formed a cloak reaching to the waist and bordered below with a broad band of tubular beads of lapis, carnelian, and gold; against the right arm were three long gold pins with lapis heads and three amulets in the form of fish, two of gold and one of lapis, and a fourth in the form of two seated gazelles, also of gold.

The head-dress, whose remains covered the crushed skull, was a more elaborate edition of that worn by the court ladies;

its basis was a broad gold ribbon festooned in loops round the hair—and the measurement of the curves showed that this was not the natural hair but a wig padded out to an almost grotesque size; over this came three wreaths, the lowest hanging down over the forehead, of plain gold ring pendants, the second of beech leaves, the third of long willow leaves in sets of three with gold flowers whose petals were of blue and white inlay; all these were strung on triple chains of lapis and carnelian beads. Fixed into the back of the hair was a golden 'Spanish comb' with five points ending in lapis-centred gold flowers. Heavy spiral rings of gold wire were twisted into the side curls of the wig, huge lunate ear-rings of gold hung down to the shoulders, and apparently from the hair also hung on each side a string of large square stone beads with, at the end of each, a lapis amulet, one shaped as a seated bull and the other as a calf. Complicated as the head-dress was, its different parts lay in such good order that it was possible to reconstruct the whole and exhibit the likeness of the queen with all her original finery in place.

For the purposes of exhibition a plaster cast was made from a well-preserved female skull of the period (the queen's own skull was too fragmentary to be used), and over this my wife modelled the features in wax, making this as thin as possible so as not to obliterate the bone structure; the face was passed by Sir Arthur Keith, who has made a special study of the Ur and all 'Ubaíd' skulls, as reproducing faithfully the character of the early Sumerians. On this head was put a wig of the correct dimensions dressed in the fashion illustrated by terracotta figures which, though later in date, probably represent an old tradition. The gold hair-ribbon had been lifted from the tomb without disturbing the arrangement of the strands, these having been first fixed in position by strips of glued paper threaded in and out between them and by wires twisted round the gold; when the wig was fitted on the head, the hair-ribbon was balanced on the top and the wires and paper bands were cut, and the ribbon fell naturally into place and required no further arranging. The wreaths were re-strung and tied on in the order noted at the time of excavation. Though the face is not an actual portrait of the queen, it gives at least the type to which she must have conformed, and the whole reconstructed head presents us with the most accurate picture we are likely ever to possess of what she looked like in her lifetime.

By the side of the body lay a second head-dress of a novel sort. On to a diadem, made apparently of a strip of soft white leather, had been sewn thousands of minute lapis lazuli beads, and against this background of solid blue was set a row of exquisitely fashioned gold animals, stags, gazelles, bulls, and goats, with between them clusters of pomegranates, three fruits hanging together shielded by their leaves, and branches of some other tree with golden stems and fruit or pods of gold and carnelian, while gold rosettes were sewn on at intervals, and from the lower border of the diadem hung palmettes of twisted gold wire.

The bodies of two women attendants were crouched against the bier, one at its head and one at its foot, and all about the

Temple of the Moon God   A view of the front court of this temple in Ur.

chamber lay strewn offerings of all sorts, another gold bowl, vessels of silver and copper, stone bowls, and clay jars for food, the head of a cow in silver, two silver tables for offerings, silver lamps, and a number of large cockle-shells containing green paint; such shells are nearly always found in women's graves, and the paint in them, presumably used as a cosmetic, may be white, black, or red, but the normal colour is green. Queen Shub-ad's shells were abnormally big, and with them were found two pairs of imitation shells, one in silver and one in gold, each with its green paint.

An Excavation at Ur A photograph of Quiet Street.

The discovery was now complete and our earlier difficulty was explained: King A-bar-gi's grave and Queen Shub-ad's were exactly alike, but whereas the former was all on one plane, the queen's tomb-chamber had been sunk below the general level of her grave-pit. Probably they were husband and wife: the king had died first and been buried, and it had been the queen's wish to lie as close to him as might be; for this end the grave-diggers had reopened the king's shaft, going down in it until the top of the chamber vault appeared; then they had stopped work in the main shaft but had dug down at the back of the chamber a pit in which the queen's stone tomb could be built. But the treasures known to lie in the king's grave were too great a temptation for the workmen;

76

the outer pit where the bodies of the court ladies lay was protected by six feet of earth which they could not disturb without being detected, but the richer plunder in the royal chamber itself was separated from them only by the bricks of the vault; they broke through the arch, carried off their spoil, and placed the great clothes-chest of the queen over the hole to hide their sacrilege.

No other explanation than this would account for the plundered vault, lying immediately below the unplundered grave of the queen. And on this showing we have two almost identical burials, the sole difference being that in the queen's case the tomb-chamber is below the level at which the other victims lie, and for this too the sentimental motive is sufficient. What the two graves tell us is quite clear so far as it goes.

To begin with, a more or less rectangular shaft was dug down into the mixed soil of the rubbish-mounds to a depth of some thirty feet; at the top the shaft might measure as much as forty-five feet by thirty; the earth walls were necessarily sloped but were kept as nearly vertical as might be, and on one side there was cut an entrance in the form of a steeply sloped or stepped passage running down from ground level. On the bottom of the shaft, but occupying only a small part of its area, the tomb-chamber was built, with stone walls and brick vaulted roof and a door in one of the longer sides. The royal body was carried down the sloping passage and laid in the chamber, sometimes, perhaps generally, inside a wooden coffin, though Queen Shub-ad lay upon an open wooden bier and another queen in the only other undisturbed burial was apparently stretched upon the floor of the tomb. Three or four of the personal attendants of the dead had their place with him or her in the tomb-chamber; thus, two were crouched by Shub-ad's bier and one lay a little apart and four shared the tomb of the other (nameless) queen; in the plundered tombs scattered bones betrayed the presence of more than one body. These attendants must have been killed, or drugged into insensibility, before the door of the tomb-chamber was walled up. The owner of the tomb was decked with all the finery befitting his station and with him in the chamber were set all such objects as we find in the graves of commoners, the only difference being that they are more numerous and of more precious material—the vessels for food and drink may be of gold and silver instead of clay—the attendants, on the other hand, while they wear what we may call their court dresses, are not laid out properly as for burial but are in the attitudes of those who serve, and they are unprovided with any grave equipment of their own; they are part of the tomb furniture.

When the door had been blocked with stone and brick and smoothly plastered over, the first phase of the burial ceremony was complete. The second phase, as best illustrated by the tombs of Shub-ad and her husband, was more dramatic. Down into the open pit, with its mat-covered floor and mat-lined walls, empty and unfurnished, there comes a procession of people, the members of the dead ruler's court, soldiers, men-servants and women, the latter in all their finery of brightly-coloured garments and head-dresses of carnelian and lapis lazuli, silver and gold, officers with the insignia of their rank, musicians bearing harps or lyres, and then, driven or backed down the slope, the chariots drawn by oxen or by asses, the drivers in the cars, the grooms holding the heads of the draught-animals, and all to take up their allotted places at the bottom of the shaft and finally a guard of soldiers forms up at the entrance. Each man and woman brought a little cup of clay or stone or metal, the only equipment needed for the rite that was to follow. There would seem to have been some kind of service down there, at least it is certain that the musicians played up to the last; then each of them drank from their cups a potion which they had brought with them or found prepared for them on the spot—in one case we found in the middle of the pit a great copper pot into which they could have dipped—and then lay down and composed themselves for death. Some-body came down and killed the animals (we found their bones on the top of those of the grooms, so they must have died later) and perhaps saw to it that all was decently in order—thus, in the king's grave the lyres had been placed on the top of the bodies of the women players, leant against the tomb wall—and when that was done earth was flung in from above, over the unconscious victims, and the filling-in of the grave-shaft was begun.

THE WORLD OF MEKET-RE'

Nearly 4,000 years ago, an Egyptian nobleman named Meket-Re was buried at Thebes on the Upper Nile. Over the years, his tomb chamber, with its gilded coffin and stone sarcophagus, had been opened and looted by thieves. But a small vault containing provisions for the nobleman's future life remained hidden and untouched until the 20th century.

On March 17, 1920, an American archaeologist, Herbert Winlock, discovered the secret burial vault of Meket-Re. His description of that amazing vault brings to life the splendiferous world of the ancient Egyptian nobility. Many of the objects Winlock and his workers found are exhibited at the Metropolitan Museum in New York City.

Excerpted from MODELS OF DAILY LIFE IN ANCIENT EGYPT,
FROM THE TOMB OF MEKET-RE AT THEBES,
(Harvard University Press, 1955) written by

H. E. WINLOCK

I HAD gotten as far on my way home as the ruins of Medinet Habu. The walls of the old temple were turning pink in the sunset glow. The water-wheel that drones and quavers all day under the palms near by was silent for the night. Way up where the purple shadows were creeping out of the valleys in the tawny mountain I could see little specks of men and boys winding down the paths from the work at the tomb. The evening meal was being prepared and the bluish smoke of cook fires was beginning to float over Gurnet Murrai, where the tombs are seething tenements of Arabs and their flocks. At the house they would be getting tea ready and I was late.

From the passers-by on the path there broke into my thoughts a cheerful voice saying: 'May thy night be happy.'

I looked around and recognized one of our workmen, Abdullahi. 'And may thine be happy and blessed,' I replied, without checking my donkey, who was far more interested in getting home to his evening clover than in stopping for wayside greetings.

Model Boat   Meket-Re' believed he would have occasion to travel in his new life. Therefore, there were several different models of boats deposited in his tomb. Meket-Re' is seated under the wicker canopy. He is sniffing a lotus flower.

But Abdullahi felt otherwise. He must shake hands—quite an uncalled-for politeness, I thought—and evidently wanted to stop and chat.

'I am going home,' he informed me, and I said that that seemed evident. 'And when I get my blankets I am going back to spend the night at the tomb.' For the life of me I couldn't remember whether we kept guards up there at night to look after the equipment, but I supposed we must, and as I started on again I laughingly hoped he had something to watch. 'The Headman Hamid says I must tell no one, but Your Honour will see something up there,' Abdullahi called after me.

He had charged his voice with all the mysteriousness he could put into it and his whole manner would have been strange enough to impress me at any other time, but I was convinced of failure, and when I remembered that Abdullahi belonged to one of the gangs which were clearing those corridors out, I knew perfectly well there could be nothing to it at all. Daressy had surely dug those corridors out, and our re-clearing to draw a plan could not possibly show up anything new.

At the house I met Lansing and Hauser coming out. They said they were going up to the work, and showed me a scrap of paper with a hastily scribbled note from Burton: 'Come *at once* and bring your electric torch. Good luck *at last.*' This seemed preposterous. Surely it was another false alarm, and we had had so many of them. However there was Abdullahi and his mysteriousness, and I decided to let my tea wait a while and go with them, but I refused to have any hopes, and the three of us got ready all sorts of sarcasms for Burton's benefit as we trudged along.

A little knot of Arabs was standing around the mouth of the tomb in the twilight. Inside in the gloom we could just make out Burton and the headmen. There was something in the air that made our sarcastic remarks sound flat. Burton pointed to a yawning black crack between the wall of the corridor and the rock floor. He said that he had tried to look in with matches but they didn't give light enough and told us to try the torches.

At least a hole here was unexpected, but we had looked into so many empty holes. Anyway, I got down flat on my stomach, pushed the torch into the hole, pressed the button, and looked in.

The beam of light shot into a little world of four thousand years ago, and I was gazing down into the midst of a myriad of brightly painted little men going this way and that. A tall slender girl gazed across at me perfectly composed; a gang of little men with sticks in their upraised hands drove spotted oxen; rowers tugged at their oars on a fleet of boats, while one ship seemed foundering right in front of me with its bow balanced precariously in the air. And all of this busy going and coming was in uncanny silence, as though the distance back over the forty centuries I looked across was too great for even an echo to reach my ears.

I was completely stupefied when I gave my torch to the others and one by one they looked in through the crack. It was almost night now and we saw that we could do nothing until the morning. While the other two went back to the house to get some sealing-wax and cord, Burton and I sat down dazedly to talk it over. He told me how he had been coming down from the mountain-top where he had been taking photographs and had stopped at the work to dismiss the men as usual. As he expected, they had cleared most of the fallen stone from the corridors, but just before he had come along one of the men in this one had noticed that the chips had an unaccountable way of trickling into a crack as fast as he dug. At first the man hadn't paid much attention. It was just one of

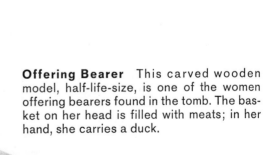

Offering Bearer This carved wooden model, half-life-size, is one of the women offering bearers found in the tomb. The basket on her head is filled with meats; in her hand, she carries a duck.

83

Stable A model stable in which cattle are being fattened for slaughter. In the stall on the right, the cattle are being force fed.

Granary As the men bring in the harvested grain for storage, scribes keep a strict accounting for tax purposes.

those crazy whims of the Americans that had made them want
to dig out such a place anyway. Still, he had called the headman of his gang and together they were scraping away the
stones from the crack when Burton had arrived.

When we left the tomb for the night the crack was stopped
up with stones and stretched across with strings securely sealed
with sealing-wax—quite a little of which was on my fingers.
The gang which was working in the corridor had received all
sorts of needless instructions about keeping someone on watch
all night. None of them slept a wink for the next three nights,
I am sure, sitting in the starlight in front of the tomb discussing
the baksheesh they hoped to get. We were no less excited.
That night we sat up late discussing what the place could be,
each one of us dwelling at length on some marvel he alone had
seen. I believe someone claimed to have seen Santa Claus
and his eight tiny reindeer—or possibly I dreamed I had seen
him. Anyway, I for one woke up in the morning with a raging
headache that was made no better by trying to seem master-
fully calm.

In the morning our work began, and three terrific days
followed. Burton rigged up mirrors to throw sunlight down
the corridor and took a photograph of the crack in the rocks.
Then we dug in front of it and found in the floor of the corridor
a little pit, about a yard square and waist-deep. It had been
carefully filled with chips of the very rock it was cut in, and
both ancient thieves and modern archæologists had taken this
filling for the living rock of the mountain and passed over it.
The side of the pit under the wall of the corridor was built up
of mud bricks, and when we had photographed them and taken
them away we were looking down into a little low chamber
about three yards square and scarcely four feet high, into which
no man had entered for four thousand years. Rock had fallen
from the roof—in doing so it had opened up the crack we had
looked into the night before—and had up-ended one of the
boats and broken others, but except for this nothing had been
disturbed. Our only fear was that as fresh air got into the
chamber more would come tumbling down, and we were torn
between a desire to get everything out safely before we had a
catastrophe and to get a complete set of photographs and plans
of everything just as we had found it. It was just luck that made
both possible, for after we were finished tons of rock began to
fall in the tomb. Still we escaped the misfortunes of our French
colleagues digging half a mile away. They had a man killed
by rock falling in a tomb chamber while we were working in
this one.

We photographed, we planned, we carefully cleared away

Gifts for the Nobleman This wooden carving shows a group of people who bear gifts for the deceased Meket-Re' to help him in his new life in the world beyond. The first man carries a wine jar on his shoulder and an incense brazier in his right hand. The next man balances linen sheets on his head. The first woman carries a goose. On her head is a basket filled with loaves of bread and sealed jars of beer. The last woman has on her head a basket filled with bread. She also carries a goose in her hand.

chips of fallen stone, and then we lifted out one or two of the boats or a group of little men and began all over again. One night will always remain a weird picture in my mind. Lansing and I had gone up to clear away more of the fallen shale to get ready for Burton's photographs in the morning. From afar off we began to halloo to the guards, for we had lent them a couple of revolvers and we were afraid of the zeal they might show in their use of them in the dark. Duly challenged, we made our way up the slope and inside the tomb' and lit candles to work by. For hours we worked away, the shadowy Arabs pattering barefooted back and forth from the flickering candle-light out into the open, where the brilliant desert stars seemed to hang right down to the mouth of the gloomy tunnel.

As we worked along through those three days and nights we began to realize what it was that we had so unexpectedly discovered. The tomb was that of a great noble of four thousand years ago. He himself had been buried in a gilded coffin and a sarcophagus of stone in a mortuary chamber deep down under the back of the corridor, where the thieves had destroyed everything ages before our day. Only this little chamber had escaped and it was turning out to be a sort of secret closet where the provisions were stored for the future life of the great man.

He could not conceive of an existence in which he would not require food and drink, clothing and housing, such as he

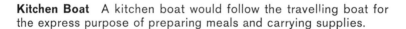

Kitchen Boat   A kitchen boat would follow the travelling boat for the express purpose of preparing meals and carrying supplies.

Garden This model garden has a copper pond which could hold water. The pond is surrounded by little wooden fig-trees and cool, shady porches. The pillars of the porches are elaborately painted.

was used to in this life, and being a rich man, naturally he wanted an estate in eternity like that which he had owned on earth. His philosophy carried him beyond that of the savage chieftain who expects a horde of servants to be slaughtered at his grave. He attained the same end by putting in his tomb a host of little wooden servants, carved and painted, at their daily tasks, working before little portraits of himself. The spirits of these little servants worked eternally, turning out spirit food or sailing ships upon a spirit Nile, and his soul could enter any one of the little portraits of himself at will to reap the harvest of their labours. In short we had found a picture of the life the great noble hoped to live in eternity, which was nothing more or less than the one he had led on earth forty centuries ago.

The first thing we had seen when we had peeped through the crack had been a big model nearly six feet long, showing a noble seated on a porch among his scribes, taking the count of his cattle as they were driven past. In the back of the room we found, under a lot of other models, neatly stacked, the stable where these same cattle were being fattened, and finally when we came to move one big boxlike affair in the far corner —a model I had tried my best to get a peep into and almost fallen headlong in the process—we found it was the butcher shop where the cattle's life history ended. The night we worked in the tomb by lamplight we got a peep into a granary where diminutive scribes sat writing down the quantity of grain being measured and carried to the bins by hard-working labourers. And later we ran across the bakery where the grain was ground and made into loaves and the brewery where the home beverage was being fermented in tall crocks and then decanted into round-bellied jugs. Lansing extracted two canoes manned by fishermen who hauled a miraculous draught of painted catfish and perch in a seine, and I picked the fallen stones out of two gardens in which copper ponds—that would hold real water—were surrounded by little wooden fig-trees and cool, shady porches. Then there was a carpenter shop and another shop where women spun thread and wove cloth. The very threads on their distaffs and spindles—frail as cobwebs though they were with age—had remained unbroken in that eternal stillness.

The business of the great man entailed a lot of travelling, and his idle hours were passed in pleasure sails or fishing trips on the Nile or on the still backwaters of the marshes. On the celestial Nile he would want to go voyaging or yachting, too, and therefore a dozen model boats were put in the chamber. We found them setting sail, the captain bossing the sailors who

Slaughter House In the model slaughter house, the men have bound the feet of two cows whose throats will be slit. The blood will be collected in vats, and the meat hung to dry. A portion of one wall of the slaughter house is completely open to allow the air to circulate freely around the drying meat.

sway on the halyards and set the backstays. A man throws his whole weight against the pole as they put off from the bank and another stands by in the bow with a fender in case they bump against another vessel. When they travel down-stream against the north wind the mast and sail are lowered and the crew man the sweeps. The noble himself sits under the awning in front of the cabin smelling a lotus flower while his son sits on deck beside him and they both listen to a singer and an old blind harper. Inside the cabin squats a steward beside the bunk, under which are shoved two little round-topped leather

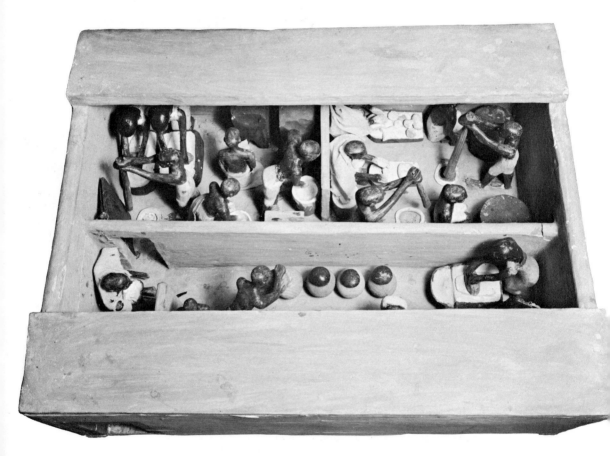

Bakery and Brewery Meket-Re' planned well for his life in his "eternal abode." Among the models found in his tomb was this model of a bakery and a brewery. These were allied industries; the production of both bread and beer required the same basic materials. In the upper portion of the photograph men are seen grinding wheat and barley for flour, and kneading dough for bread. In the lower portion, men are grinding and storing grain in jars; the grain will ferment to make beer.

trunks. A kitchen-boat follows, and the cooks get ready a meal to be served when evening comes and they are moored to the bank. There were yachts, to be sailed with the wind or paddled against it, and a low raking skiff, from the bow of which two men are casting harpoons while others land an enormous fish over the side.

Thus had the great man lived and so did he expect to live after he had gone to his 'eternal abode', as he called it. Finally, the funeral day had come. His body was brought across the river from Thebes, through the green fields, where the wondering peasants leaned on their hoes to watch it pass, and then up through the rocky gorges to his tomb. A long procession followed him, each model borne on the head of one of his serfs, and a crowd of peasant girls and women from his estates brought baskets of wine and beer and baked meats for the funeral banquet. Even their contributions were expected to go on for ever, and statues of two of them, half life-sized, had been made to go with the models in the chamber. There we found them towering above the horde of miniature men and beasts, looking over at us with grave, wide-open eyes. Four thousand years they had stood thus silent—if only we could have broken that silence and got from them the secret of the pattern their tightly clinging dresses were made on, we were sure we could have made a killing in the suit and clothing trade in the New York of today.

Four thousand years is an eternity. Just saying it over and over again gives no conception of the ages that have gone by since that funeral. Stop and think of how far off William the Conqueror seems. That takes you only a quarter of the way back. Julius Cæsar takes you half-way back. With Saul and David you are three-fourths of the way, but there remains another thousand years to bridge with your imagination. Yet in that dry, still, dark little chamber those boats and statues had stood indifferent to all that went on in the outer world, as ancient in the days of Cæsar as Cæsar is to us, but so little changed that even the finger-prints of the men who put them there were still fresh upon them. Not only finger-prints but even fly-specks, cobwebs, and dead spiders remained from the time when these models were stored in some empty room waiting for the day of death and burial. I even suspect that some of his grandchildren had sneaked in and played with them while they were at that house in ancient Thebes, for some of them were broken in a way that is hard to explain otherwise. Possibly that is a wild guess, but at any rate there is no doubt of what had happened to them in the little chamber in the tomb on the day of the funeral. After all of the models had been stowed away and the masons had come to brick up the doorway, they had found one of the boats in their way. So one of them picked it up and laid it to one side on top of the granary, and under bow and stern he left a great smear of the mud he had just been mixing for mortar. There those smears still remain.

The little models had to be parted after all these ages together. Half of them went to the Egyptian Government, under the terms of our concession, and are now on view in the museum in Cairo. The others can be seen in the Metropolitan Museum in New York. If any reader should see them there in their glass cases he will get a far better first view of them than we did with our electric torches flashing through that crack in the rock—but none of us would swap places with him. They meant too much to us that evening when we were wondering where we would dig next.

STONEHENGE: A PREHISTORIC TEMPLE

Its massive stones silhouetted against the sky, Stonehenge in Salisbury Plain is one of the most impressive and puzzling of prehistoric monuments. No one knows how it was used or just when it was built. But most scholars agree that it served as some kind of ceremonial building, perhaps a great religious structure for ancient peoples. And excavations by two archaeologists, Stuart Piggott and R. J. C. Atkinson, indicate that building and rebuilding at Stonehenge probably occurred over a period of 500 years, between 1900 and 1400 B.C.

Like many archaeological finds, one important discovery by Atkinson was made quite by accident. In examining the stones in 1953, he noticed on some of them prehistoric carvings of axes and daggers—carvings that had been overlooked by the many previous scholars who had studied the Stonehenge monument. In this excerpt, Atkinson describes the carvings and discusses their significance. He also discusses the remarkable feat by which the huge stones were transported from Pembrokeshire to Stonehenge, a distance of 135 miles as the crow flies and almost twice as far by any feasible route.

Excerpted from STONEHENGE, *(Hamish Hamilton, 1956) written by*

R. J. C. ATKINSON

STONEHENGE stands on Salisbury Plain, about eight miles north of Salisbury and a little more than two miles west of Amesbury. To the visitor who approaches the monument for the first time, particularly from the direction of Amesbury, the first glimpse is often keenly disappointing, for the stones, vast though they are, seem entirely dwarfed by the even vaster background of rolling Wiltshire downland. It is not until one approaches more closely, so that the stones are silhouetted against the sky, that the true size of the place becomes apparent, and begins to communicate to even the most casual and unfeeling visitor something of the awe and wonder with which it has for so many centuries been invested. . . .

To the enquiring observer the signs of man's handiwork are everywhere apparent: the squared and tapering forms of the stones; the severely functional shapes of the mortice and tenon joints on uprights and lintels; and the delicate rippled fluting of their tooled surfaces, like wave-patterns left on the sand by an ebbing tide. Yet these things, though they betray the hand of the mason, and alone allow us to confer upon Stonehenge the dignity of architecture, are nowhere obtrusive. Everywhere these specifically man-made forms are being etched and gnawed by remorseless time, so that the stone, having once yielded itself to the builders and suffered shaping to their purpose, now seems to be reasserting its own essential nature by the gradual obliteration of their handiwork. To me at least this stubborn yet imperceptible battle between the works of man and of nature, in which nature must inevitably triumph in the end, gives to Stonehenge a quality of immemorial antiquity and, at the same moment, of timeless performance, that is lacking from all our other early prehistoric monuments, whose stones have only been chosen, but not shaped, by man. . . .

There is hardly a single sarsen-stone at Stonehenge which does not bear at least one inscription of a personal name or initials. One of the most deeply engraved, and probably also the earliest, is on the inner face of stone 53, a little above eye height. It reads IOH: LVD: DEFERRE.* It was while I was preparing to photograph this inscription one afternoon in July 1953 that I had the good fortune to notice the prehistoric carvings immediately beneath it.

The principal carvings on this stone consist of a hilted dagger, point downwards, and four axe-heads, cutting-edge upwards. In addition there are a number of other axe-heads, less deeply cut or more severely weathered, and several vaguer markings, almost certainly artificial but too much eroded for even the most conjectural identification.

A few days after this initial discovery David Booth, the ten-year-old son of one of our helpers at Stonehenge, discovered the first of an even larger group of axe-carvings on the outer face of stone 4; and during the succeeding weeks Mr. R. S. Newall, while engaged in taking casts of these, found a number of shallower and more weathered axes on the same stone, and three quite well-defined axes on the lower part of the adjacent stone 3.

*That is, Johannes Ludovicus (or John Louis) de Ferre. I have not been able to trace anyone bearing this name in the seventeenth century, the period to which the style of lettering and the degree of weathering are appropriate. The

During the same season Mr. Newall also made a rubbing of the rather vague sub-rectangular marking on the inner (now the upper) face of stone 57. Its existence had long been recognized, but until the discovery of the dagger and axes no particular attention had been paid to it, and it had usually been assumed to be of recent date. The rubbing, however, revealed a feature of the carving which had not previously been observed, since it is very shallow, and has in any case been largely obliterated by the shoes (and not infrequently the hob-nailed boots) of generations of visitors. This feature is a rounded extension of the upper margin of the design. As soon as its presence was realized, Mr. Newall at once saw the close similarity of the design to certain carvings, which occur in Brittany in chambered tombs and on standing stones of Neolithic date. French archæologists have termed these symbols 'shield-escutcheons' (*boucliers-écussons*), but this is merely a conventional name which should not be taken literally, particularly as there is no other evidence for the use of rectangular shields in Europe at the period when these carvings were made. It is much more probable that they, and the Stonehenge specimen, are conventional representations of a cult-figure, possibly a mother-goddess. . . . Whatever its precise significance, however, there is no reason to doubt that the carving on stone 57 is of prehistoric origin. As the visitor can see for himself, it has already been seriously damaged by the feet of visitors in the century and a half since the stone fell, and its future preservation is a matter of some concern. Indeed, the only satisfactory way of ensuring its safety is to re-erect the stone on which it is carved, or for that matter the whole of the fallen trilithon; and it is gratifying to know that this action has been recommended to the Minister of Works by the Ancient Monuments Board as part of a strictly limited restoration of Stonehenge. . . .

Few people who have seen the Stonehenge dagger will deny that, once one knows where to look, it is perfectly obvious; indeed when the sun is shining across the face of the stone, it can be seen from the gate of the Stonehenge enclosure, over a hundred yards away. Yet during the past three centuries hundreds of thousands of visitors must have looked at the dagger (to say nothing of the other carvings) without actually *seeing* it. Nothing could demonstrate better that one sees only what one is expecting to see. I do not pretend for a moment, of course, that I was expecting to see the dagger at the time

letter E is executed in the form of a Greek Σ, an academic affectation which has misled more than one visitor into supposing that the whole inscription is in Greek.

that I found it. But I am convinced that I should not have seen it, had not my attention been engaged at the time upon *carvings*, though admittedly modern ones. If these remarkable carvings can have escaped notice for so long in the most frequented of all British antiquities, archæologists may well ruefully ask themselves how many similar surprises may yet lie in wait for them in less celebrated monuments.

One final carving at Stonehenge deserves to be mentioned, if only because it forms a trap for those who care to search (and may there be many of them) for further carved symbols. On the east side (originally the underside) of the fallen lintel of the great trilithon (stone 156) is a deeply incised outline in the form of a question-mark, the upper loop of which encloses the letters LV. On more than one occasion in the past this has been claimed to be of prehistoric date, and the sickle-like form of the main outline has invited the inevitable attribution to the Druids. It has been conclusively proved, however, that this design was cut by an itinerant workman, probably a stone-mason, about the year 1829.

Having described the carvings, I must add an appeal to the visitor *not to finger them*. Admittedly the stone is exceptionally hard, and fingers are soft. But one need look no further than the recumbent effigies in Salisbury Cathedral to see what constant fingering can do; and there is no need to add wilfully to the effacement already wrought by time.

THE BLUESTONES

The bluestones of Stonehenge form two settings which repeat the plan of the sarsens: a circle of uprights within the sarsen circle and a horseshoe of uprights within the horseshoe of sarsen trilithons. They are so called from their colour, which in dry weather is a bluish-grey. But when they are wet after rain they acquire a noticeably blue tinge, especially where the constant abrasion of the feet and hands of visitors has smoothed and even polished their surfaces. . . .

The source of the majority of the bluestones has been narrowed down, by petrological identifications, to an area of about one square mile at the eastern end of the Prescelly Mountains in north Pembrokeshire. There can be no question of the stones having been carried even part of the way towards southern England by ice during the Pleistocene period, and their appearance at Stonehenge can only be explained as the result of deliberate transport by man. The question to be

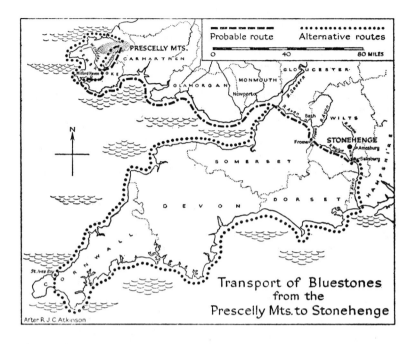

Transport of Bluestones
from the
Prescelly Mts. to Stonehenge

answered is therefore quite clear: by what route, and by what means, were these eighty-odd stones, weighing up to four tons apiece, brought from Prescelly to Stonehenge, a distance as the crow flies of some 135 miles? Of the alternative answers of a land and water route, it is safe to say that the second is overwhelmingly the more probable.

The enormous growth of rail and road transport in the last half-century has tended to obscure the fact that carriage by boat, either coastwise or on inland waterways, is by far the most economical means of moving bulky material from one place to another. The decline in such traffic (neglect of our inland waterways apart) is due chiefly to the fact that it is much slower than the alternatives of road and rail. In pre-historic times the undoubted advantages of water transport would have been even more apparent, for not only was time, relatively speaking, of little importane, but in addition there were not alternatives, as there are today. During the second millennium B.C., at any rate, there were no wheeled vehicles or even pack-animals. The only beast of burden was man himself. Under these circumstances water transport was the sole means of moving goods, and above all heavy goods, with relative speed and economy. That this was widely realized in prehistoric times is amply demonstrated by the relation of the

99

pattern of settlement to the river systems of the country, and more particularly by the very large numbers of objects, of all dates from the Neolithic onwards, which have been dredged in modern times from the rivers themselves.

It is thus inherently probable that the builders of Stonehenge II would seek to convey the bluestones from Pembrokeshire as far as possible by water, since this would mean a great saving in labour. The number of men required to move a stone of a given weight is discussed in detail below, but it may be said here by way of illustration that to haul a stone weighing four tons on a sledge and rollers would need about forty men

Stonehenge   Remains of a prehistoric temple erected between 1900 and 1400 B.C. on the Salisbury Plain of Southern England.

for the actual pulling, and another twenty to handle the rollers and steer the sledge by means of guide-ropes. To carry the same stone by boat or raft would need a crew of only twelve men at the most, and in sheltered waters as few as half a dozen. The saving in man-power through the use of water transport is thus of the order of eighty per cent.

Admittedly the journey by water is somewhat longer than the shortest overland route, but the difference is only fifty miles. Moreover the land route is one of exceptional difficulty, for over the greater part of its length, from Prescelly to the crossing of the Severn somewhere in the region of Gloucester, it involves climbing and descending the slopes of the innumerable valleys of streams and rivers flowing southwards from the mountains of southern Wales to the sea. Even if the route kept as close to the coast as possible, a detour would be necessary whenever a river mouth was encountered, in order to find a crossing where the stream was narrow and the banks sufficiently firm. Indeed it is very doubtful whether a stone could be hauled even as far as Gloucester without the use of boats or rafts, and these would certainly be required for the crossing of the Severn. If water transport had thus to be used occasionally in any case, it seems certain that, because of its manifest advantages, it would have been used as far as possible throughout.

What then is the most probable route for the carriage of the bluestones from Prescelly to Stonehenge, using boats or rafts wherever practicable? From the source of the stones themselves, at the east end of the Prescelly Mountains, the shortest route to the sea is north-westwards down the valley of the River Nevern, some of whose tributary streams actually rise within sight of the outcrops from which the stones are derived. From these outcrops to the mouth of the river at Newport is about eight miles, and over this distance the stones would have been hauled on sledges, since the stream is too shallow to allow the use of boats until very near its mouth.

In fact, however, it is most improbable that this route to the sea was used, since it involves a very dangerous passage round the western peninsula of Pembrokeshire. From Newport Bay to the mouth of Milford Haven, a distance of some fifty miles, the coast is exceptionally forbidding, with steep cliffs and numerous submerged rocks offshore; while off St. David's Head and in the sounds between the mainland and the islands of Ramsey, Skomer and Skokholm there are fierce tide-races of up to five knots, and dangerous whirlpools and eddies, to which any sensible navigator of today gives a wide berth. The distribution of prehistoric coastal settlement in Britain shows that then, too, the navigators of much frailer craft preferred at all costs to avoid such dangerous headlands, even to the point of making a portage overland. We may be quite sure that the carriers of the bluestones, borne down alike by the weight of their cargo and by their heavy responsibility for its safety, are not likely to have hazarded it, and their own lives, at the very outset of their journey.

The alternative routes from Prescelly to the sea are longer, but would make it possible to load the stones in sheltered waters at a starting-point well to the east of the most dangerous parts of the Pembrokeshire coast. There are in fact two possible routes, both leading to Milford Haven. The first follows the line of the present Cardigan-Tenby road (A.478), which passes less than two miles from the source of the stones. About two miles north of Narberth it joins the road from Carmarthen to Haverfordwest (A.40), which runs westwards to cross the Eastern Cleddau River at Canaston Bridge. The bridge marks approximately the highest point to which the river is navigable by even shallow-draught boats, for above this it soon becomes a fast-flowing shallow mountain stream.

The second route follows the crest of the Prescelly Mountains westwards to the point where they are crossed by the road from Cardigan to Haverfordwest (B.4329), and then joins this road to where it crosses the Western Cleddau River at the latter town, again at the highest navigable point. The two Cleddau Rivers flow southwards from these points for about six miles, and then unite to form the upper reaches of Milford Haven.

The existence of these two routes was originally pointed out by Mr. W. F. Grimes, F.S.A. It is impossible to say which was the one chosen, though for what it is worth the concentration of prehistoric antiquities is somewhat greater along the first than on the second. But it seems certain that in either case the stones were shipped out from Milford Haven, since the only two varieties of foreign stone at Stonehenge which do *not* come from Prescelly have both been identified with outcrops on its shores. The micaceous sandstone of the Altar Stone occurs in the Cosheston Beds on the north bank, near Langwm, about two miles below the head of the estuary; while a second variety of micaceous sandstone, known at Stonehenge from chips only, can be matched very closely at Mill Bay, a narrow inlet on the south shore, four miles lower down. The occurrence of these rocks so close to each other, combined with the fact that the estuary and its tributary rivers do form the nearest *practicable* approach by water to the source of the stones, makes it overwhelmingly probable that Milford Haven was the starting-point of the sea journey to England.

From here the next and longest stage of the journey must have been coastwise along the shores of South Wales to the estuary of the Severn. There are admittedly a number of stretches of rocky cliffs along this coastline, particularly between the mouth of Milford Haven and Tenby. But there are also numerous gently shelving sandy beaches where boats or rafts could put in, and except for this initial stage there is hardly more than five miles of coast at a stretch in which there is no possibility of landing to wait for the passing of rough weather. Provided that it was possible to wait for fair conditions (and it must be remembered that this was the universal practice of all early navigators), there is no reason to suppose that this long coastwise journey would involve any special hazards, nor even any extraordinary efforts. For the spring tides along this coast average about three knots, and the prevailing wind is westerly. So long as there was no urgency, much of the journey could have been accomplished using the wind and tides, leaving to human effort only the task of keeping the vessels far enough offshore to avoid submerged rocks and the more violent currents and eddies round the headlands.

From the estuary of the Severn there are two possible water routes to Stonehenge. The first, and by far the longer, follows the north coasts of Somerset, Devon, and Cornwall to St. Ives Bay, then by land across the neck of the Penwith peninsula from Hayle to Marazion, to avoid the dangerous sea passage round Land's End, and thence up the south coast to the mouth of the Hampshire Avon at Christchurch, and so up the Avon itself to Amesbury.

The second route, which is not only some four hundred miles shorter but also follows sheltered inland waters all the way, is up the Bristol Avon from its mouth to a point about seven miles above Bath, where the Frome joins it; then up the latter river to the town of Frome; thence overland to the headwaters of the River Wylye at Warminster, a distance of six miles; and finally down the Wylye to its confluence with the Avon at Salisbury, and so again to Amesbury and Stonehenge.

For every reason the second of these routes is to be preferred, and there is indeed some evidence that this was the route actually used. On the chalk downs which form the northwestern margin of Salisbury Plain, to the east of Westbury and Warminster, there are a number of Long Barrows, the characteristic burial-places of the Windmill Hill [Neolithic] people. One of these, Boles Barrow, lies in the parish of Heytesbury about

Stonehenge One of the most mysterious of men's ancient ruins. For years historians and archaeologists have tried to establish who built Stonehenge, how, and for what purpose, but the mystery is still not definitely solved.

three miles north of the River Wylye. It was partially excavated in 1801 by William Cunnington, who remarked that the central core of the mound was composed of piled boulders, chiefly of sarsenstone, among which was one of 'the Blue hard Stone also, ye same to some of the upright Stones in ye inner circle at Stonehenge'. This stone, with others, was removed by Cunnington to his house at Heytesbury, and after many vicissitudes is now preserved in Salisbury Museum. Petrological examination has confirmed that it is of the same characteristic spotted dolerite from Prescelly that occurs at Stonehenge.

The occurrence of this boulder in a Long Barrow, which could well have been built at or after the time of the transport of the bluestones to Stonehenge, provides good reason for supposing that the River Wylye lay on the route. It cannot be *proved*, of course, that this boulder did not come from Stonehenge itself. But it is much less likely that the builders of the Long Barrow would have stolen it from there, in itself a dangerous act of desecration, and dragged it for fourteen miles (it weighs at least 600 lb.), than that they should have gathered it from the neighbourhood, where it may well have been discarded as useless by the original carriers after some accidental damage to a larger block.

If it is accepted that the bluestones were brought to Wiltshire by water, what type of craft was used? The alternatives are rafts, made of suitable solid logs lashed together, or true boats, either dug-outs hollowed out from the solid or composite boats formed of a skin hull stretched on an articulated wooden frame. For the sea journey the raft has some marked advantages over the boat, in that it is unsinkable and cannot be swamped in rough weather. On the other hand a raft to support a given weight is very much larger and heavier than a boat, or composite vessel of several boats lashed together to carry the same burden, and is therefore more difficult to propel by paddling, and far less manœuvrable in an emergency. Moreover, while it is possible that rafts were used at sea, it is very doubtful if they would be practicable for the inland part of the journey.

The minimum size of raft required is determined by the weight of the heaviest stone together with that of the appropriate crew. In their present dressed state the largest of the Stonehenge foreign stones is the Altar Stone, with a weight of $6\frac{1}{4}$ tons. One may assume that in its original state, before dressing, it weighed in the region of 7 tons, and would need a crew of a dozen men averaging 11 stone apiece. The total burden to be supported by the raft is thus about 17,500 lb.

The lightest timber likely to be available in quantity is pine, which when dry weighs about 35 lb. per cubic foot. A cubic foot of water weighs about 60 lb., so that floating pinewood will support a maximum load of about 25 lb. per cubic foot. The required raft must therefore contain not less than 700 cubic feet to carry the calculated load with its upper surface just awash. A log raft must necessarily consist of at least two layers of logs, one laid at right-angles to the other, and to keep its dimensions to a minimum it must be square in plan. It follows, therefore, that a raft to carry the Altar Stone and its crew, if built of logs with an average diameter of one foot, would measure 21 ft. square, with a draught of 2 ft. if built in two layers, or 17 ft. square, with a draught of 3 ft. if built in three layers. In practice these dimensions would have to be rather greater, both to give some free-board (that is, to raise the surface of the raft above water-level) and to allow for the gradual waterlogging of the wood after prolonged immersion.

It can be said quite confidently that even today it would be impossible to navigate rafts of this size along the suggested course of the Avons and the Wylye; for if the draught is kept small enough to avoid grounding in shallow places the width becomes too great, while if the width is reduced to a practicable figure the draught immediately becomes impossibly large. If such navigation is ruled out today, it would certainly be impossible in prehistoric times, when the depth of the rivers was more variable and in general shallower, owing to the existence in many places of multiple channels, many of which have today been artificially suppressed or controlled.

For the inland part of the journey, therefore, boats must have been used. What kind of boats were they? Fortunately we have plenty of evidence, in the form of actual remains dredged from the beds of rivers, for the use of dug-out canoes in Britain from Neolithic times onwards, and indeed before. It is not impossible that skin boats were used as well, though no actual remains survive. The Eskimo *umiak*, the Irish curragh and on a smaller scale the Welsh coracle are all modern representatives of the type. It need not be considered further here, however, as it is structurally unsuitable for carrying the loads envisaged.

The dug-out canoes were made by splitting a large tree-trunk longitudinally and hollowing out the interior, probably with the help of fire in the initial stages, until a one-piece hull was obtained with walls some 2-3 in. thick. The size and shape of such boats is determined by the available raw material, which is usually oak. Exceptional examples have been recorded with a total length of 55 ft., but for present purposes it will be wise to assume a maximum length of 35 ft., a beam of 4 ft., and a depth of 2 ft. The shape of these vessels resembles that of an unusually deep punt, with a more or less flat bottom and vertical sides.

Theoretically, a single canoe of this size will carry a weight of about 8,700 lb. with a displacement of half its depth. Two such boats lashed side by side could therefore support the Altar Stone and a crew of at least ten men, with a free-board of 1 ft. In fact, however, three or more boats would make a more satisfactory composite vessel. With two boats only, the load on each gunwale would be of the order of $1\frac{3}{4}$ tons, and this load would be concentrated in the central half of the vessel, measured longitudinally, so that there would be a tendency both for the sides of the individual canoes to spread or buckle and for the vessel as a whole to break its back in the middle. Three canoes, each of the same beam and draught, but only 24 ft. in length, would carry the same weight far more safely distributed. The stone would rest, of course, on bearers extending the full width of the vessel, so that the load was evenly divided between the six gunwales. These same bearers would also serve to lock the three canoes together, and if they were notched to fit over the gunwales would at the same time act as stretchers preventing the sides from spreading under the applied load.

The practicability of this arrangement was proved in an experiment devised by the writer and his colleagues in collaboration with Mr. Paul Johnstone of the B.B.C. Television Service, which formed part of a television programme on Stonehenge broadcast in July, 1954. Three 'canoes', built of elm boarding and measuring 12 ft. by 2 ft. 3 in. by 1 ft. 6 in., were fixed together by four transverse bearers and floated on the River Avon near Salisbury. A replica of a bluestone in reinforced concrete, measuring 7 ft. 6 in. by 2 ft. by 1 ft. 6 in., was lowered on to the vessel by a mobile crane. The total load, including a crew of four boys from Bryanston School, was about 3,600 lb. and gave a draught of 9 in. The crew punted the loaded vessel up and down a stretch of the Avon with the greatest ease, and it was clear that it could have been propelled, at least in slow-flowing water, by a single man. Indeed, the operation had much in common with the pleasant pastime of punting agreeable companions (built happily upon less uncompromisingly monolithic lines) upon the quiet waters of the Cherwell or the Cam.

This practical trial leaves very little doubt that some such arrangement of dug-out canoes was used for the inland part of the voyage from Prescelly. The possibility of using the same craft *at sea* is another matter, and has not so far been put to the test. There is every reason to suppose that such canoes were used at sea in prehistoric times, though not usually with so heavy a load. But in any case, as we have seen, rafts could have been used for this part of the journey, and would have some advantage over boats.

The route suggested above includes at least twenty-four miles of land transport: sixteen miles from Prescelly to Canaston Bridge, six miles between Frome and Warminster, and two miles up the Avenue (processional way) from the Avon to Stonehenge. Over these distances the stones must have been dragged on sledges.

The almost universal use of wheeled vehicles today makes us forget that sledges are not merely for use in snow, but are also by far the best way of carrying heavy or bulky goods over dry ground, where wheeled vehicles or pack-animals are not available. Indeed there are still farms in Wales and Ireland today where the horse-drawn sledge is the main, and sometimes the only, vehicle. One can safely assume the existence of such dry-ground sledges in prehistoric Britain (but drawn by men, not animals), though owing to the perishable nature of their timbers no certain example has survived. What may be the remains of such a sledge, however, were found by the writer, in a condition so decayed as to render identification uncertain, in a grave near Dorchester-on-Thames, where it had apparently been used to transport the body of the dead man from a distance. Significantly, perhaps, he belonged to the Beaker culture, to which the earliest bluestone structure should probably be assigned.

The practicability of sledging the bluestones was also tested successfully in the television programme referred to above. A sledge was made to the writer's specification of roughly squared 6-inch timbers, with an overall length of 9 ft. and a width of 4 ft., and the replica of the bluestone was lashed in place upon it. The loaded sledge was then dragged over the down immediately south of Stonehenge by a party of thirty-two schoolboys, arranged in ranks of four along a single hauling-rope, each rank holding at chest level a wooden bar to whose centre the rope was fastened. It was found that this party could just haul the sledge, weighing some 3,500 lb. in all, up a slope of about 4° (1 in 15), though it is doubtful whether they could have continued this effort for long. The sledge slid easily over the long rank grass, and left no sign of its passage apart from some slight crushing.

The use of wooden rollers under the runners of the sledge allowed the hauling-party to be reduced from thirty-two to fourteen, that is, by fifty-six per cent., and it is certain that if the rollers had been more carefully selected for roundness a further reduction to a dozen or even less could have been made. The saving in man-power is not quite as great as it looks, however, because a separate party is needed to shift the rollers as they emerge from behind the sledge, and lay them again some distance in front of it, so that there is always a sufficient number in place to form a track. Moreover as soon as rollers are used the problem of steering the sledge arises, as especially when climbing a slope obliquely it has a natural tendency to slip sideways off the rollers. To counteract this, guide-ropes were fixed to the four corners of the sledge and each was manned by two people. These ancillary tasks occupied at least a dozen people, so that the total number required to move the stone *with rollers* would be twenty-four, against thirty-two *without rollers*.

The experiment was carried out with senior schoolboys from Canford School, who were naturally unaccustomed to this particular activity; and the figures given are critical figures, that is, the *minimum* number necessary to move the stone. It seems safe to assume, however, that if the same numbers of *trained and experienced men* were employed, the stone could be moved continuously for several miles a day without undue exertion. The total required is thus in the region of sixteen men per ton weight, or about 110 men for the Altar Stone, the heaviest of the foreign stones.

There is no means of telling, of course, how many of the bluestones were transported at one time, nor how long a journey took. But for the sea and river voyage, at least, it is probable that there were convoys of perhaps up to a dozen vessels, whose crews would provide a body of men sufficiently large to ensure that help could rapidly be given to any individual vessel that found itself in difficulties.

A CACHE OF PHARAOHS

By the time of Ramses IX (d. 1123 B.C.) the grandeur of Egypt and the magnificence of the Pharaohs was but a dream. The priests of Amon at Thebes controlled the kings like puppets and grew fat on the wealth that flowed into the treasuries of the gods.

For 500 years before Ramses' time the Pharaohs and their queens and families had been laid to rest in splendor not far from the temples of Amon. But now in the days of decadence the royal tombs were being robbed. And when at last the line of Ramses collapsed and the High Priests of Amon seized power the spoliation was complete.

From inscriptions we know that although the priests shut their eyes to the looting they still felt some glimmer of responsibility for the preservation of the actual mummies. Successive records inscribed on the royal coffins tell of their removal from one hiding place to another, and speak eloquently of the decadence of the age. At last a disused tomb at Deir el-Bahari was chosen as a depository for many of the old illustrious dead. Here they were packed in unceremoniously with what remained of their funerary offerings. The passage to this grave was sealed early in the XXIInd dynasty, not long after the year 940 B.C. Here the great kings of Egypt slept unmolested for nearly 3,000 years until about 1871 or 1872, when robbers discovered the place and again began plundering the royal bodies.

In the following extract the French archaeologist Gaston Maspero gives a vivid account of how he found this cache of Pharaohs and saved the mummies from modern tomb robbers. Today the kings rest in Cairo. The beautiful alabaster sarcophagus of Seti I is in Sir John Soane's Museum in London. Giovanni Battista Belzoni found it in 1815 in the original tomb of the Pharaoh from which everything else had been stolen long before.

Excerpted from a free translation from the French of LES MOMIES ROYALES
DE DEIR EL-BAHARI, MEMOIRES: MISSION ARCHEOLOGIQUE
FRANCAISE AU CAIRE, 1881-84, *(Ernest Leroux, Paris, 1884) written by*

GASTON MASPERO

DURING the summer of 1871, an Arab of Gournah, in search of antiques, discovered a tomb full of coffins piled in confusion one upon the other. Most of them were covered with cartouches and carried the uræus (the symbol of the sacred serpent). The grave robbers at Thebes had known for a long time that these were the marks of royal dignity, and this man knew his job too well not to realize at first glance that luck had bestowed upon him a vault *full of pharaohs.* Never had such a thing been seen in the memory of man!

But the discovery, however precious it might be, was certainly going to be difficult to exploit. The coffins were numerous and heavy; it would need at least a dozen workmen to remove them. In order to empty the burial chambers of its precious contents, a shaft would have to be sunk and a scaffolding of beams and ropes erected over the gaping hole which would be impossible to disguise. He realized also that it would be necessary to take the neighbours into his confidence, and even to divide the treasure with them. Even so, he could not be sure that one of his associates, discontented with his share, might not go to the *moudir* of the district, or the Director of Antiquities and reveal all.

The Arab resigned himself for the moment to taking only a limited helping of the windfall that had come his way. Two of his brothers and one of his sons helped him to unwrap several mummies, to remove two or three cases of figurines, scarabs, canopic jars, painted wooden figures of Osiris, half a dozen papyri, and a collection of objects easy to carry away and to hide. Only three times in ten years did they venture to go down to their hidden tomb, and then only at night and for a few hours. Their precautionary measures had been so successful that no outsider had a suspicion of the importance of their discovery. Each winter they sold some of the plunder they had brought back from these expeditions to the tourists; and for the disposal of the rest they hoped to meet some official who had been commissioned by his Government to acquire Egyptian antiques, or a tourist rich enough to be able to buy

Seti I This is a drawing of the alabaster sarcophagus of Seti I, found by Giovanni Battista Belzoni in 1815 in the tomb of the Pharaoh. The sarcophagus is now on exhibition in Sir John Soane's Museum in London.

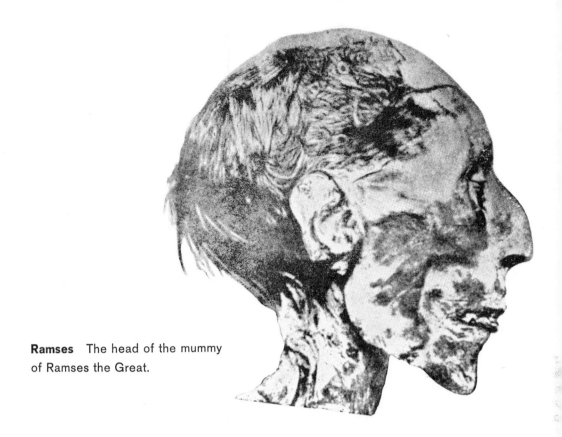

Ramses The head of the mummy of Ramses the Great.

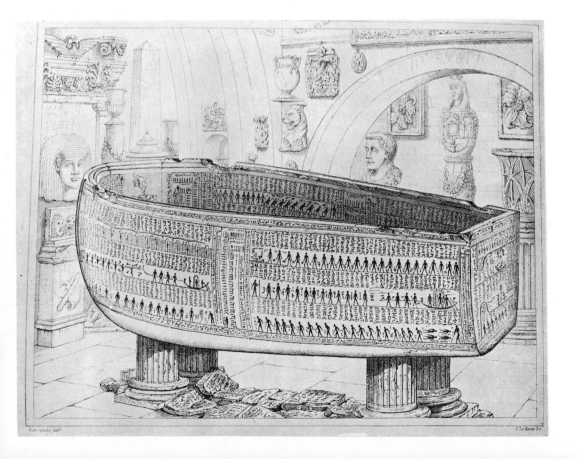

Royal Head This red granite
statue is possibly Tuthmosis III.

Statue of Amenophis III This piece of
sculpture is carved from black granite.

the royal mummies *en bloc* and to negotiate their clearance through the Egyptian customs.

However, in due course some of the objects which they had sold, found their way to Europe. About 1874 several figurines, of rough workmanship but coated with a charming blue enamel, made their appearance on the Paris market. Those that I saw there at that time were not stamped with a royal name, but carried merely the title Kheperkhare, which was attributed to at least two of the Pharoahs, namely Sesostris II of the XIIth dynasty and the more recent Pinedjem of the XXIst. All things considered, I decided that the inscription referred to the latter, and later indications soon proved that I was right. In the spring of 1876 an English general of the name of Campbell showed me a papyrus of the hieratic Ritual of the High Priest of Amon, Pinedjem, which he had bought at Thebes for four hundred pounds. In 1877 Monsieur de Saulcy sent me the photograph of a long papyrus which had belonged to Queen Nedjamet, the end portion of which is now in the Louvre and other fragments in both England and Bavaria. It was said that it had originally belonged to a Syrian dragoman who had come by it in Luxor. Monsieur Mariette had already acquired a papyrus of the same type in Suez which had been copied by order of Queen Tiuhathor Henutani. And in 1878 Rogers-Bey exhibited a wooden tablet in Paris upon which was written the following warning: 'The god Amon has issued a decree safeguarding the body of Princess Neskhous.' In short, by the year 1878 I felt sure that the Arabs had somewhere discovered one or more vaults of a hitherto unknown group of royal tombs of the XXIst dynasty.

To hunt for this site was one of the principal objects of my journey to Upper Egypt in the months of March and April, 1881. I had no expectation that methodical digging would reveal the precise spot whence all the tell-tale objects had come—the task was much more difficult than that: it would, I knew, be necessary to extract from the fellahin, by finesse, or by force, the secret they had so carefully guarded for so long.

A long and patient enquiry among the European tourists and other purchasers had taught me one important fact, namely that the principal vendors of royal antiques were a certain Abder Rassoul Ahmed, his brother Mohammed Abder Rassoul of the village Sheikh Abd-el-Gournah, and Moustapha Agha Ayat, the consular agent in Luxor for the English, Belgian and Russian Governments. The approach to this last man would not be easy, since he was covered by diplomatic immunity and could thus escape awkward interrogation. I decided to proceed vigorously against the brothers Abder

Rassoul. On April 4th I sent an order to the Chief of Police at Luxor to arrest Abder Rassoul Ahmed. I also sent a telegram to Daoud Pasha, *moudir* of Qénéh, who was also the superintendent of Public Works in the district, demanding his authorization of an immediate enquiry into the actions of the principal inhabitants of the village of Shéikh Abd-el-Gournah.

Abder Rassoul Ahmed was seized by two policemen when he was returning from an excursion in the hills and brought aboard my boat. As I do not yet speak fluent Arabic, I had him interrogated in my presence first by Monsieur Emile Brugsch, at that time Joint Curator of the Boulaq Museum, and then by Monsieur Rochementeix, Sub-Administrator of the Commission of State Lands, who were kind enough to give me the benefit of their experience and to act as interpreters. Abder Rassoul denied all knowledge of the doings I imputed to him— despite the unanimous testimony of the tourists who had bought the antiques. And he also denied having contravened Turkish law which prohibited clandestine digging, the unauthorized sale of papyri and funerary statuettes, the breaking open of mummy-cases, and the sale of objects of art or ancient Egyptian curiosities, all of which were deemed to be the property of the State. I accepted the offer he made that I should search his house, less in the hope of finding anything compromising as of giving him an opportunity of revising his attitude and of coming to some understanding with us. Soft speech, threats and offers of money were alike unsuccessful and on April 6th, the order having been received to start the official enquiry, I sent the prisoner and one of his brothers, Hussein-Ahmed, to Qénéh, where the *moudir* was waiting to investigate the case.

The business was gone into with great thoroughness. Interrogations were conducted by the magistrates of the *Moudîriyéh* in the presence of our delegate, the Inspector of Deudérah, Ali Effendi Halîl, which had, as their sole result, the sole production of innumerable witnesses in favour of the accused. The notables and elders of Gournah affirmed repeatedly and on oath that Abder Rassoul was the loyaliest and most disinterested man in Egypt, who never had excavated and never would excavate anything, and was incapable of misappropriating the very smallest antique object, let alone of violating a royal tomb. One noticed the insistence with which Abder Rassoul Ahmed proclaimed that he was the servant of Moustapha Agha Ayat, and that he lived under this personage's roof. He clearly believed that by allowing it to be known that he enjoyed this domestic association with a consular agent he shared the privileges attached to diplomatic status and that, in some way, he had become a Belgian, Russian and British

Head of a Queen This colossal statue is made of limestone.

Wooden Figure of a King

Hawk-headed Limestone Sphinx

protégé. Moustapha Agha had carefully fostered this belief, not only in Abder Rassoul Ahmed, but in all his accomplices; also, he had persuaded them that behind the screen of official protection they were beyond the reach of the local administration. Thanks to this artifice, he had succeeded in concentrating in his own hands the entire trade in antiques in the area round Thebes.

Abder Rassoul Ahmed was provisionally set at liberty under the guarantee of his two friends, Ahmed Serour and Ismaïl Sayid Nagîb. He returned home about the middle of May having been invested by the notables of Gournah with a reputation of unblemished integrity. However, his arrest, the two months of imprisonment that he had endured, and the vigour with which the inquiry had been conducted by Daoud Pasha, had demonstrated the powerlessness of Moustapha Agha to protect even the most faithful of his associates. Moreover, it was known that I proposed to return to Thebes during the winter and to reopen the inquiry from my side, whilst the *moudir* would continue his investigations as well. A few timid disclosures began to filter into the Museum. Some fresh information reached us from abroad; and, what was still more valuable, discord developed in the family of Abder Rassoul. Some members believed that the danger had passed never to return, and that the Museum administrators had been foiled, whilst others contended that it would be much more prudent to come to an understanding with the authorities and to divulge the secret to them.

At the same time Abder Rassoul claimed that the group owed him compensation for the months he had spent in prison; and also demanded that in future he should receive half the treasure as his portion, instead of the fifth, with which he had so far been content. If the others were to refuse to give way to this demand he threatened to go to the *moudir* and tell him everything about the illicit excavations.

After a month of discussions and quarrels, the elder of the brothers, Mohammed Abder Rassoul, seeing that betrayal by his relatives was imminent, decided to get in first. He went secretly to Qénéh on June 25th, and announced to the *moudir* that he knew the whereabouts of the site for which they had searched so long and so fruitlessly.

Daoud Pasha immediately notified the Minister of the Interior, who sent the dispatch to the Khedive. I had spoken to the Khedive when I returned from Upper Egypt, and he recognized at once the importance of this declaration and demanded precise details. A second telegram arrived the next day which left no doubt as to the magnitude of the discovery.

119

It read: 'In verifying the site discovered at Gournah on 25th of the current month of June, we have found it to be extensive and to contain more than thirty sarcophagi and many other objects such as statuettes, marbles, etc., and most of the mummy cases are covered with inscriptions. The images of serpents, and the ornaments one can see, prove it to be the site of royal burials. It is impossible to say how many antique objects there are in the chambers without bringing them up from underground.'

The Curator, Vassalli-Bey, was away on holiday, and I was on the point of departure for Europe, on private business; so I gave Monsieur Émile Brugsch the necessary powers and instructed him to take over. On June 27th, upon receipt of a second telegram, the Khedive ordered him to proceed to Thebes in company with Messrs. Thadeos Matafian, since nominated Inspector of the Area of the Pyramids, Ahmed Effendi Kamal, Secretary-Inspector of the Museum, and Mohammed Abdessalam, the pilot of the *Menshiéh*, the boat belonging to the Excavation Service.

The little party set out on the evening of Friday, July 1st. Upon arrival at Qénéh on the afternoon of Monday the 4th, a surprise awaited them. Daoud Pasha had received various valuable objects from Mohammed Abder Rassoul, among other things the four canopic jars of Queen Aahmes Nefertari, and three funerary papyri—those of Queen Mâkerî, Queen Isimkhobion, and of Princess Insikhonsou. This was a start calculated to encourage the team; and to ensure the success of the delicate task they were about to commence, Daoud Pasha put at their disposal his *wêkîl* (agent), Mohammed-Bey el-Bédaoui, and several other employees of the *Moudîriyéh*, who, by their zeal and vigilance, were to render outstanding service.

On Wednesday, 6th, Mohammed Bey, Emile Brugsch, Ahmed Effendi Kamal and Thadeos Matafian were conducted by Abder Rassoul to the entrance of the rock-cut tomb. The ancient Egyptian grave-diggers had taken all possible precautions: never was a burial place more effectively disguised. The chain of hills, which here separates Bab el-Molouk from the plain of Thebes, forms a series of natural amphitheatres, separated one from the other by buttresses of rock varying in thickness between eighty and two hundred metres. At the foot of these cliffs was a long slope of yellow sand formed by the erosion of the rock above. The surface stone, dried and baked by the sun for thousands of years, had lost its consistency and disintegrated at the slightest touch. In less than twenty minutes I was able to crumble away a block of about half a square

Sandstone Statue of an Ape This work of art was found in the great hall of the temple of Ramses II (c. 1304-1237 B.C.) at Abu Simbel.

Stone Coffin Religious scenes cover this sepulchre which dates from the late period after 600 B.C.

metre with my bare hands without using a knife or an instrument of any sort. There was difficulty in driving galleries and excavating chambers in such friable material, and so the ancient diggers had not made any serious attempt to tunnel in these particular cliffs until the end of the XXth dynasty. The tomb of the royal mummies had finally been cut in the harder rock of the north-west face of the buttress which separates this Amphitheatre from the Valley of Deir el-Baharî.

(*The tomb consists of a shaft twelve metres deep and two long galleries, twenty-three and thirty metres respectively, separated from each other by a flight of steps. At the far end of the second gallery there is a small chamber.*)

The whole was filled with wooden coffins containing mummies, and with grave goods of all kinds. Near the entrance a white and yellow coffin, with the name of Nibsni, barred the way. Beyond it was the massive mummy case of Tiouâqen, in the style of the XVIIth dynasty; then those of Queen Tiuhathor Henutani and of Seti I. Along the side, on a bed of dried flowers, were boxes of funerary statuettes, canopic jars, bronze libation bowls, and right at the end, in the corner of the passage was a leather cover, presumably from a dais which had belonged to Queen Isimkhobion. It was crumpled and had been thrown carelessly in a heap, as though of no value. Possibly some official, in his hurry to be gone, had thus discarded it. The whole length of the passage was in the same chaotic state. . . . The coffins, seen in the fitful light of candles, bore historic names—Amenhotpou I, Thutmose II, Ahmose I and his son Siamon, the Queen Ahhotpou, Aahmes Nefertari, Pinedjem—for whom we had searched so long and earnestly and many others.

In the chamber at the far end of the galleries the objects reached to the roof; but one glimpse showed that the contents had belonged to the XXth and XXIst dynasties. These amazing discoveries surpassed all expectation. Where I had hoped to find perhaps two or three obscure kinglets, the fellahin had discovered whole families of Pharaohs. And what Pharaohs! Possibly the most illustrious ever to have reigned over Egypt: those who had delivered her from the Hyksos invaders: Sounounri and Ahmose I, the conquerors of Syria and of Ethiopia; Thutmose III, Seti I, and even Ramses II, who had been immortalized by Greek historians under the name of Sesostris.

The brothers Abder Rassoul had guarded their secret so well that even the inhabitants of Luxor and Gournah were as surprised as were the Europeans by the number and importance of the royal mummies. Already their imaginations were on fire:

they spoke of caskets full of gold, of necklaces of diamonds and rubies, and of talismans. It was necessary to take immediate action in order to protect the treasure from the possibility of theft, or even of armed raiding. Two hundred Arabs were quickly assembled by the efforts of the *wêkîl* and were set to work. The Museum boat had not yet arrived, although it had been summoned, but Mohammed Abdessalam's small vessel was available.

He, Mohammed Abdessalam, took up his station at the bottom of the shaft and undertook to superintend the extraction of the contents of the galleries. Emile Brugsch and Ahmed Effendi Kamal received the objects as they were brought to the surface and had them taken down the slope, where they were arranged side by side. Brugsch and Kamal never for one instant relaxed their vigilance. It took forty-eight hours of hard work to clear the galleries and chamber; but the task was only half completed: it remained to transport the treasure across the plain of Thebes and ship it across the Nile to Luxor. It took twelve and sometimes sixteen men seven or eight hours to carry the heavy coffins from the slopes of the hills to the river bank. It is easy to imagine what this journey must have been like in the dust and heat of July.

The small objects were so numerous that many of the Arabs to whom they had been entrusted attempted to steal some of them, hoping the loss would not be noticed. But the *wêkîl* had his eye upon them all: energetic measures brought prompt restitution and everything that had been purloined was recovered, except for one basket which had held some fifty blue enamel figurines. At last, by eleven o'clock at night, mummies, coffins and grave goods were all at Luxor.

Three days later the *Menshiéh* arrived, was loaded with her cargo of Kings, and set off again at full speed for Boulaq.

TUT·ANKH·AMEN: EGYPTIAN KING

"We made a discovery that far exceeded our wildest dreams."

In the following extract the British Egyptologist Howard Carter tells of one of the most spectacular archaeological discoveries of modern times: the discovery of the tomb of a young Egyptian Pharaoh, Tut·ankh·Amen, who ruled Egypt for a few years beginning in 1357 B.C.

The ancient Egyptians believed that they must take with them into the next world all the paraphernalia that had made their life on earth enjoyable. The tombs of Egyptian kings became magnificent treasure troves with riches so great that they were often plundered within a few years of their completion. Because the tomb of Tut·ankh·Amen was in the discreet Valley of the Kings on the Upper Nile, it had remained undiscovered and intact until Carter and his patron, the Earl of Carnarvon, opened it in 1922. The treasures it contained are now in the Cairo Museum.

Excerpted from THE TOMB OF TUT·ANKH·AMEN *(Cassell, 1927) written by*

HOWARD CARTER & A. C. MACE

THIS was to be our final season in The Valley. Six full seasons we had excavated there, and season after season had drawn a blank; we had worked for months at a stretch and found nothing, and only an excavator knows how desperately depressing that can be; we had almost made up our minds that we were beaten, and were preparing to leave The Valley and try our luck elsewhere; and then—hardly had we set hoe to ground in our last despairing effort than we made a discovery that far exceeded our wildest dreams. Surely, never before in the whole history of excavation has a full digging season been compressed within the space of five days.

Let me try and tell the story of it all. It will not be easy, for the dramatic suddenness of the initial discovery left me in a dazed condition, and the months that have followed have been so crowded with incident that I have hardly had time to think. Setting it down on paper will perhaps give

Entrance to the Tomb The large opening at the bottom corner leads to the tomb of Tut·ankh·Amen. Just above, going straight into the mountain, is the entrance to the tomb of Rameses VI. The tomb of Tut·ankh·Amen was not plundered for so many years because the tomb of Rameses VI was built on top of the former. The later construction hid the lower tomb.

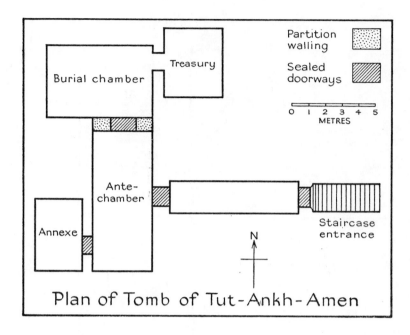

Plan of Tomb of Tut-Ankh-Amen

me a chance to realize what has happened and all that it means.

I arrived in Luxor on 28th October, and by 1st November I had enrolled my workmen and was ready to begin. Our former excavations had stopped short at the north-east corner of the tomb of Rameses VI, and from this point I started trenching southwards. It will be remembered that in this area there were a number of roughly constructed workmen's huts, used probably by the labourers in the tomb of Rameses. These huts, built about three feet above bed-rock, covered the whole area in front of the Ramesside tomb, and continued in a southerly direction to join up with a similar group of huts on the opposite side of The Valley, discovered by Davis in connexion with his work on the Akh·en·Aten cache. By the evening of 3rd November we had laid bare a sufficient number of these huts for experimental purposes, so, after we had planned and noted them, they were removed, and we were ready to clear away the three feet of soil that lay beneath them.

Hardly had I arrived on the work next morning (4th November) than the unusual silence, due to the stoppage of the work, made me realize that something out of the ordinary had happened, and I was greeted by the announcement that a steep cut in the rock had been discovered underneath the very first hut to be attacked. This seemed too good to be true, but a short amount of extra clearing revealed the fact that we were actually in the entrance of a steep cut in the rock, some thirteen feet below the entrance to the tomb of Rameses VI, and a similar depth from the present bed level of The Valley. The manner of cutting was that of the sunken stairway entrance so common in The Valley, and I almost dared to hope that we had found our tomb at last. Work continued feverishly throughout the whole of that day and the morning of the next, but it was not until the afternoon of 5th November that we succeeded in clearing away the masses of rubbish that overlay the cut, and were able to demarcate the upper edges of the stairway on all its four sides.

It was clear by now, beyond any question, that we actually had before us the entrance to a tomb, but doubts, born of previous disappointments, persisted in creeping in. There was always the horrible possibility, suggested by our experience in the Thotmes III Valley, that the tomb was an unfinished one, never completed and never used; if it had been finished there was the depressing probability that it had been completely plundered in ancient times. On the other hand, there was just the chance of an untouched or only partially plundered tomb, and it was with ill-suppressed excitement that I watched the descending steps of the staircase, as one by one they came to light. The cutting was excavated in the side of a small hillock, and, as the work progressed, its western edge receded under the slope of the rock until it was, first partially, and then completely, roofed in, and became a passage, ten feet high by six feet wide. Work progressed more rapidly now; step succeeded step, and at the level of the twelfth, towards sunset, there was disclosed the upper part of a doorway, blocked, plastered, and sealed.

A sealed doorway—it was actually true, then! Our years of patient labour were to be rewarded after all, and I think my first feeling was one of congratulation that my faith in The Valley had not been unjustified. With excitement growing to fever-heat I searched the seal impressions on the door for evidence of the identity of the owner, but could find no name: the only decipherable ones were those of the well-known royal necropolis seal, the jackal and nine captives. Two facts, however, were clear: first, the employment of this royal seal was certain evidence that the tomb had been constructed for a person of very high standing; and second, that the sealed door was entirely screened from above by workmen's huts of the Twentieth Dynasty was sufficiently clear proof that at least from that date it had never been entered. With that for the moment I had to be content.

While examining the seals I noticed, at the top of the doorway, where some of the plaster had fallen away, a heavy wooden lintel. Under this, to assure myself of the method by which the doorway had been blocked, I made a small peephole, just large enough to insert an electric torch, and discovered that the passage beyond the door was filled completely from floor to ceiling with stones and rubble—additional proof, this, of the care with which the tomb had been protected.

It was a thrilling moment for an excavator. Alone, save for my native workmen, I found myself, after years of comparatively unproductive labour, on the threshold of what might prove to be a magnificent discovery. Anything, literally anything, might lie beyond that passage, and it needed all my self-control to keep from breaking down the doorway, and investigating then and there.

One thing puzzled me, and that was the smallness of the opening in comparison with the ordinary Valley tombs. The design was certainly of the Eighteenth Dynasty. Could it be the tomb of a noble buried here by royal consent? Was it a royal cache, a hiding-place to which a mummy and its equipment had been removed for safety? Or was it actually the tomb of the king for whom I had spent so many years in search?

Once more I examined the seal impression for a clue, but on the part of the door so far laid bare only those of the royal necropolis seal already mentioned were clear enough to read. Had I but known that a few inches lower down there was a perfectly clear and distinct impression of the seal of Tut·ankh· Amen, the King I most desired to find, I would have cleared on, had a much better night's rest in consequence, and saved myself nearly three weeks of uncertainty. It was late, however, and darkness was already upon us. With some reluctance I reclosed the small hole that I had made, filled in our excavation for protection during the night, selected the most trustworthy of my workmen—themselves almost as excited as I was—to watch all night above the tomb, and so home by moonlight, riding down The Valley.

Naturally my wish was to go straight ahead with our clearing to find the full extent of the discovery, but Lord Carnarvon was in England, and in fairness to him I had to delay matters until he could come. Accordingly, on the morning of 6th November, I sent him the following cable: 'At last have made wonderful discovery in Valley; a magnificent tomb with seals intact; re-covered same for your arrival; congratulations.'

Antechamber Treasure The antechamber as it appeared upon discovery. Overturned chariots are piled in one corner with two gilt couches, some small caskets, several chairs, and a stack of white oviform boxes. The chariots had been dismantled in order to get them through the door. The oviform boxes contained food.

My next task was to secure the doorway against interference until such time as it could finally be reopened. This we did by filling our excavation up again to surface level, and rolling on top of it the large flint boulders of which the workmen's huts had been composed. By the evening of the same day, exactly forty-eight hours after we had discovered the first step of the staircase, this was accomplished. The tomb had vanished. So far as the appearance of the ground was concerned there never had been any tomb, and I found it hard to persuade myself at times that the whole episode had not been a dream.

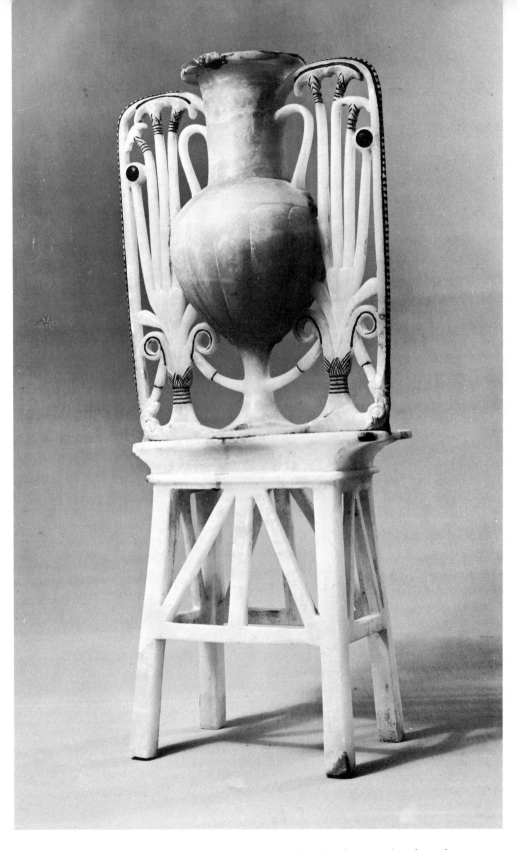

Jar This elaborate stone jar for oil was found in the antechamber of King Tut·ankh·Amen's tomb.

I was soon to be reassured on this point. News travels fast in Egypt, and within two days of the discovery congratulations, inquiries, and offers of help descended upon me in a steady stream from all directions. It became clear, even at this early stage, that I was in for a job that could not be tackled single-handed, so I wired to Callender, who had helped me on various previous occasions, asking him if possible to join me without delay, and to my relief he arrived on the very next day. On the 8th I had received two messages from Lord Carnarvon in answer to my cable, the first of which read: 'Possibly come soon,' and the second, received a little later: 'Propose arrive Alexandria 20th.'

We had thus nearly a fortnight's grace, and we devoted it to making preparations of various kinds, so that when the time of reopening came, we should be able, with the least possible delay, to handle any situation that might arise. On the night of the 18th I went to Cairo for three days, to meet Lord Carnarvon and make a number of necessary purchases, returning to Luxor on the 21st. On the 23rd Lord Carnarvon arrived in Luxor with his daughter, Lady Evelyn Herbert, his devoted companion in all his Egyptian work, and everything was in hand for the beginning of the second chapter of the discovery of the tomb. Callender had been busy all day clearing away the upper layer of rubbish, so that by morning we should be able to get into the staircase without any delay.

By the afternoon of the 24th the whole staircase was clear, sixteen steps in all, and we were able to make a proper examination of the sealed doorway. On the lower part the seal impressions were much clearer, and we were able without any difficulty to make out on several of them the name of Tut·ankh·Amen. This added enormously to the interest of the discovery. If we had found, as seemed almost certain, the tomb of that shadowy monarch, whose tenure of the throne coincided with one of the most interesting periods in the whole of Egyptian history, we should indeed have reason to congratulate ourselves.

With heightened interest, if that were possible, we renewed our investigation of the doorway. Here for the first time a disquieting element made its appearance. Now that the whole door was exposed to light it was possible to discern a fact that had hitherto escaped notice—that there had been two successive openings and reclosings of a part of its surface: furthermore, that the sealing originally discovered, the jackal and nine captives, had been applied to the reclosed portions, whereas the sealings of Tut·ankh·Amen covered the untouched part of the doorway, and were therefore those with which the

Gilt Couch One of the three gilt couches which were in the ante-chamber of the tomb of Tut·ankh·Amen. The animals forming the couches are mythological composites. Underneath the couch is a hole made by a plunderer. Evidently the thieves were interrupted, for little or nothing was taken from the tomb.

tomb had been originally secured. The tomb then was not absolutely intact, as we had hoped. Plunderers had entered it, and entered it more than once—from the evidence of the huts above, plunderers of a date not later than the reign of Rameses VI—but that they had not rifled it completely was evident from the fact that it had been re-sealed.

Then came another puzzle. In the lower strata of rubbish that filled the staircase we found masses of broken potsherds and boxes, the latter bearing the names of Akh·en·Aten, Smenkh·ka·Re and Tut·ankh·Amen, and, what was much more upsetting, a scarab of Thotmes III and a fragment with

134

the name of Amen·hetep III. Why this mixture of names? The balance of evidence so far would seem to indicate a cache rather than a tomb, and at this stage in the proceedings we inclined more and more to the opinion that we were about to find a miscellaneous collection of objects of the Eighteenth Dynasty kings, brought from Tell el Amarna by Tut·ankh· Amen and deposited here for safety.

So matters stood on the evening of the 24th. On the following day the sealed doorway was to be removed, so Callender set carpenters to work making a heavy wooden grille to be set up in its place. Mr. Engelbach, Chief Inspector of the Antiquities Department, paid us a visit during the afternoon, and witnessed part of the final clearing of rubbish from the doorway.

On the morning of the 25th the seal impressions on the doorway were carefully noted and photographed, and then we removed the actual blocking of the door, consisting of rough stones carefully built from floor to lintel, and heavily plastered on their outer faces to take the seal impressions.

This disclosed the beginning of a descending passage (not a staircase), the same width as the entrance stairway, and nearly seven feet high. As I had already discovered from my hole in the doorway, it was filled completely with stone and rubble, probably the chip from its own excavation. This filling, like the doorway, showed distinct signs of more than one opening and reclosing of the tomb, the untouched part consisting of clean white chip, mingled with dust, whereas the disturbed part was composed mainly of dark flint. It was clear that an irregular tunnel had been cut through the original filling at the upper corner on the left side, a tunnel corresponding in position with that of the hole in the doorway.

As we cleared the passage we found, mixed with the rubble of the lower levels, broken potsherds, jar sealings, alabaster jars, whole and broken, vases of painted pottery, numerous fragments of smaller articles, and water-skins, these last having obviously been used to bring up the water needed for the plastering of the doorways. These were clear evidence of plundering, and we eyed them askance. By night we had cleared a considerable distance down the passage, but as yet saw no sign of a second doorway or of a chamber.

The day following (26th November) was the day of days, the most wonderful that I have ever lived through, and certainly one whose like I can never hope to see again. Throughout the morning the work of clearing continued, slowly perforce, on account of the delicate objects that were mixed with the filling. Then, in the middle of the afternoon, thirty feet down from the outer door, we came upon a second sealed doorway, almost an exact replica of the first. The seal impressions in this case were less distinct, but still recognizable as those of Tut·ankh·Amen and of the royal necropolis. Here again the signs of opening and reclosing were clearly marked upon the plaster. We were firmly convinced by this time that it was a cache that we were about to open, and not a tomb. The arrangement of stairway, entrance passage, and doors reminded us very forcibly of the cache of Akh·en·Aten and Tyi material found in the very near vicinity of the present excavation by Davis, and the fact that Tut·ankh·Amen's seals occurred there likewise seemed almost certain proof that we were right in our conjecture. We were soon to know. There lay the sealed doorway, and behind it was the answer to the question.

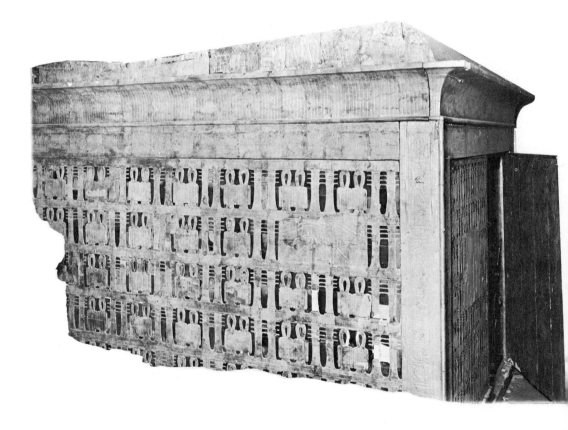

Shrine This is the outermost of three shrines in which the stone sarcophagus and the three coffins of Tut·ankh·Amen were enclosed.

Effigy of a Young Pharaoh A second coffin was found within the first. The golden effigy of the young boy king is rigged for removal from the tomb.

Slowly, desperately slowly it seemed to us as we watched, the remains of passage debris that encumbered the lower part of the doorway were removed, until at last we had the whole door clear before us. The decisive moment had arrived. With trembling hands I made a tiny breach in the upper left-hand corner. Darkness and blank space, as far as an iron testing-rod could reach, showed that whatever lay beyond was empty and not filled like the passage we had just cleared. Candle tests were applied as a precaution against possible foul gases, and then, widening the hole a little, I inserted the candle and peered in, Lord Carnarvon, Lady Evelyn, and Callender standing anxiously beside me to hear the verdict. At first I could see nothing, the hot air escaping from the chamber causing the candle flame to flicker, but presently, as my eyes grew accustomed to the light, details of the room within emerged slowly from the mist, strange animals, statues, and gold—everywhere the glint of gold. For the moment—an eternity it must have seemed to the others standing by—I was struck dumb with amazement, and when Lord Carnarvon, unable to stand the suspense any longer, inquired anxiously, 'Can you see anything?' it was all I could do to get out the words, 'Yes, wonderful things.' Then widening the hole a little further, so that we both could see, we inserted an electric torch.

I suppose most excavators would confess to a feeling of awe —embarrassment almost—when they break into a chamber closed and sealed by pious hands so many centuries ago. For the moment, time as a factor in human life has lost its meaning. Three thousand, four thousand years maybe, have passed and gone since human feet last trod the floor on which you stand, and yet, as you note the signs of recent life around you—the half-filled bowl of mortar for the door, the blackened lamp, the finger-mark upon the freshly painted surface, the farewell garland dropped upon the threshold—you feel it might have been but yesterday. The very air you breathe, unchanged throughout the centuries, you share with those who laid the mummy to its rest. Time is annihilated by little intimate details such as these, and you feel an intruder.

That is perhaps the first and dominant sensation, but others follow thick and fast—the exhilaration of discovery, the fever of suspense, the almost overmastering impulse, born of curiosity, to break down seals and lift the lids of boxes, the thought—pure joy to the investigator—that you are about to add a page to history, or solve some problem of research, the strained expectancy—why not confess it?—of the treasure-seeker. Did these thoughts actually pass through our minds at the time, or have I imagined them since? I cannot tell. It was the discovery that my memory was blank, and not the mere desire for dramatic chapter-ending, that occasioned this digression.

Surely never before in the whole history of excavation had such an amazing sight been seen as the light of our torch revealed to us. The reader may get a better idea of it by reference to the photograph, but this was taken afterwards when the tomb had been opened and electric light installed. Let him imagine how they appeared to us as we looked down upon them from our spy-hole in the blocked doorway, casting the beam of light from our torch—the first light that had pierced the darkness of the chamber for three thousand years—from one group of objects to another, in a vain attempt to interpret the treasure that lay before us. The effect was bewildering, overwhelming. I suppose we had never formulated exactly in our minds just what we had expected or hoped to see, but certainly we had never dreamed of anything like this, a roomful—a whole museumful it seemed—of objects, some familiar, but some the like of which we had never seen, piled one upon another in seemingly endless profusion.

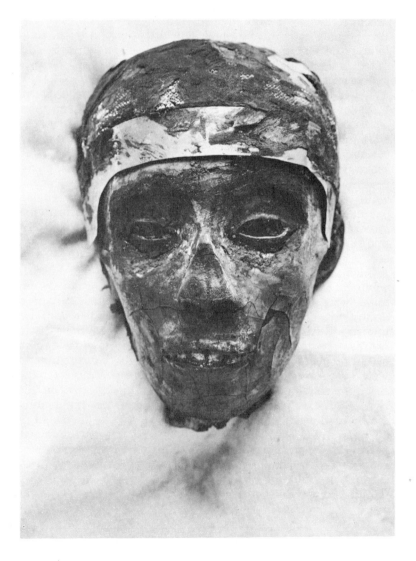

Mummy The mummy of Tut·ankh·Amen as it was found under the gold mask in the innermost casket. Everything has been removed from the mummy except a skull cap of thin sheet gold. There is a thin layer of linen and bead work on the skull cap.

Gradually the scene grew clearer, and we could pick out individual objects. First, right opposite to us—we had been conscious of them all the while, but refused to believe in them —were three great gilt couches, their sides carved in the form of monstrous animals, curiously attenuated in body, as they had to be to serve their purpose, but with heads of startling realism. Uncanny beasts enough to look upon at any time: seen as we saw them, their brilliant gilded surfaces picked out of the darkness by our electric torch, as though by limelight, their heads throwing grotesque distorted shadows on the wall behind them, they were almost terrifying. Next, on the right, two statues caught and held our attention; two life-sized figures of a king in black, facing each other like sentinels, gold kilted, gold sandalled, armed with mace and staff, the protective sacred cobra upon their foreheads.

These were the dominant objects that caught the eye at first. Between them, around them, piled on top of them, there were countless others—exquisitely painted and inlaid caskets; alabaster vases, some beautifully carved in open-work designs; strange black shrines, from the open door of one a great gilt snake peeping out; bouquets of flowers or leaves; beds; chairs beautifully carved; a golden inlaid throne; a heap of curious white oviform boxes; staves of all shapes and designs; beneath our eyes, on the very threshold of the chamber, a beautiful lotiform cup of translucent alabaster; on the left a confused pile of overturned chariots, glistening with gold and inlay; and peeping from behind them another portrait of the king.

Such were some of the objects that lay before us. Whether we noted them all at the time I cannot say for certain, as our minds were in much too excited and confused a state to register accurately. Presently it dawned upon our bewildered brains that in all this medley of objects before us there was no coffin or trace of a mummy, and the much-debated question of tomb or cache began to intrigue us afresh. With this question in view we re-examined the scene before us, and noticed for the first time that between the two black sentinel statues on the right there was another sealed doorway. The explanation gradually dawned upon us. We were but on the threshold of our discovery. What we saw was merely an antechamber. Behind the guarded door there were to be other chambers, possibly a succession of them, and in one of them, beyond any shadow of doubt, in all his magnificent panoply of death, we should find the Pharaoh lying.

Funerary Mask This mask was placed directly on the mummy of Tut·ankh·Amen inside the innermost coffin. It is made of solid gold with inlays of glass and semi-precious stones.

We had seen enough, and our brains began to reel at the thought of the task in front of us. We reclosed the hole, locked the wooden grille that had been placed upon the first doorway, left our native staff on guard, mounted our donkeys and rode home down The Valley, strangely silent and subdued.

It was curious, as we talked things over in the evening, to find how conflicting our ideas were as to what we had seen. Each of us had noted something that the others had not, and it amazed us next day to discover how many and how obvious were the things that we had missed. Naturally, it was the sealed door between the statues that intrigued us most, and we debated far into the night the possibilities of what might lie behind it. A single chamber with the king's sarcophagus? That was the least we might expect. But why one chamber only? Why not a succession of passages and chambers, leading, in true Valley style, to an innermost shrine of all, the burial chamber? It might be so, and yet in plan the tomb was quite unlike the others. Visions of chamber after chamber, each crowded with objects like the one we had seen, passed through our minds and left us gasping for breath. Then came the thought of the plunderers again. Had they succeeded in penetrating this third doorway—seen from a distance it looked absolutely untouched—and, if so, what were our chances of finding the king's mummy intact? I think we slept but little, all of us, that night.

Next morning (27th November) we were early on the field, for there was much to be done. It was essential, before proceeding further with our examination, that we should have some more adequate means of illumination, so Callender began laying wires to connect us up with the main lighting system of The Valley. While this was in preparation we made careful notes of the seal-impressions upon the inner doorway and then removed its entire blocking. By noon everything was ready and Lord Carnarvon, Lady Evelyn, Callender and I entered the tomb and made a careful inspection of the first chamber (afterwards called the Antechamber). The evening before, I had written to Mr. Engelbach, the Chief Inspector of the Antiquities Department, advising him of the progress of clearing, and asking him to come over and make an official inspection. Unfortunately he was at the moment in Kena on official business, so the local Antiquities Inspector, Ibrahim Effendi, came in his stead.

By the aid of our powerful electric lamps many things that had been obscure to us on the previous day became clear, and we were able to make a more accurate estimate of the extent of our discovery. Our first objective was naturally the sealed

Dagger and Sheath   The influence on Egyptian art by the Minoan civilization is evident in the decoration of this dagger and sheath. Animals in flight and the use of palms were not common to the Egyptians.

door between the statues, and here a disappointment awaited us. Seen from a distance it presented all the appearance of an absolutely intact blocking, but close examination revealed the fact that a small breach had been made near the bottom, just wide enough to admit a boy or a slightly built man, and that the hole made had subsequently been filled up and re-sealed. We were not then to be the first. Here, too, the thieves had forestalled us, and it only remained to be seen how much damage they had had the opportunity or the time to effect.

Our natural impulse was to break down the door, and get to the bottom of the matter at once, but to do so would have entailed serious risk of damage to many of the objects in the Antechamber, a risk which we were by no means prepared to face. Nor could we move the objects in question out of the way, for it was imperative that a plan and complete photographic record should be made before anything was touched, and this was a task involving a considerable amount of time, even if we had had sufficient plant available—which we had not—to carry it through immediately. Reluctantly we decided to abandon the opening of this inner sealed door until we had cleared the Antechamber of all its contents. By doing this we should not only ensure the complete scientific record of the outer chamber which it was our duty to make, but should have a clear field for the removal of the door-blocking, a ticklish operation at best.

(They clear the Antechamber.)

When we entered the Burial Chamber we found, lying beside a small hole made by the robbers through the masonry of the door, which had been subsequently reclosed by the ancient Egyptian officials, portions of two necklaces dropped by a thief. Around the four sides of the great shrine, which occupied almost the entire area of the chamber, were divers objects and emblems. . . .

At the eastern end of the shrine were two massive folding doors closed with ebony bolts shot into copper staples, their panels decorated with strange figures—headless demon guardians of the caverns of the Underworld. Before these doors stood an exquisite triple-lamp of floral form, carved out of a single block of translucent calcite, in shape three lotiform cups, with stems and leaves springing from a single circular base. . . .

In front, standing along the east wall, was Amen's sacred

Child Rulers in Garden   This fine work of art, found on the back of a chair is decorated with inlay and gold leaf. This wooden carving depicts the young Pharaoh Tut·ankh·Amen and his wife ankh·Es·En·Amen.

goose of wood, varnished black, and swathed in linen; beside it were two rush-work baskets collapsed with age, and a wine-jar bearing the legend: 'Year 5, wine of the house of (?) Tut·ankh·Amen, from the Western river Chief of the Vintners, Kha.'

Resting upon the ground, between the shrine and the north wall, were magic oars to ferry the king's barque across the waters of the Nether World. . . .

Ornamental Box This beautifully carved container was probably used by the young king, Tut·ankh·Amen.

When we drew back those ebony bolts of the great shrine, the doors swung back as if only closed yesterday, and revealed within yet another shrine, in type like the first, save for the blue inlay. It had similarly bolted doors, but upon them was a seal intact, bearing the name of Tut·ankh·Amen and a recumbent jackal over Egypt's nine foes. Above the shrine drooped a linen pall. This bespangled linen pall, brown with age, still hanging on its curious wooden supports, was rent by the weight of the gilt bronze marguerites sewn to its fabric. The shrine, dazzling from the brilliance of its gold, was decorated with scenes wrought, in beautiful incised-relief, from the book *Of that which is in the Underworld*—that guide to the Hereafter, which points out to the deceased the road he should take, and explains to him the various malefic powers he must meet during his subterranean journey. According to this book two routes led him to the Land of the Blessed, one by water, the other by land, and it further shows that there were byways leading to seething rivers of fire by which he must not travel.

The pall made us realize that we were in the presence of a dead king of past ages. The unbroken seal upon the closed doors of the second shrine gave us the data we were seeking. Had the tomb robbers, who had entered the Antechamber, its Annexe, the Burial Chamber and its Store-room, by any chance reached the king? The shrine was intact, its doors bore their original seal uninjured, indicating that the robbers had not reached him. Henceforth, we knew that, within the shrine, we should be treading where no one had entered, and that we should be dealing with material untouched and unharmed since the boy king was laid to rest nearly three thousand three hundred years ago. . . .

On either side, between the two shrines, stacked in the right and left corners, were numerous ceremonial maces, sticks, staves and bows, some carefully wrapped in linen. Perhaps the choicest of them all were the gold and silver sticks, made of two thin tubular shafts supporting tiny statuettes of the youthful monarch, cast and chased in their respective metals. . . .

The doors of this second shrine were bolted top and bottom, and carefully fastened with cord tied to metal staples and sealed. The clay seal upon this cord was intact. It bore impressions of two distinct seals, one bearing Tut·ankh·Amen's prenomen, Kheperu·neb·Re, surmounting 'A Jackal over nine Foes', the second bore the device of the Royal Necropolis Seal, 'The Jackal over nine Foes', without other distinguishing mark or royal insignia. Here was a great piece of luck, as manifestly behind those two seals we should be dealing with

147

Battle Scene   This ivory linen chest shows Tut·ankh·Amen leading his troops against aggressors. As was common in this type of scene, the forces of the Pharaoh are in strict order while those of the enemy are in complete chaos. According to at least one authority, it is unlikely that this battle ever took place.

material unharmed since the burial of the king. It was with great care that the cords were severed, and those folding doors opened which, when swung back, revealed yet a third shrine, also sealed and intact—the seal-impressions upon this third shrine being identical to those on the second.

At this point of our undertaking we realized that it would now be possible, by opening those further doors, to solve the secret the shrines had so jealously guarded throughout the centuries. I therefore decided before any other procedure to make the experiment. It was an exciting moment in our arduous task that cannot easily be forgotten. We were to witness a spectacle such as no other man in our times had been privileged to see. With suppressed excitement I carefully cut the cord, removed that precious seal, drew back the bolts, and opened the doors, when a fourth shrine was revealed, similar in design and even more brilliant in workmanship than the last. The decisive moment was at hand! An indescribable moment for an archæologist! What was beneath and what did that fourth shrine contain? With intense excitement I drew back the bolts of the last and unsealed doors; they slowly swung open, and there, filling the entire area within, effectually barring any further progress, stood an immense yellow quartzite sarcophagus, intact, with the lid still firmly fixed in its place, just as the pious hands had left it. It was certainly a thrilling moment, as we gazed upon the spectacle enhanced by the striking contrast—the glitter of metal—of the golden shrines shielding it. Especially striking were the outstretched hand and wing of a goddess sculptured on the end of the sarcophagus, as if to ward off an intruder. It symbolized an idea beautiful in conception and, indeed, seemed an eloquent illustration of the perfect faith and tender solicitude for the well-being of their loved one, that animated the people who dwelt in that land over thirty centuries ago.

We were now able to profit by the experience we had acquired and had a much clearer conception of the operation immediately before us: the three remaining shrines would have to be taken to pieces and removed before the problem of the sarcophagus could be contemplated.

The tackle for raising the lid of the sarcophagus was in position. I gave the word. Amid intense silence the huge slab, broken in two, weighing over a ton and a quarter, rose from its bed. The light shone into the sarcophagus. A sight met our eyes that at first puzzled us. It was a little disappointing. The contents were completely covered by fine linen shrouds. The lid being suspended in mid-air, we rolled back those covering

Model Ship A pleasure craft found in the tomb of Tut•ankh•Amen.

shrouds, one by one, and as the last was removed a gasp of wonderment escaped our lips, so gorgeous was the sight that met our eyes: a golden effigy of the young boy king, of most magnificent workmanship, filled the whole of the interior of the sarcophagus. This was the lid of a wonderful anthropoid coffin, some seven feet in length, resting upon a low bier in the form of a lion, and no doubt the outermost coffin of a series of coffins, nested one within the other, enclosing the mortal remains of the king. Enclasping the body of this magnificent monument were two winged goddesses, Isis and Neith, wrought in rich gold-work upon gesso, as brilliant as the day the coffin was made. To it an additional charm was added, by the fact that, while this decoration was rendered in fine low bas-relief, the head and hands of the king were in the round,

151

in massive gold of the finest sculpture, surpassing anything we could have imagined. The hands, crossed over the breast, held the royal emblems—the Crook and the Flail—encrusted with deep blue faience. The face and features were wonderfully wrought in sheet-gold. The eyes were of aragonite and obsidian, the eyebrows and eyelids inlaid with lapis lazuli glass. There was a touch of realism, for while the rest of this anthropoid coffin, covered with feathered ornament, was of brilliant gold, that of the bare face and hands seemed different, the gold of the flesh being of different alloy, thus conveying an impression of the greyness of death. Upon the forehead of this recumbent figure of the young boy king were two emblems delicately worked in brilliant inlay—the Cobra and the Vulture—symbols of Upper and Lower Egypt, but perhaps the most touching by its human simplicity was the tiny wreath of flowers around these symbols, as it pleased us to think, the last farewell offering of the widowed girl queen to her husband, the youthful representative of the 'Two Kingdoms'.

Among all that regal splendour, that royal magnificence—everywhere the glint of gold—there was nothing so beautiful as those few withered flowers, still retaining their tinge of colour. They told us what a short period three thousand three hundred years really is—but Yesterday and the Morrow. In fact, that little touch of nature made that ancient and our modern civilization kin.

Thus from stairway, steep descending passage, Antechamber and Burial Chamber, from those golden shrines and from that noble sarcophagus, our eyes were now turned to its contents—a gold encased coffin, in form a recumbent figure of the young king, symbolizing Osiris or, it would seem, by its fearless gaze, man's ancient trust in immortality. Many and disturbing were our emotions awakened by that Osiride form. Most of them voiceless. But, in that silence, to listen—you could almost hear the ghostly footsteps of the departing mourners.

Our lights were lowered, once more we mounted those sixteen steps, once more we beheld the blue vault of the heavens where the Sun is Lord, but our inner thoughts still lingered over the splendour of that vanished Pharaoh, with his last appeal upon his coffin written in our minds: 'Oh Mother Nût! spread thy wings over me as the Imperishable Stars.'

153

Writing Implements These were the writing implements of King Tut. Each case holds several pens and two pieces of solid ink.

MUMMIES

Giovanni Battista Belzoni won dubious fame as a collector of antiquities during the early 1800's. He had left his native Italy for England, where he earned his living in a number of ingenious ways—one of which was as a "strong man" at carnivals. Pictures of the time show him, all muscles and moustache, in the conventional attitude: feet planted on the floor, knees out, arms wide, supporting tier upon tier of young men balanced above him.

From England, Belzoni went to Egypt where he began to collect antiquities for the government. His methods were brutal and careless, yet surprisingly successful. In discussing his tomb-robbing techniques, archaeologists have written that they turn "green with envy, then red with shame, and then white with rage."

Excerpted from NARRATIVE OF THE OPERATIONS AND RECENT DISCOVERIES IN EGYPT AND NUBIA, *(John Murray, 1820) written by*

G. B. BELZONI

PREFACE TO BELZONI'S ACCOUNT OF HIS WORK IN EGYPT AND NUBIA

AS I made my discoveries alone, I have been anxious to write my book by myself, though in so doing, the reader will consider me, and with great propriety, guilty of temerity; but the public will perhaps gain in the fidelity of my narrative, what it loses in elegance. I am not an Englishman, but I prefer that my readers should receive from myself, as well as I am able to describe them, an account of my proceedings in Egypt, in Nubia, on the coast of the Red Sea, and in the Oasis; rather than run the risk of having my meaning misrepresented by another. If I am intelligible, it is all that I can expect. I shall state nothing but the plain matters of fact, as they occurred to me in these countries, in 1815–16–17–18 and –19. A description of the means I took in making my researches, the difficulties I had to encounter, and how I overcame them, will give a tolerably correct idea of the manners and customs of the people I had to deal with. Perhaps I have spoken too much of the obstacles thrown in my way, by the jealousy and intriguing spirit of my adversaries, without considering that the public will care little about my private quarrels, which to me, of course, appeared of the greatest consequence on the spot, in these countries. But I hope that a little indulgence may be allowed to my mortified feelings, particularly when I reflect that it was through them that I was compelled to leave Egypt before I had completed my plans.

I must apologize also for the few humble observations I have ventured to give on some historical points; but I have become so familiar with the sight of temples, tombs, and pyramids, that I could not help forming some speculation on their origin and construction. The scholar and learned traveller will smile at my presumption, but do they always agree themselves in their opinions on matters of this sort, or even on those of much less difficulty? Much has been written on Egypt and Nubia by the travellers of the last century, by Denon, and the French *sçavans*, whose general account of these countries has scarcely left anything unnoticed; and by Mr. Hamilton, to the accuracy of the latter of whom I can bear the most ample testimony. But what can I say of the late Sheik Burckhardt, who was so well acquainted with the language of these people, that none of them suspected him to be an European? His account of the tribes in these countries is so minutely correct that little or nothing remains for observation in modern Egypt and Nubia.

I have, however, one more remark to make on myself, which I am afraid the reader will think very vain: it is this, that no traveller had ever such opportunities of studying the customs of the natives as were afforded to me, for none had ever to deal with them in so peculiar a manner. My constant occupation was searching after antiquities, and this led me in the various transactions I had with them, to observe the real character of the Turks, Arabs, Nubians, Bedoweens, and Ababdy tribes. Thus I was very differently circumstanced from a common traveller, who goes merely to make his remarks on the country and its antiquities, instead of having to persuade these ignorant and superstitious people to undertake a hard task, in labours, with which they were previously totally unacquainted.

My native place is the city of Padua: I am of a Roman family, which has resided there for many years. The state and troubles of Italy in 1800, which are too well known to require any comment from me, compelled me to leave it; and from that time I have visited different parts of Europe, and suffered many vicissitudes. The greater part of my younger days I passed in Rome, the former abode of my ancestors, where I was preparing myself to become a monk; but the sudden entry of the French army into that city altered the course of my education, and being destined to travel, I have been a wanderer ever since. My family supplied me occasionally with remittances; but as they were not rich, I did not choose to be a burthen to them, and contrived to live on my own industry, and the little knowledge I had acquired in various branches. I turned my chief attention to hydraulics, a science that I had learned in Rome, which I found much to my advantage, and which was ultimately the very cause of my going to Egypt. For I had good information that a hydraulic machine would be of great service in that country, to irrigate the fields, which want water only to make them produce at any time of the year. But I am rather anticipating. In 1803 I arrived in England, soon after which I married, and, after residing in it nine years, I formed the resolution of going to the South of Europe. Taking Mrs. Belzoni with me, I visited Portugal, Spain and Malta, from which latter place we embarked for Egypt, where we remained from 1815 to 1819. Here I had the good fortune to be the discoverer of many remains of antiquity of that primitive nation. I succeeded in opening one of the two famous Pyramids of Ghizeh, as well as several of the Tombs of the Kings at Thebes. Among the latter, that which has been pronounced by one of the most distinguished scholars of the age to be the tomb of Psammuthis, is at this moment the principal, the most perfect and splendid monument in that country. The celebrated bust of young Memnon, which I brought from Thebes, is now in the British Museum; and the alabaster sarcophagus, found in the Tombs of the Kings, is on its way to England.

Near the second cataract of the Nile, I opened the temple of Ybsambul; then made a journey to the coast of the Red Sea, to the city of Berenice, and afterwards an excursion in the western Elloah, or Oasis. I now embarked for Europe, and after an absence of twenty years, returned to my native land, and to the bosom of my family; from whence I proceeded to England.

On my arrival in Europe I found so many erroneous accounts had been given to the public of my operations and discoveries in Egypt, that it appeared to be my duty to publish a plain statement of facts; and should anyone call its correctness in question, I hope they will do it openly, that I may be able to prove the truth of my assertions.

NARRATIVE OF THE OPERATIONS AND RECENT DISCOVERIES
IN EGYPT AND NUBIA

G. B. BELZONI

... Gournow is a tract of rocks, about two miles in length, at the foot of the Libyan mountains, on the west of Thebes, and was the burial place of the great city of a hundred gates. Every part of these rocks is cut out by art, in the form of large and small chambers, each of which has its separate entrance; and though they are very close to each other, it is seldom that there is any interior communication from one to the other. I can truly say, it is impossible to give any description sufficient to convey the smallest idea of those subterranean abodes, and their inhabitants. There are no sepulchres in any part of the world like them; there are no excavations or mines, that can be compared to these truly astonishing places; and no exact description can be given of their interior, owing to the difficulty of visiting these places. The inconvenience of entering into them is such, that it is not everyone who can support the exertion.

A traveller is generally satisfied when he has seen the large hall, the gallery, the staircase, and as far as he can conveniently go: besides, he is taken up with the strange works he observes cut in various places, and painted on each side of the walls: so that when he comes to a narrow and difficult passage, or to have to descend to the bottom of a well or cavity, he declines taking such trouble, naturally supposing that he cannot see in these abysses anything so magnificent as what he sees above, and consequently deeming it useless to proceed any farther. Of some of these tombs many persons could not stand the suffocating air, which often causes fainting. A vast quantity of dust rises, so fine that it enters into the throat and nostrils, and chokes the nose and mouth to such a degree, that it requires great power of lungs to resist it and the strong effluvia of the mummies. This is not all: the entry or passage where the bodies are is roughly cut in the rocks, and the falling of the sand from the upper part or ceiling of the passage causes it to be nearly filled up. In some places there is not more than the vacancy of a foot left, which you must contrive to pass through in a creeping posture like a snail, on pointed and keen stones, that cut like glass. After getting through these passages, some of them two or three hundred yards long, you generally find a more commodious place, perhaps high enough to sit. But what a place of rest! Surrounded by bodies, by heaps of mummies in all directions; which, previous to my being accustomed to the sight, impressed me with horror. The blackness of the wall, the faint light given by the candles or torches for want of air, the different objects that surrounded me, seeming to converse with each other, and the Arabs with the candles or torches in their hands, naked and covered with dust, themselves resembling living mummies, absolutely formed a scene that cannot be described. In such a situation I found myself several times, and often returned exhausted and fainting, till at last I became inured to it, and indifferent to what I suffered, except from the dust, which never failed to choke my throat and nose; and though fortunately I am destitute of the sense of smelling, I could taste that the mummies were rather unpleasant to swallow. After the exertion of entering into such a place, through a passage of fifty, a hundred, three hundred, or perhaps six hundred yards, nearly overcome, I sought a resting place, found one, and contrived to sit; but when my weight bore on the body of an Egyptian, it crushed it like a bandbox. I naturally had recourse to my hands to sustain my weight, but they found no better support; so that I sunk altogether among the broken mummies, with a crash of bones, rags, and wooden cases, which raised such a dust as kept me motionless for a quarter of an hour, waiting till it subsided again. I could not remove from the place, however, without increasing it, and every step I took I crushed a mummy in some part or other. Once I was conducted from such a place to another resembling it, through a passage of about twenty feet in length, and no wider than that a body could be forced through. It was choked with mummies, and I could not pass without putting my face in contact with that of some decayed Egyptian; but as the passage inclined downwards, my own weight helped me on; however, I could not avoid being covered with bones, legs, arms and heads rolling from above. Thus I proceeded from one cave to another, all full of mummies piled up in various ways, some standing, some lying, and some on their heads. The purpose of my researches was to rob the Egyptians of their papyri; of which I found a few hidden in their breasts, under their arms, in the space above the knees, or on the legs, and covered by the numerous folds of cloth, that envelop the mummy. The people of Gournow, who made a trade of antiquities of this sort, are very jealous of strangers, and keep them as secret as possible, deceiving the travellers by pretending, that they have arrived at the end of the pits, when they are scarcely at the entrance. I could never prevail on them to conduct me into these places till my second voyage, when I succeeded in obtaining admission into any cave where mummies were to be seen.

159

My permanent residence in Thebes was the cause of my success. The Arabs saw that I paid particular attention to the situation of the entrance into the tombs, and that they could not avoid being seen by me when they were at work digging in search of a new tomb, though they are very cautious when any stranger is in Gournow not to let it be known where they go to open the earth; and as travellers generally remain in that place a few days only, they used to leave off digging during that time. If any traveller be curious enough to ask to examine the interior of a tomb, they are ready to show him one immediately, and conduct him to some of the old tombs, where he sees nothing but the grottoes in which mummies formerly had been deposited, or where there are but few, and these already plundered; so that he can form but a poor idea of the real tombs, where the remains were originally placed.

The people of Gournow live in the entrance of such caves as have already been opened, and by making partitions with earthen walls, they form habitations for themselves, as well as for their cows, camels, buffaloes, sheep, goats, dogs, etc. I do not know whether it is because they are so few in number, that the Government takes so little notice of what they do; but it is certain that they are the most unruly people in Egypt. At various times many of them have been destroyed, so that they are reduced from three thousand, the number they formerly reckoned, to three hundred, which form the population of the present day. They have no mosque, nor do they care for one; for though they have at their disposal a great quantity of all sorts of bricks, which abound in every part of Gournow, from the surrounding tombs, they have never built a single house. They are forced to cultivate a small tract of land, extending from the rocks to the Nile, about a mile in breadth, and two and a half in length; and even this is in part neglected; for if left to their own will, they would never take a spade in their hands, except when they go to dig for mummies; which they find to be more profitable employment than agriculture. This is the fault of travellers, who are so pleased the moment they are presented with any piece of antiquity, that, without thinking of the injury resulting from the example to their successors, they give a great deal more than the people really expect. Hence it has arisen, that they now set such an enormous price on antiquities, and in particular on papyri. Some of them have accumulated a considerable sum of money, and are become so indifferent, that they remain idle, unless whatever price they demand to be given them; and it is to be observed, that it is a fixed point in their minds, that the Franks would not be so liberal, unless the articles were worth ten times as

Khnum-hotep This mummy pre-dates the period when the Egyptians began to make coffins in the shape of the human body. Khnum-hotep has, however, a gilded funerary mask covering his face.

much as they pay for them. . . .

After having described the tombs, the mummies, the rocks and the rogues of Gournow, it is time to cross the Nile and return to Carnak. . . . My daily employment kept me in continual motion. In the morning I used to give my directions for the works at Carnak. The Arabs generally come to work at the rising of the sun, and leave off from noon till two or three o'clock. When I had many employed, I divided them into parties, and set an overseer over each, to see that they worked at the proper hours, and on the allotted spots of ground, which I had previously marked out; but generally some of our people were obliged to be there, for no trust is to be reposed in the Arabs, if they should find any small pieces of antiquity. Before noon I used to cross the river and inspect the works at Gournow. Having been there the year before, and had dealings with these people, I was at home in every part of Thebes, knew every Arab there, and they knew me as well. Mr. Beechy had taken possession of the temple at Luxor, without requesting permission from the gods, and we made a dwelling place of one of the chambers: I believe it must have been the *sekos*. By the help of some mats we procured a very tolerable accommodation, but could not prevent the dust from coming on our beds, and clothes to which for my part I had long before become indifferent. We could not sleep any longer in the boat; for in consequence of the provision we had on board, such quantities of large rats accompanied us all the way to Luxor, that we had no peace day or night, and at last they succeeded in fairly dislodging us. We thought to have been a match for them, however, for we caused all the provision to be taken out, and the boat to be sunk at Luxor, but as they were good swimmers, they saved their lives, and hid themselves in the holes of the pier; and when the provision had been put on board again, they all returned cheerfully, a few excepted, and were no doubt grateful to us for having given them a fresh appetite and a good bathing.

In Gournow our researches continued among the mummies. The Arabs had become quite unconcerned about the secret of the tombs; for they saw it was their interest to search, as they were rewarded for what they found, and those who were duly paid were indifferent whether we or their brethren found a tomb. The men were divided into two classes. The most knowing were making researches on their own account, employing eight or ten to assist them. They indicated the ground where they hoped to find a tomb, and sometimes were fortunate enough to hit on the entrance of a mummy pit in the first attempt. At other times after spending two or three days, they often found only a pit filled with mummies of the inferior class, which had nothing among them worthy of notice: so that, even to the most skilful explorer, it was a mere chance what he should find. On the other hand, in some of the tombs of the better class they found very good specimens of antiquity, of all sorts. I met with some difficulty at first in persuading these people to work in search of tombs, and receive a regular daily payment; for they conceived it to be against their interest, supposing I might obtain the antiquities at too cheap a rate: but when they saw, that sometimes they received their pay regularly, and I had nothing for it, they found it was rather in their favour, to secure twenty paras (three pence) a day, than run the risk of having nothing for their labour, which often happened with those who worked at adventure.

It was from these works that I became better acquainted with the manner in which the Egyptians regulated their burial places; and I plainly saw the various degrees and customs of the divers classes, from the peasant to the king. The Egyptians had three different methods of embalming their dead bodies, which, Herodotus informs us, were according to the expense the persons who presented the dead bodies to the mummy-makers chose to incur. This father of history thus expresses himself on the subject:

Certain persons were appointed by the laws to the exercise of this profession. When a dead boy was brought to them, they exhibited to the friends of the deceased different models, highly finished in wood. The most perfect of these, they said, resembles one, whom I do not think it religious to name on such an occasion; the second was of less price, and inferior in point of execution; the other was still more mean. They then inquired after which model the deceased should be represented. When the price was determined, the relations retired, and the embalmers proceeded in their work. In the most perfect specimens of their art, they extracted the brain through the nostrils, partly with a piece of crooked iron, and partly by the infusion of drugs. They then, with an Ethiopian stone, made an incision in the side, through which they drew out the intestines. These they cleaned thoroughly, washing them in palm-wine, and afterwards covering them with pounded aromatics. They then filled the body with powder of pure myrrh, cassia, and other spices, without frankincense. Having sewn up the body, it was covered with nitre for the space of seventy days, which time they were not allowed to exceed. At the end of this period, being first washed, it was closely wrapped in bandages of cotton, dipped in gum, which the Egyptians use as a glue. It was then returned to the relations, who enclosed the body in a case of wood, made to resemble a human figure, and placed it against the wall in the repository of their dead. This was the most costly mode of embalming.

For those who wished to be at less expense, the following method was adopted. They neither drew out the intestines, nor made any incision in the dead body, but injected a liniment made from the cedar. After taking proper means to secure the injected oil within the body, it was covered with nitre for the time above specified. On the last day they withdrew the liquid before introduced, which brought with it all the intestines. The nitre dried up and hardened the flesh, so that the corpse appeared little but skin and bone. In this state the body was returned, and no further care taken concerning it.

There was a third mode of embalming, appropriated to the poor. A particular kind of lotion was made to pass through the body, which was afterwards merely left in nitre for the above space of seventy days and then returned.

Such is the account given us by Herodotus.

Nothing can more plainly distinguish the various classes of people, than the manner of their preservation: but there are many other remarks that may be made to the same effect. I shall describe how I found the mummies of the principal class untouched, and hence we may judge how they were prepared and deposited in their respective places. I am sorry that I am obliged to contradict my old guide, Herodotus; for in this point, and many others, he was not well informed by the Egyptians. In the first place, speaking of the mummies in their cases, he mentions them as erect: but it is somewhat singular, that in so many pits as I have opened, I never saw a single mummy standing. On the contrary, I found them lying regularly, in horizontal rows, and some were sunk into a cement, which must have been nearly fluid when the cases were placed on it. The lower classes were not buried in cases: they were dried up, as it appears, after the regular preparation of the seventy days. Mummies of this sort were in the proportion of about ten to one of the better class, as near as I could calculate by the quantity I have seen of both; and it appeared to me, that, after the operation of the nitre, adopted by the mummy-makers, these bodies may have been dried in the sun. Indeed for my own part, I am persuaded it was so; as there is not the smallest quantity of gum or anything else to be found on them. The linen in which they are folded is of a coarser sort, and less in quantity; they have no ornaments about them of any consequence, and they are piled up in layers so as to crowd several caves excavated for the purpose in a rude manner. In general these tombs are to be found in the lower grounds, at the foot of the mountains of Gournow; and some extend as far as the border to which the inundation reaches. They are to be entered by a small aperture, arched over, or by a shaft four or five feet square, at the bottom

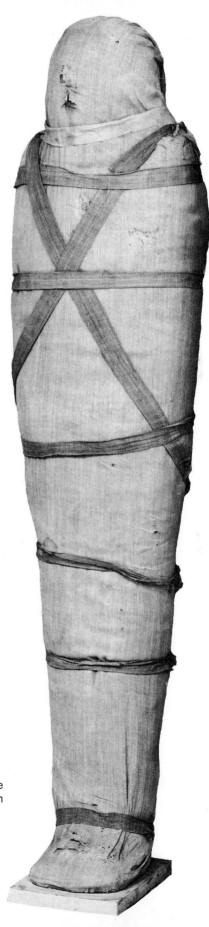

Kharu-shery This mummy of the XXII-XXIII Dynasty derives from Sheik Abd El Kurna, Thebes.

of which are entrances into various chambers, all choked up with mummies: and though there is scarcely anything to be found on them, many of these tombs have been rummaged, and left in the most confused state.

I must not omit that among these tombs we saw some which contained the mummies of animals intermixed with human bodies. There were bulls, cows, sheep, monkeys, foxes, bats, crocodiles, fishes, and birds in them; idols often occur; and one tomb was filled with nothing but cats, carefully folded in red and white linen, the head covered by a mask representing the cat, and made of the same linen. I have opened all these sorts of animals. Of the bull, the calf, and the sheep there is no part but the head which is covered with linen, and the horns projecting out of the cloth; the rest of the body being represented by two pieces of wood, eighteen inches wide and three feet long, in an horizontal direction, at the end of which was another, placed perpendicularly, two feet high, to form the breast of the animal. The calves and sheep are of the same structure, and large in proportion to the bulls. The monkey is in its full form, in a sitting posture. The fox is squeezed up by the bandages, but in some measure the shape of the head is kept perfect. The crocodile is left in its own shape, and after being well bound round with linen, the eyes and mouth are painted on this covering. The birds are squeezed together, and lose their shape, except the ibis, which is found like a fowl ready to be cooked, and bound round with linen like all the rest.

It is somewhat singular that such animals are not to be met within the tombs of the higher sort of people; while few or no papyri are to be found among the lower order, and if any occur they are only small pieces stuck upon the breast with a little gum or asphaltum, being probably all that the poor individual could afford to himself. In those of the better classes other objects are found. I think they ought to be divided into several classes, as I cannot confine myself to three. I do not mean to impute error to Herodotus when he speaks of the three modes of embalming; but I will venture to assert that the high, middling and poorer classes, all admit of farther distinction. In the same pit where I found mummies in cases, I found others without; and in these, papyri are most likely to be met with. I remarked, that the mummies in the cases have no papyri; at least I never observed any: on the contrary, in those without cases they are often obtained. It appears to me that such people as could afford it would have a case to be buried in, on which the history of their lives was painted; and those who could not afford a case, were contented to have their lives written on papyri, rolled up and placed above their knees. Even in the appearance of the cases there is a great difference: some are exceedingly plain, others more ornamented, and some very richly adorned with figures well painted. The cases are generally made of Egyptian sycamore: apparently this was the most plentiful wood in the country, as it is usually employed for the different utensils. All the cases have a human face, male or female. Some of the large cases contain others within them, either of wood or of plaster, painted. The inner cases are sometimes fitted to the body of the mummy: others are only covers to the body, in form of a man or woman, easily distinguishable by the beard and the breast, like that on the outside. Some of the mummies have garlands of flowers, and leaves of the acacia, or stunt tree, over their heads and breasts. This tree is often seen on the banks of the Nile, above Thebes, and particularly in Nubia. The flower when fresh is yellow, and of a very hard substance, appearing as if artificial. The leaves also are very strong, and though dried and turned brown, they still retain their firmness. In the inside of these mummies are found lumps of asphaltum, sometimes so large as to weigh two pounds. The entrails of these mummies are often found bound up in linen and asphaltum. What does not incorporate with the fleshy part, remains of the natural colour of the pitch; but that which does incorporate becomes brown, and evidently mixed with the grease of the body, forming a mass, which on pressure crumbles into dust. The wooden case is first covered with a layer or two of cement, not unlike plaster of Paris; and on this are sometimes cast figures in *basso rilievo*, for which they make niches cut in stone. The whole case is painted; the ground generally yellow, the figures and hieroglyphics blue, green, red and black. The last is very seldom used. The whole of the painting is covered with a varnish, which preserves it very effectually. Some of the colours, in my humble opinion, were vegetable, for they are evidently transparent; besides, I conceive it was easier for the Egyptians to produce vegetable colours than mineral, from the great difficulty of grinding the latter to such perfection.

The next sort of mummy that drew my attention, I believe I may with reason conclude to have been appropriate to the priests. They are folded in a manner totally different from the others, and so carefully executed as to show the great respect paid to those personages. The bandages are strips of red and white linen intermixed, covering the whole body and forming a curious effect from the two colours. The arms and legs are not enclosed in the same envelope with the body, as in the common mode, but are bandaged separately, even the fingers and toes being preserved distinct. They have sandals of painted leather on their feet, and bracelets on their arms and wrists. They are always found with their arms across the breast, but not pressing it; and though the body is bound with such a quantity of linen, the shape of the person is carefully preserved in every limb. The cases in which mummies of this sort are found are somewhat better executed, and I have seen one, that had the eyes and eyebrows of enamel, beautifully executed in imitation of nature. . . .

The tombs containing the better classes of people are of course superior to the others. There are some more extensive than the rest, having various apartments, adorned with figures representing different actions of life. Funeral processions are generally predominant. Agricultural processes, religious ceremonies, and more ordinary occurrences such as feasting, etc. are to be seen everywhere. . . . It would be impossible to describe the numerous little articles found in them, which are well adapted to show the domestic habits of the ancient Egyptians. It is here the smaller idols are occasionally found, either lying on the ground, or in the cases of the mummies. Vases are sometimes found containing the embalmed entrails of the mummies. These are generally made of baked clay, and painted over; their sizes differ from eight inches to eighteen; their covers represent the head of some divinity, bearing either the human form, or that of a monkey, fox, cat, or some other animal. I met with a few of these vases of alabaster in the Tombs of the Kings, but unfortunately they were broken. A great quantity of pottery is found, and also wooden vessels in some of the tombs as if the deceased had resolved to have all he possessed deposited along with him. The most singular among these things are the ornaments, in particular the small works in clay and other composition. I have been fortunate to find many specimens of their manufactures, among which is leaf gold, beaten nearly as thin as ours. The gold appears to me extremely pure and of a finer colour than is generally seen in our own. . . .

THE WINGED LIONS OF NIMRUD

A British lawyer and statesman, Austen Layard, became fascinated with the history of ancient Assyria. From 1845 to 1847 he conducted excavations of Assyrian cities, leaving vivid records of his pioneer work. Not only did he discover the treasures contained in Assyrian mounds, but he also worked with Arab tribesmen who still lived and fought with all the gusto of their age-old customs.

In the following extract Layard tells how he brought two huge human-headed animals from the Palace at Nimrud back to England. These great creatures guarded the entrance to one of the principal apartments of the palace of Ashur-nasir-pal II, completed in 879 B.C.

Excerpted from NINEVEH AND BABYLON, *(John Murray, 1853) written by*

SIR AUSTEN LAYARD

THE gigantic human-headed lions, first discovered in the north-west palace at Nimrud, were still standing in their original position. Having been carefully covered up with earth previous to my departure in 1848, they had been preserved from exposure to the effects of the weather, and to wanton injury on the part of the Arabs. The Trustees of the British Museum wishing to add these fine sculptures to the national collection, I was directed to remove them entire. A road through the ruins, for their transport to the edge of the mound, was in the first place necessary, and it was commenced early in December. They would thus be ready for embarkation as soon as the waters of the river were sufficiently high to bear a raft so heavily laden, over the rapids and shallows between Nimrud and Baghdad. This road was dug to the level of the pavement or artificial platform, and was not finished till the end of February, as a large mass of earth and rubbish had to be taken away to the depth of fifteen or twenty feet. . . .

By 28th. January, the colossal lions forming the portal to the great hall in the north-west palace of Nimrud were ready to be dragged to the river-bank. The walls and their sculptured panelling had been removed from both sides of them, and they stood isolated in the midst of the ruins. We rode one calm cloudless night to the mound, to look on them for the last time before they were taken from their old resting-places. The moon was at her full, and as we drew nigh to the edge of the deep wall of earth rising around them, her soft light was creeping over the stern features of the human heads, and driving before it the dark shadows which still clothed the lion forms. One by one the limbs of the gigantic sphinxes emerged from the gloom, until the monsters were unveiled before us. I shall never forget that night, or the emotions which those venerable figures caused within me. A few hours more and they were to stand no longer where they had stood unscathed amidst the wreck of man and his works for ages. It seemed almost sacrilege to tear them from their old haunts to make them a mere wonder-stock to the busy crowd of a new world. They were better suited to the desolation around them; for they had guarded the palace in its glory, and it was for them to watch over it in its ruin. Sheikh Abd-ur-Rahman, who had ridden with us to the mound, was troubled with no such reflections. He gazed listlessly at the grim images, wondered at the folly of the Franks, thought the night cold, and turned his mare towards his tents. We scarcely heeded his going, but stood speechless in the deserted portal until the shadows again began to creep over its hoary guardians.

Beyond the ruined palaces a scene scarcely less solemn awaited us. I had sent a party of Jebours to the bitumen springs, outside the walls to the east of the enclosure. The Arabs, having lighted a small fire with brushwood, awaited our coming to throw the burning sticks upon the pitchy pools. A thick heavy smoke, such as rose from the jar on the seashore when the fisherman had broken the seal of Solomon, rolled upwards in curling volumes, hiding the light of the moon, and spreading wide over the sky. Tongues of flame and jets of gas, driven from the burning pit, shot through the murky canopy. As the fire brightened, a thousand fantastic forms of light played amidst the smoke. To break the cindered crust, and to bring fresh slime to the surface, the Arabs threw large stones into the springs; a new volume of fire then burst forth, throwing a deep red glare upon the figures and upon the landscape. The Jebours danced round the burning pools, like demons in some midnight orgy, shouting their war-cry, and brandishing

Winged Lion One of the two Winged Lions which guarded the Palace of Ashur-nasir-pal II (885-860 B.C.) at Nimrud. The pair was removed from their original positions over one hundred years ago by Sir Austen Layard. This statue is now in the British Museum in London. The other is exhibited in the Metropolitan Museum of Art, New York City.

A WINGED MAN-HEADED LION FROM A DOORWAY IN THE PALACE OF ASSUR-NASIR-PAL, KING OF ASSYRIA, B.C. 885-860.
EXCAVATED BY SIR H. LAYARD, 1847

their glittering arms. In an hour the bitumen was exhausted for the time, the dense smoke gradually died away, and the pale light of the moon again shone over the black slime pits.

The colossal lions were moved by still simpler and ruder means than those adopted on my first expedition. They were tilted over upon loose earth heaped behind them, their too rapid descent being checked by a hawser, which was afterwards replaced by props of wood and stone. They were then lowered, by levers and jackscrews, upon the cart brought under them. A road paved with flat stones had been made to the edge of the mound, and the sculpture was, without difficulty, dragged from the trenches.

Beneath the lions, embedded in earth and bitumen, were a few bones, which, on exposure to the air, fell to dust before I could ascertain whether they were human or not. The sculptures rested simply upon the platform of sun-dried bricks without any other sub-structure, a mere layer of bitumen, about an inch thick, having been placed under the plinth.

Owing to recent heavy rains, which had left in many places deep swamps, we experienced much difficulty in dragging the cart over the plain to the riverside. Three days were spent in transporting each lion. The men of Naifa and Nimrud again came to our help, and the Abou-Salman horsemen, with Sheikh Abd-ur-Rahman at their head, encouraged us by their presence. The unwieldy mass was propelled from behind by enormous levers of poplar wood; and in the costumes of those who worked, as well as in the means adopted to move the colossal sculptures, except that we used a wheeled cart instead of a sledge, the procession closely resembled that which in days of yore transported the same great figures, and which we see so graphically represented on the walls of Kouyunjik. As they had been brought so were they taken away.

It was necessary to humour and excite the Arabs to induce them to persevere in the arduous work of dragging the cart through the deep soft soil into which it continually sank. At one time, after many vain efforts to move the buried wheels, it was unanimously declared that Mr. Cooper, the artist, brought ill luck, and no one would work until he retired. The cumbrous machine crept onwards for a few more yards, but again all exertions were fruitless. Then the Frank lady would bring good fortune if she sat on the sculpture. The wheels rolled heavily along, but were soon clogged once more in the yielding soil. An evil eye surely lurked among the workmen or the bystanders. Search was quickly made, and one having been detected upon whom this curse had alighted, he was ignominiously driven away with shouts and execrations. This impediment having been removed, the cart drew nearer to the village, but soon again came to a standstill. All the Sheikhs were now summarily degraded from their rank and honours, and a weak ragged boy having been dressed up in tawdry kerchiefs, and invested with a cloak, was pronounced by Hormuzd to be the only fit chief for such puny men. The cart moved forwards, until the ropes gave way, under the new excitement caused by this reflection upon the character of the Arabs. When that had subsided, and the presence of the youthful Sheikh no longer encouraged his subjects, he was as summarily deposed as he had been elected, and a greybeard of ninety was raised to the dignity in his stead. He had his turn; then the most unpopular of the Sheikhs were compelled to lie down on the ground, that the groaning wheels might pass over them, like the car of Juggernaut over its votaries. With yells, shrieks, and wild antics the cart was drawn within a few inches of the prostrate men. As a last resource I seized a rope myself, and with shouts of defiance between the different tribes, who were divided into separate parties and pulled against each other, and amidst the deafening *tahlel* of the women, the lion was at length fairly brought to the water's edge.

The winter rains had not yet swelled the waters of the river so as to enable a raft bearing a very heavy cargo to float with safety to Baghdad. It was not until the month of April, after I had left Mosul on my journey to the Khabour, that the floods, from the melting of the snows in the higher mountains of Kurdistan, swept down the valley of the Tigris. I was consequently obliged to confide the task of embarking the sculptures to Behnan, my principal overseer, a Mosuleean stonecutter of considerable skill and experience, Mr. Vice-consul Rassam kindly undertaking to superintend the operation. Owing to extraordinary storms in the hills, the river rose suddenly and with unexampled rapidity. Mr. and Mrs. Rassam were at the time at Nimrud, and the raftsmen had prepared the rafts to receive the lions. It was with difficulty that they escaped before the flood, from my house in the village to the top of the ruins. The Jaif was one vast sea, and a furious wind drove the waves against the foot of the mound. The Arabs had never seen a similar inundation, and before they could escape to the high land many persons were overwhelmed in the waters.

When the flood had subsided, the lions on the river bank, though covered with mud and silt, were found uninjured. They were speedily placed on the rafts prepared for them, but unfortunately during the operation one of them, which had previously been cracked nearly across, separated into two parts. Both sculptures were doomed to misfortune. Some person, uncovering the other during the night, broke the nose. I was unable to discover the author of this wanton mischief. He was probably a stranger, who had some feud with the Arabs working in the excavations.*

The rafts reached Baghdad in safety. After receiving the necessary repairs they floated onwards to Busrah. The waters of the Tigris throughout its course had risen far above their usual level. The embankments, long neglected by the Turkish government, had given way, and the river, bursting from its bed, spread itself over the surrounding country in vast lakes and marshes. One of the rafts was dragged into a vortex which swept through a sluice newly opened in the crumbling bank. Notwithstanding the exertions of the raftsmen, aided by the crew of a boat that accompanied them, it was carried far into the interior, and left in the middle of a swamp, about a mile from the stream. The other raft fortunately escaped, and reached Baghdad without accident.

For some time the stranded raft was given up for lost. Fortunately it bore the broken lion, or its recovery had probably been impossible. Captain Jones, with his usual skill and intrepidity, took his steamer over the ruined embankment, and into the unexplored morass. After great exertion, under a burning sun in the midst of summer, he succeeded in placing the two parts of the sculpture on large boats provided for the purpose, and in conveying them to their destination.*

* Both sculptures have, however, been completely restored in the British Museum.

* These accidents, and even still more the carelessness afterwards shown in bringing them to this country, have much injured these fine specimens of Assyrian sculpture, which now stand in a great hall of the British Museum.

CHICHEN ITZA: WELL OF SACRIFICE

In Mexico, in north central Yucatan, stand the remains of one of the greatest of America's ancient cities—Chichen Itza. Its life was a long one, perhaps the longest of any of the cities of the New World. Founded about the eighth century A.D. by the Maya, Chichen Itza led a checkered life until it was finally destroyed in 1451. Then the city became a religious center for pilgrims, and its Sacred Well was used for offerings of treasure to the gods and for human sacrifices.

At the beginning of the 16th century, the Spaniards conquered Yucatan. But even at that date, although the power of Chichen Itza as a town had vanished, the Sacred Well drew pilgrims from far and wide. In the waters of the Well, or Cenote as it is called, the gifts to the gods lay hidden for more than 300 years until archaeologists dredged the place and recovered much of the treasure and the sacrificial bones.

Alfred M. Tozzer was a leader in the field of Middle American studies. The following is his fascinating account of the rituals of the Sacred Well.

Excerpted from CHICHEN ITZA AND ITS CENOTE OF SACRIFICE,
Memoirs of the Peabody Museum of Archaeology and Ethnology,
(Harvard University, Vols. XI and XII, 1957) written by

A. M. TOZZER

WE do not know the actual date when Bishop Landa was at Chichen Itza. He arrived in Yucatan in 1549 and remained here until 1563. It was during this first period of residence that he was at Chichen. He went back to Spain for ten years before he returned as Bishop. Six years later (1579) he died in Merida. . . .

Of Chichen Itza he writes: 'At some distance in front of the staircase on the north [side of the Castillo], there were two small stages of hewn stone, [each] with four staircases, paved on the top, where they say that farces were represented, and comedies for the pleasure of the public.' These two structures are now known respectively, as the Tomb of the Chac Mool or the Temple of the Eagles, and the Temple of the Cones, the latter standing almost in the very centre of the court.

The third structure in the court, near and north of the Chac Mool tomb, is called Mausoleum II or Temple of the Skulls. . . .

'From the court in front of these stages,' observes Landa, 'a wide and handsome causeway runs, as far as a well which is

Sacrificial Well   The huge well at Chichen Itza into which human sacrifices were thrown to appease the gods.

about two stones' throw off.' This road, which starts about 300 feet north of the Temple of the Cones, is built on a rubble foundation and is paved; it is about 33 feet wide and is raised slightly above ground level. The road runs for about 900 feet to the south side of the small structure which stands on the very brink of the well. At the north end on the east side is a paved platform from which the victims of sacrifice are supposed to have been hurled. . . .

This sacred well is about 168 feet in north-south diameter, over 200 feet east-west. . . . The walls are practically vertical except on the south side. Unlike the grand cenote or Xtoloc Cenote which is south of the Castillo and from which the natives obtained their water, there is no path or other means of reaching the water. The water level in the well evidently fluctuates; it has been reported anywhere from 60 to 80 feet below the rim. The greatest depth of water lies near the centre and averages about 36 feet; this decreases gradually toward the sides. Between 30 and 60 feet of accumulated detritus, mud, and blue silt rest on the uneven bottom of the well. Landa writes of 'the very green water and I think that the groves with which it is surrounded cause this'. . . .

On the south side of the pool the wall overhangs 14 feet measured from the surface of the water. From about 70 feet along the east side the upper portion of the wall projects in a great shelf-like edge about 20 feet above the water. The walls are made up of projecting ledges, due to the varying degrees of hardness of the strata. There is a slightly northward dip of the rock. On the west side a narrow beach has formed upon a ledge, almost level with the water. On this grow a number of native cork trees. . . .

The appearance of the Sacred Cenote in 1904 is well described in the field notes of Cole (1910), who was good enough to place them at my disposal. He writes:

> The impression, as one comes suddenly upon these deep 'wells' in the middle of a dense forest, is a memorable one. They look like circular quarries, 150 feet or so in diameter. The sides are practically vertical, sometimes overhanging, with the trees hanging out over the space at the top and a few here and there where they can find a hold on the walls. In the bottom is water, which has a brownish green appearance apparently on account of organisms in it. . . . The walls are weathered unevenly, leaving holes of greater or less size in which live iguanas, and other lizards may often be seen clambering about over the rocky sides. . . .

We come next to the Maya and early Spanish accounts of the ritual practised at the Cenote. Unlike most archæological sites in the New World, Chichen has a relatively abundant literature, without which we would have little information on the ceremonial side of the life of the people other than that offered by the specimens recovered from the well. Accounts of the Cenote as a place of sacrifice date, with two exceptions, from the days during or immediately following the Spanish conquest (from about 1536 to 1588); most of them indicate that the ritual at the Cenote still flourished when the descriptions were written. . . .

The earliest Spanish references to the Sacred Cenote at Chichen Itza are to an attempted native pilgrimage (1536) to supplicate the rain gods in a time of drought. This ended in a holocaust. . . .

Landa was perhaps the most dramatic and the most important single figure connected with the early Spanish history of Yucatan. He was called the *historiador primordial* of this country. He was born 'of noble parents' in Cifuentes, Toledo, in 1524. At the age of sixteen he joined the Franciscan Order in his native town and was one of the first friars brought to Yucatan by Nicolas de Albalate, the Procurador, in 1549. At once his zeal was recognized and he held a long succession of offices in the Church, ending, after many vicissitudes, as Bishop. His work and methods of christianization have been variously estimated. He has been regarded 'as a saint and an odious persecutor', as an impetuous and ardent servant of the Lord who won approbation of the multitudes, and as a cruel zealot. He has been described as dying 'in the odour of sanctity . . . and he is stigmatized as a fanatical, extravagant and cruel man'. In some respects both extremes seem to be true. The *auto da fé* held by him at Mani in 1562 brought down upon his head the denunciation of Bishop Torao, and Landa was forced to return to Spain for examination where he was finally exonerated. It was while he was there that he probably wrote his famous *Relación de las Cosas de Yucatan* (1566). . . .

Probably the most important information conveyed by the Bishop are various entries regarding the Cenote of Sacrifice. One of these concerns the vain attempt of the Xiu to make a pilgrimage to the well. Three other entries are given here. . . .

We will tell about the well into which they threw living men in sacrifice, as well as other beautiful things. . . .

Sometimes they threw living victims into the well of Chichen Itza, believing that they would come out on the third day, although they never appeared again. . . .

Into this well, they have had, and then had, the custom of throwing men alive as a sacrifice to the gods, in times of drought, and they believed that they did not die though they never saw them

View of Chichen Itza

again. They also threw into it a great many other things, like precious stones and things which they prized. And so if this country had possessed gold, it would be this well that would have the greater part of it, so great was the devotion which the Indians showed for it.

Next in importance to Landa's references is the account of the ritual at the Cenote of Sacrifice given in the *Relación de Valladolid*:

In this Cenote the lords and important men of all these provinces of Valladolid were accustomed to fast for sixty days without raising their eyes in this time even to look upon their wives nor upon those who brought them food, and this they did as a preliminary to, upon reaching the mouth of that Cenote, throwing into it at break of dawn some Indian women belonging to each of those lords, whom they had told to ask for a good year and all those things which seemed best to them [the lords]. And thus these Indian women having been thrown in without being bound, but flung down as from a cliff, they fell into the water striking it with great force. And at exactly midday the one who was to come out shouted for them to throw her a rope to take her out, and when she came up above half-dead, they made great fires around her, censing her with copal. And when she came to, she said that there were many of their race below, men as well as women, who received her, and that when she raised her head to look at some one of them, they gave her severe blows on the neck so that she would keep her head bowed down, all of which occurred within the water in which they say there were many hollows and holes. And they replied to her whether they would have a good or bad year according to the questions which the Indian woman put. And if the demon was angry with one of the lords of those who threw in the Indian women, they already knew that [her] not asking to be taken out on the point of noon was because he was angry with them, and such a one never came out. This seems a likeness to what happened in the cave of Salamanca. Then, having seen that she did not emerge, all the Lord's people and he himself threw large stones into the water and with a great hue and cry took flight from there.

Thomas Lopez Medel (1612) was a Franciscan, auditor and judge of the Audiencia of Guatemala and the Confines and, later, one of the judges to sit at the trial of Landa. He finally absolved Landa in regard to the inquisition inaugurated by him. His *Ordinances* were probably written about 1552; the *Relación* is dated 1612. The latter furnishes material on the victims offered at the well and discusses the sacrifice both for rain and for divination. His account of the ritual follows:

Among other sacrifices which the devil had taught them in those provinces of Yucatan was one of which they made use in time of necessity, and when they were in need of rain for their maize, which sacrifice they made with the death and offering of one or two Indian virgins (*doncellas*) or the number they wished. In this way they chose the virgin as seemed best to them and they took her to Chichen Itza, where the lodging of all the lords was and where the priests were and the principal *cu* and place of sacrifice, and from there they all went in procession with her by a paved causeway, all of slabs, which came to an end at a large and deep Cenote which was there. . . . And they placed her in a shrine which was near there, where the priests withdrew with her. And they instructed her and informed her concerning what she was to ask there from their demons and false gods. And they brought her forth from there, and having tied her with a long rope, they lowered her down to the depth of the water, ducking her many times until they drowned her, all the people charging her and asking her when they threw her in to be a good mediator with their false gods in order that they might send them rain. And in this manner the sacrifice was completed,

Chichen Itza   This heavily sculptured wall is on the west side of one of the buildings in the ruins of Chichen Itza.

leaving her drowned in the Cenote. Some old Indians of that province affirmed that they sometimes saw in these sacrifices a fierce and frightful dragon, which they represented as a large crocodile, which came out upon those waters as if to receive that sacrifice which they sent him there. And, certainly, considering the nature of the place, nothing else can be thought except that that was some demon, because a crocodile or dragon could not live there, the nature of the water opposing it; nor has such a thing been seen in any of the other Cenotes, nor do I believe it possible there. . . .

The *Relación* of Landa gave the impetus for two attempts to dredge the famous well, for he observed: 'They also threw into it a great many other things, like precious stones and things which they prized. And so if this country has possessed gold it would be in this well.' The hope of verifying the Bishop's words was uppermost in the minds of those who planned the dredging of the well, along with the lure of finding some of those 'things' which the Maya 'prized'.

Landa's account of the Cenote of Sacrifice, written about 1566 but first published in 1864, failed to arouse any of the early explorers to action until 1882, when Désiré Charnay visited Chichen. Of his unsuccessful attempt to dredge the sacred well he writes, 'Aware of the treasures the cenote might contain, I had provided myself with two automatic Toselli sounding-machines, one of which is capable of bringing up half a cubic metre of deposit; but unfortunately I could not get it to work, owing to the height of the walls, the depth of the water, and the enormous detritus of several centuries.'

A second attempt, this time successful, was made to dredge the well by Edward H. Thompson, resident of Yucatan from 1885 to 1923. In 1894 he acquired the hacienda of Chichen Itza, a property previously owned by the historian Crescencio Carrillo y Ancona, Delia Morena Canton, Emilio Garcia Fajardo and Leopoldo Canton Frexes. . . .

Thompson's most important and spectacular work was the dredging of the Sacred Cenote at Chichen. Stephen Salisbury of Worcester and Charles P. Bowditch of Boston were the main instigators and most generous supporters of Thompson's work, which was done almost exclusively under the private direction of Mr. Bowditch and of Professor F. W. Putnam, then Director of the Peabody Museum. With two exceptions, the result of all Thompson's explorations and excavations, consisting of objects, photographs, moulds, and other data, were presented to the Peabody Museum by Bowditch, and the greater part of his publications were brought out by the Museum.

After numerous negotiations and delays in obtaining the

necessary machinery, dredging began on 5 March 1904. The first campaign ended on 1 July 1907. Between these two dates the work was by no means continuous. . . .

Leon J. Cole, then a graduate student in biology at Harvard University, was present at the beginning of the operations. His notes, kindly made available by him, state:

On 26 February 1904, the road was cleared to the Cenote and a rope ladder was made for getting down to the level of the water, where a platform was built, and a raft was constructed and launched from the small beach on the west side of the pool.

Just east of the ruined structure on the southern edge of the well, a place was cleared of debris and a stiff-legged derrick erected, having a twenty-foot upright and a boom, thirty feet in length. This was operated by a double-handed winch, two or four men working it. The dredge was a Harwood orange-peel bucket of a capacity of two and a half cubic feet. Around the perimeter of the pool a series of numbered stations was established and a divided arc at the foot of the derrick corresponded to these stations. Dredging was first started in the radius allowed by the thirty-foot boom. To reach outside of this sector, a rope was attached to the top of the dredge, and this ran around a pulley in one of the numbered stations on the perimeter of the pool on the opposite side of the Cenote, and ended at the base of operations. By using this rope the dredge could be pulled to any place between the home station and that opposite. By changing the position of the pulley the dredging could theoretically reach anywhere within the well. As a matter of fact, Thompson argued that all the various offerings were probably thrown into the pool from the place where the derrick was erected, to the east of the 'shrine'.

One of Cole's favourite stories concerned his making a dummy of the shape and the average weight of a human body, and noting how far into the pool he could throw it. Only an area with a radius of about thirty feet from the dredge was actually covered by the operations. This was, of course, only a very small part of the expanse of the well.

The dredge was first operated on 5 March 1904. On March 10th the Cole diary reads:

They made ten hauls in the morning and six or eight in the afternoon. In the fifth haul in the morning Rafael found a human humerus and, in the next, what appeared to be a finger bone. . . . March 11th: During the day the dredge brought up a number of bones . . . also several pieces of pottery. These things came from nearly fourteen feet down in the mud (so the mechanic in charge told me).

The first pieces of copal incense arrived on March 12th. Wooden objects soon put in an appearance. The first piece of jade, a round bead, came up on the 19th. It was not until May 28th that any

The Great Ball Court This sculptured wall remains in the Great Ball Court which was used in playing the ancient ball game, tlachti. The court had two parallel walls. A small temple stood at each end. About 20 feet above the ground projecting from the center of each side wall was a huge stone ring four feet in diameter. The object of the game was to throw the ball through these rings without touching the ball with the hands or with the feet, using only the elbows, knees, or thighs.

Chac-Mool On the top platform of the Temple of Warriors stands this Chac-Mool—a human figure reclining on its back, with knees drawn up and head turned sharply to one side.

metal was recovered. On this date two copper bells appeared. Up to June 1st, practically no stone objects were encountered. It was not until early November that jade and pottery objects came out in any quantities. The next month marked the appearance of the first gold specimens other than a small gold mask on a wooden sceptre which had come up some time before. . . .

By means of a rough boat, many light objects, especially the balls of copal, were recovered; removed from the mud by the dredge, they usual floated on the surface of the water.

The dredge would be brought up and swung over the land. All large objects and many of the smaller ones were removed before the dredge was opened. The remainder, freed by opening the dredge, were allowed to fall in a pile. This was gone over carefully for smaller objects but, unfortunately, only a portion of this debris was sifted either when it was wet or after it had dried. The objects were usually washed in clear water to free them from the mud immediately after removal from the dredge. The wooden material was kept wet by immersion in water.

It was soon found that no possibility of stratification could be noted as the heavier objects had sunk to the lower levels when they were thrown in.

It should be admitted that the nature of the operations precluded the possibility of the care usually taken in the excavation of a terrestrial site. By ordinary archæological standards, the work could not be considered either exhaustive or complete. There is every reason to suppose that the well, and even the debris, still contains objects of archæological interest.

In a letter to Thompson dated 20 September 1905, Bowditch proposed an engine to operate the winch. This was tried, and in the following March, Thompson reported:

I have had to abandon the use of the engine and for a cause that I do not think anyone could imagine or foresee. To explain, the wall surface of the whole Cenote is built up of consecutive layers of rock of varying degrees of hardness, separated by thick layers of a finely divided flour-like substance, called by the natives *kut*. . . . The trepidation of the engine and the trembling force of the rapidly up-rising heavily laden bucket caused such a downpour of this substance . . . that the whole water surface of the Cenote became of a milky colour and finally pieces of the ledge itself . . . commenced to fall.

A coffer-dam was suggested as a possible means of working the fertile zone near the shrine without the water hazard. This was declared impracticable as the sides and bottom of the Cenote are porous and it would have been found most difficult if not impossible to keep the portion protected by the dam free

187

from water. Pumping the well dry was practically hopeless for the same reasons.

As early as December 1905 Thompson wrote, 'I think that when I do commence work I shall decide to use the diving outfit. I shall, however, meanwhile prove the outfit practically and can then determine definitely.' There is no further reference to making use of diving during this first campaign ending in 1907. It was in May 1909 that the quotation regarding diving operations is found; in the final agreement of November 1909 Bowditch refers to diving for the first time in the correspondence now available and states that Thompson 'will make the exploration of the Cenote with a diver's apparatus to be furnished by him, and that he will superintend the work in person'. It seems quite evident that the work done by means of diving yielded very meagre results as, in 1910, Thompson suggests rigging up the dredge again.

In spite of a difficult terrain and with techniques which to-day would seem crude, this accomplishment, started fifty years ago, was of the greatest consequence. . . .

There are three aspects of the Cenote material which give it unique significance in archæological study. First, the objects were offered to the gods of rain by a native population in elaborate religious rites that are explained by an abundant literature. Second, these objects thrown into the huge sink-hole represent a great span both in time and in area. This is particularly true of the jades; the metals come all the way from Guerrero and Oaxaca in the north, to British Honduras and Honduras, southward to Veraguas and Cocle in Panama, and even to Colombia in South America. Third, the objects preserved here under water are of perishable material that usually survives only at archæological sites in arid countries. There is perhaps no other single collection in New World archæology that has offered so comprehensive a view of the æsthetic life of an ancient people. The amount and diversity of the articles are evidence of the Cenote's importance in the religion of the Maya toward the end of their existence as an independent people untouched by European culture. . . .

Landa's report not only fills out the picture at almost every turn, but inspired the dredging of the pool, an operation that has verified his observation on what the well contained in every respect except one. The country did have gold, brought in by trade, however, in the form of bells, amulets, and plates; much of it seems to have found its way into the natural reservoir at Chichen Itza. . . .

According to the Sotuta-Homun testimony, only at this site were the victims thrown in while still living. This, of course, confirms Landa's account. Even at Chichen, according to the 1562 witnesses, only nine men at this time seem to have been actually drowned in the pool. At three other sacrifices here five men were put to death, their hearts extracted, and their dead bodies thrown into the Cenote. The early literary sources offer us a fairly complete picture of the ritual which probably took place at Chichen. . . .

There is little question but that the beginnings of these ceremonies at the Cenotes for rain do not go back to the great

Temple of Warriors   This immense pyramidal construction is surmounted by many elaborately carved pillars.

Mayan Painting .This mural is found in the Inner Chamber of the Great Ball Court.

period of Maya culture, which ended in Yucatan about the year 1000. Until recently it was commonly thought that the ritual connected with the sacred wells was brought into the country along with other types of human sacrifice and idolatry by Quetzalcoatl and his followers about the year 1000, the beginning of Tula-Toltec Chichen and the Itza. . . .

There seems little doubt that there were two main purposes of the ancient Cenote ritual: the first was intercession for rain, the second was divination of future crops.

In 1536, the Xiu pilgrimage was an attempt to worship at Chichen in order to bring rain when 'a famine fell upon them and they were reduced to eating the bark of trees'. Landa notes that the natives made a sacrifice at Chichen in times of drought. The desire for rain again appears in the account of a rite in a Cenote of Tixpayan: 'And they made them [the idols of the gods] that sacrifice in order to be provided with sustenance and good rainy spells and because of some days it had not rained and the *milpas* were drying up. . . .'

A request for rain is implied in some of the prayers to the gods recorded in the 1562 testimony of 'idolatrous practices'. One runs, 'Lord god all powerful, provide us with what we need and give us water and that which is necessary for our sustenance'; a second asks 'for good rainy seasons'; and a third desires 'life and temporal goods'. . . .

The importance of prognostication among the Maya and Mexican peoples can be understood if one realizes that a great part of many of their pre-Columban manuscripts have to do with the sacred period of 260 days, usually called in Aztec, the *tonalpohualli* or *tonalamatl*, 'Book of the Days', a device to determine the auspicious periods in which to undertake ceremonials, go on journeys, plant and harvest fields, and engage in other secular occupations.

From the importance of the prophecy in the early manuscripts it is not, therefore, any surprise to find divination as the second main purpose of the Cenote ritual. This comes out most clearly in the famous description of the rites in the *Relación* of Valladolid, where meditation is also seen. We learn that some Indian women belonging to each of the lords were thrown into the well, and they were told that they were to ask for a good year and all those things which seemed best to them. The victim was supposed to come out of the water, shout to be rescued, and then relate to the assembled group whether the future was to be propitious. Landa was sceptical regarding the actual return of the victim. . . .

The apotheosis of the martyr is not uncommon in primitive religions. There are references among the Aztec to the belief that the persons to be sacrificed are identified as gods and, before the actual offering, are treated as deities. The Maya, so far as our testimony goes, do not seem to share this idea.

Among the Maya there seem to have been two categories of people who were given to the gods. 'Some,' according to Lopez, 'were offered and sacrificed of their own free will, while others were forced to undergo the death. The first were inhabitants and natives of the *pueblos* where they were sacrificed.'

It seems clear that offering made by the victim himself is rare. Lopez continues:

Those who were sacrificed by their own free will were few. . . . Some did it in time of necessity and on account of their pride and vainglory in order to leave that memory of themselves; and for that reason not only was the memory of those who thus killed themselves perpetually celebrated but those of that lineage were highly esteemed. The day when one of those sacrifices was offered was celebrated greatly and one of the most important holy spectacles they thought they had. There was a special place for this and it was performed with much pomp and solemnity. In the first place the sacrificial victim offered himself to the priests and made manifest to them his intention and vow, and the day on which it was to take place having been designated, the unfortunate wretch ascended to that place, which was very high, and, the people having gathered to see so sad a spectacle, he made an oration in which he gave an account of his motive and intention and he praised that kind of sacrifice and started to tell of all those of his lineage who had offered themselves in that way, and speaking and reaching the point of counting himself among the number of the others, he threw himself down there below, dashing himself to pieces, the people at once hastening with great devotion to take a piece of that flesh in order to eat it, a thing they held in great devotion and veneration.

The most frequent victims seem to have been boys and girls. As in Mexico, children were especially acceptable to the gods of rain and of agriculture. In the Sotuta and Homun testimony there are constant references to children, often five or six years of age, being offered to the gods. Of the 168 persons who are mentioned by the witnesses in the trials as having been sacrificed, eighty per cent are boys or men and twenty per cent girls or women.

The children offered were obtained in several ways. Some were bought. We read of a boy 'whom they bought from the Cupuls who was about four years old'; again 'two bought from the Cupuls'. In another purchase the price is given as 'five red *cuentas* (beads) for each boy'. The cost of a boy seems to have run from five to ten beads. In two places, a fathom-length of thickbeads was paid for each of two boys.

The Red House   A building in the ruins of Chichen Itza, a Mayan city, founded in the 4th or 5th Century A.D. The city was abandoned in 698 and reoccupied in 964. Chichen Itza grew large and powerful during the tenth and eleventh centuries. Rivalry among the cities of the Mayan civilization led to a civil war in which Chichen Itza was subjugated (1194) by Mayapan. The period of Mayapan's domination was ended by a revolt of the Maya lords under the leadership of Uxmal (1441). The New Empire civilization then began to decline and the great cities were abandoned.

There seem to have been certain persons whose office or profession it was to obtain children for sacrifice by capture. Among the Indians of the New Kingdom, according to Lopez, children were 'taken and seized from their enemies and opponents in their wars'. We shall see later that these were put to death in a special way.

Orphans formed a class which furnished food for the gods. Some of these seem to have been taken into the houses of rich men to be brought up and later contributed by their patrons.

Temple of Warriors   At the top of a staircase stands this carving of a standard bearer, atop a projecting snake head.

Others may have been the offspring of deceased male relatives and slave women. Little time was lost in sacrificing a child after both parents were dead: 'They killed and sacrificed a girl named Ix Chable . . . daughter of Nahasio Chable and of his wife, natives of Sahcaba, already dead, and when they killed the said girl her mother had been dead five or six days.'

Among this category of victims may have been the offspring of deceased male relatives and slave women just mentioned. Palacio (1576) gives a vivid description of the sacrifice of a boy among the Pipil in Guatemala and also of '*bastoardos nacidos entre ellos*'.

Landa records: ' . . . Some in their devotion gave their little children who were made much of, and feasted up to the day [of the festival], and they were well guarded, so that they should not run away or pollute themselves with any carnal sin. And in the meanwhile they led them from town to town dancing, while the priests, *chilans*, and other officers fasted. And when the day arrived, they all came together in the court of the temple. . . .'

Herrera tells us that when slaves were lacking, 'they were so devout that they gave their little nephews and even their sons'.

Children were donated by pious men and also presented by one *cacique* to another: 'And the same Lorenzo Iuit told the other *caciques* that the *cacique* of Cansahcab, who is called Francisco Chel, had sent these girls, whom they said were from Cah which is their name for the province of Izamal, because such was the custom in ancient times that some *caciques* sent boys and girls as presents to other *caciques* for sacrifice, which was formerly called *quymchich* (*cim cich*).'

Certain writers have assumed that the girls who were sacrificed in the Cenote were all virgins. The worst offenders in this interpretation were the Englishmen Arnold and Frost (1909), who claimed, quite incorrectly, that all the skulls recovered were those of young females from twelve to sixteen. They add: '[They were] hurled by the priests into the chasm, possibly after defilement by the high priests in the small building at the pool's edge, thus symbolizing the simultaneous surrender of virginity and life to the Rain Deity.' At the time these statements were made regarding the status and treatment of the girls thrown into the Cenote, there was little basis for attempting to establish either their virginity or pre-sacrificial defilement. Now that the Spanish text of the *Relación* of Lopez is available, we find he uses the term *doncellas* to describe Indian women who were sacrificed, and he notes, 'And they placed her in a shrine which was near there, where the priests withdrew with her.' Here, perhaps, is a late justification for Arnold and Frost's statement made in 1909. In the testimony collected at Sotuta and Homun regarding human sacrifice the victims are usually called *muchachos* and *muchachas*. Sometimes the girls are called *niñas*. In a few places their names are given in full and preceding each name is the Maya feminine prefix *ix*.

All the skeletal material recovered from the Cenote has been studied by Hooton, whose report is significant in view of the above statements. He writes:

Certainly, or almost certainly, thirteen of the skulls, belonged to adult males, and four of the six pelves represented the same sex. The males ranged in age from sub-adult (eighteen to twenty-one years) to old (fifty-five years and over). Only one of the females was middle-aged (thirty-five to fifty-four years); of the other seven, six were young adults (twenty-one to thirty-four years) and the other a sub-adult (eighteen to twenty). There are seven skulls of children between ten and twelve years. Of the fourteen skulls of younger children, nine were estimated to have been aged four to six years, one six to eight years, one three to four years, one eighteen months. The other two were represented only by fragments.

In so very short a series as twenty-one adults, there is no statistical value. However, of the twenty-one adults, sixty-two per cent were male and thirty-eight per cent female. As Hooton remarks, 'All of the individuals involved (or rather immersed) may have been virgins but the osteological evidence does not permit a determination of this nice point.'

Of the many references to the sacrifice of virgins in other regions, we note the account by Cortés of the people of Teutiercas in Acalan dedicating their principal temple presumably to the goddess Ix Chel. In her 'they had much faith and hope'. In her honour, 'they sacrificed only maidens who were virgins and very beautiful; and if they were not such, she became very angry with them'.

The Lopez *Relación* states that those who were compelled to be sacrificed were 'captives and men taken in the wars'. In a *Relación* dated 1579 we read of a Cupul, lord of Ekbalam, who had a war with a *pueblo* called Yalcoba and 'those whom they captured remained slaves and the others they sacrificed to their idols'. There seems to have been some class distinction in those captured, as Landa notes: 'If they made a prisoner of some distinguished man, they sacrificed him immediately, not wishing to leave any one alive who might injure them afterwards. The rest of the people remained captive in the power of those who had taken them.' Here one might assume the sacrifice was for policy rather than for religious purposes, but in the

Chichen Itza Sculpture This stone piece was
found in the Guards Room.

Chi Manuscript we read, 'Those who were captured in war
. . . if they were men of rank, [they sacrificed them to the
idols, although some of them] were ransomed.' Less distinguished captives were held as slaves, and Cogolludo adds that
such slaves were very severely treated.

Another point of view regarding the social significance of the
prisoner is brought out in a passage from Herrera: 'Their
greatest desire was to seize important men to sacrifice, because
the greater the quality of the victim, the more acceptable the
service they did to the god seemed to them.'

One of the many descriptions of the ill-fated outcome of the
Valdivia Expedition of 1511 is that given by Cervantes de
Salazar in 1560. We read of the Spaniards under Valdivia,
wrecked on the north-east coast of Yucatan, and captured by a
cruel lord of the country who offered Valdivia and four others
to his idols, afterwards eating them, 'making a feast' according
to the custom of the country. Geronimo de Aguilar, Gonzalo
Guerrero, and a few others 'remained in a coop in order that,
for another festival that was approaching, being fatter, we
might solemnize their banquet with our flesh'. Aguilar and
Guerrero escaped, the former eventually to join Cortés, while
Guerrero, refusing this opportunity, 'went native', serving
faithfully one of the lords of the country and helping him in
resisting the Spaniards and native enemies. After one of their
victorious encounters with another band of Maya, 'they took
many *principales* prisoners, whom they afterwards sacrificed'.

We have already seen in Landa's description of the attempted
Xiu pilgrimage that they 'brought them [the idols], slaves of
both sexes to throw them into the well of Chichen Itza'. . . .

There seems no doubt but that the one to be offered to the
gods was usually stripped of his clothes and anointed with a blue
colour. It seems clear that blue is the colour of sacrifice and
associated both with the priests and with the persons and
objects offered to the gods. Both the *nacom*, the sacrificer, and
the *chacs*, who hold the victim, appear with bluish-black bodies
in the representation of the rite on the fresco in the Temple of
the Warriors at Chichen.

We continue with Landa's description of the dress of the
martyr. They 'put a *coroza* on his head'. In another place this is
described as of feathers and seems to refer to a head-dress, a
pointed cap, or mitre. The priest also 'wore a sort of *coroza*',
as we have seen. The same term is used to refer to 'a coronet
worn as a mark of infamy' and was imposed by the Catholic
priests on the natives as a kind of punishment and mark of
infidelity to the new religion. In the testimony in the trial of

the idolaters the victim of sacrifice is described as having his hands tied behind his back, as 'without a shirt, wearing breeches, his eyes covered with a white cloth'.

In four places, Landa speaks of a ceremonial progress along a road that had 'been cleaned and adorned with arches and greens'; 'by a path which was very clean and ornamented, they went all together with their accustomed devotion'. . . .

We are fortunate in having an account of the actual procession over the causeway to the Cenote. From the court in front of the Castillo, according to Lopez, the priests 'went in procession with her [the victim] by a paved causeway, all of slabs, which came to an end at a large and deep Cenote which was there'. Accompanying the priests with their elaborate raiment and those to be sacrificed, there were undoubtedly musicians, singers, and dancers. The bas-reliefs at Chichen, even with little colour left, give some idea of the splendour of the ancient processionals.

On arrival at the platform beside the well, there must have been some ritual at the very edge of the well in the little temple or shrine there. Lopez says: 'And they placed her in a shrine which was near there, where the priests withdrew with her. And they instructed her and informed her concerning what she was to ask there from their demons and false gods. . . .'

As the final act before the victim was actually thrown into the well there seems, in some cases at least, to have been a homily directed to the one to be sacrificed. In the Sotuta testimony it states: 'Diego Pech, *cacique*, said to the one whom they wished to kill who was weeping, "Take courage and console yourself since we are not doing you harm now nor are we casting you into a bad region nor into hell but into heaven and glory in the manner of our ancestors who were accustomed to do so." '

THE GRAVE OF A SCYTHIAN KING

Between the seventh and second centuries B.C., Scythian nomads roved the natural grasslands of Asia and Europe. They lived a turbulent and free existence: forever on horse-back, hunting, fighting, and guarding their animals. But despite the apparent wildness of their lives, they were artists who loved to live well. Since they were nomadic and possessed no temples, their burial grounds were revered beyond all else, and here costly and elaborate ceremonies for the dead took place. The rich tombs of the royal Scyths are located in southern Russia, north of the Black Sea.

Although not as elaborate as some, the grave at Solokha has given the world incomparable treasures. And the Golden Comb found there demonstrates most beautifully the instinctive delight of the Scythian people in the use of animal forms for decoration.

The following article is written by the finder of the Golden Comb of Solokha.

Excerpted from THE GOLDEN COMB OF SOLOKHA,
(London Calling, 7 May 1953) written by

COUNT ALEXIS BOBRINSKOY

THE heat was intense on that afternoon in July when my father and I left the railway carriage and stepped out on to the platform of a small railway station some twelve miles north of Nicopol, a small town in South Russia. The temperature rose to about 110 degrees Fahrenheit and all life was at a standstill. A small cart drawn by two horses was expecting us at the exit. Father and I took our kit-bags and got into the cart. The sleepy horses started off in a lazy but regular trot on a journey of some thirty miles over perfectly flat, sun-baked ground.

My father had had a telegram which made him jump to his feet and order an immediate departure from our comfortable, quiet home hundreds of miles away. 'Have terminated preliminary excavations very important sepulchral mound stop expecting your immediate arrival before digging king's tomb. Professor Wesselovsky.'

My father, as President of the Imperial Archæological Commission, assisted by a staff of some sixteen learned archæologists and historians, was for many years directing the research work in the field of Russian archæology. One of his colleagues was Professor Wesselovsky, the eminent Orientalist, author of many learned books, who was now supervising the excavation of a barrow built over the remains of some unknown Scythian chieftain in the vast plains of South Russia, in the fifth or fourth century before our era.

Since the barrow was in the heart of the mysterious country of the Scythians described by Herodotus himself, Professor Wesselovsky's telegram roused my father's curiosity. He dared not hope that this particular tomb was untouched by the hands of robbers. Could such luck now reward the toils of the scientists?

At last, towards sunset, our usually silent coachman said: 'I can see Solokha, the barrow, on the horizon,' and pointed it out to us with his whip. Indeed, we also were able to see the small hill in the distance: our monotonous journey was coming to an end. We did not cross a single village; on a stretch of thirty miles we did not see a single house. As we were getting nearer and nearer to the site of the excavations we could get a glimpse of the workmen busy with their wheelbarrows filled with earth, and at last Professor Wesselovsky met us with an outstretched hand and a broad smile: 'I am so glad you were able to come.' he said. 'To-morrow morning we will start digging the king's tomb.'

Suddenly, in the middle of the night, we were startled by terrific thunder and lightning. Rain started falling in torrents. In a few minutes our tent was soaked through. We felt helpless and miserable. Our scanty belongings were swimming in mud. My father said, philosophically: 'Well, my friends, no wonder! The king protests against our intrusion. He does not want us to molest his last abode.' Gradually the storm calmed down, and the rain stopped, but we had spent a sleepless night, full of terrible discomforts.

Dawn came and the sun rose in a pink, cloudless sky. We had our early-morning cup of tea and felt a little better. 'Indeed,' said Professor Wesselovsky, with his usual kind smile, 'only a very powerful king can send such thunder out of the blue. But this heavy fall of rain will soften the ground and it will be easier for us to dig. In my opinion the spirit of the king

Scythian Tomb Ancient monuments on the graves of the Polovtz and Scythian-Sarmatians who at one time inhabited the broad expanses of the Southern Ukraine.

intends to help us find all his treasures. Shall we start?'

'Yes, of course, let us start,' said my father, 'with the help of God let us start; but remember that people for some reason call this barrow Solokha, and Solokha means a witch . . . !'

We went to the open barrow. First we had to clear the passage to the actual grave and carefully investigate all its approaches. This operation, before we actually started digging the chieftain's grave, took us quite two hours of time to complete. Then came the real thing. We spread newspapers on the ground so as to place on them all the objects which were now to be unearthed from the grave itself. Gently, very gently, my father and Professor Wesselovsky started scraping the surface of the grave with their sharp trowels, and throwing the earth into a sieve.

Many minutes passed: the expectation was tense. I stood respectfully aside, just in case my help would suddenly be wanted. Familiar thuds and knocks were heard now and again, as the archæologists came across various little metal objects with their trowels. These were the sharp, bronze arrow-heads, but the wooden shafts of the arrows had decayed into dust centuries ago. Next came earthenware cups and small vases made for the Scythian king by his Greek prisoners.

At last we came to the skeleton of the king himself, and had to proceed with utmost care not to damage or break the golden ornaments with which he had been adorned on his death-bed. There he lay, in all his magnificence, untouched by robbers or any other hand for twenty-four centuries. We removed the earth, little by little, taking away the pieces of what was left of the wooden structure of his burial chamber. The king—now there was no longer any possible doubt that this was a king—was literally covered with golden plaques, sewn into his silk cloak.

As we removed the earth, inch by inch, we could see the traces of the silk fabric, the threads of most vivid colours—red, crimson, emerald green, and lilac. But no sooner were these frail tissues exposed to the action of the air than they immediately faded away and left only colourless dust in our hands. Only the golden ornaments, which had once adorned this bright cloak, survived in all their beauty.

We found over three hundred such golden plaques, each about a square inch in size. Near the king's skeleton lay two swords, one of which had a gold-plated sheath, handle, and guard; then we discovered a quiver plated with silver gilt, a bronze helmet, a bronze corslet of scales, which the king wore under his silk cloak; then came several bronze scimitars and other weapons.

Round the king's neck was a large, heavy, massive, twisted necklace of solid gold, ten inches in diameter—a masterpiece of Greek jewellery of the best period. At the ends of this necklace were two heads of lions facing each other and holding a Gordian knot in their mouths. Another golden necklace, a chain of golden tubes with golden pendants, five bracelets of solid gold were put across his wrists, and near by was a golden round dish ornamented with scenes of fighting lions, at least forty of them, executed by Greek prisoners, in high relief. At the king's side were buried seven circular silver bowls ornamented with scenes of galloping horsemen spearing lions pursued by mastiffs, and other hunting scenes so dear to the heart of the Scythians. At the king's feet were three large copper cauldrons and more vases for wine and oil. The sight of so many wonderful treasures coming one after another out of the king's grave made us giddy with surprise and excitement.

As time went on and the king's tomb was at last completely emptied of all its treasures, my father and Professor Wesselovsky could at last straighten their backs and take a short rest from their strenuous work. It was getting late, and we all felt very hungry. Professor Wesselovsky took my father by the arm, and they left the site of the excavations and proceeded towards our camp, where a meal was ready for us. As regards myself, I was still so excited by the wonderful treasures which were unearthed that I simply could not tear myself away from the king's grave. There I sat bewildered, as in a spell, as if attached by some hidden magnet to this freshly dug grave now entirely empty of its precious contents. With my little sharp trowel I went on scraping and digging at the hard, black earth without any precise reason, as if attracted by the ground which would not let me leave it.

Suddenly, my little trowel struck something solid. Was it a stone? Or a piece of particularly hard earth? I gave another jab with the trowel, and saw something glitter in the hard ground. I plunged my trowel deeper and brought to light a large, solid, square, heavy, golden object with long spikes sticking down from an ornamented carved upper part. It was a golden comb.

I shouted at the top of my voice: 'Father, come back quickly, I have found a comb, a comb, quick, come back, look at it . . .' and I took the comb into my hands. The distance between my father and myself was quite a hundred yards, and he shouted back: 'Don't touch it, you will break it, for God's sake don't touch it, leave it!'

'I can't break it,' I retorted, 'it is heavy, it is of solid gold. . . .' In another moment he was kneeling by my side, speechless with bewilderment. Indeed, it was a golden comb, the only golden comb of that size and artistic quality in existence, the magnificent, the now world-famous golden comb of Solokha. After 2,300 years I was the first human being to touch it. Perhaps the ghost of the king of the Scythians, wishing to play a prank on the two learned men, chose me, an ignorant boy, as a medium for the great discovery; or was it the mysterious witch, the legendary Solokha, who mischievously put such a treasure into my hands?

Golden Comb of Solokha For 2300 years the comb had been buried until quite by accident young Count Bobrinskoy dug it up. The comb was large and heavy, made of solid gold and decorated with animal forms.

BEHISTUN: A KEY TO HISTORY

From 521 B.C. to 485 B.C., the mighty Persian Empire was ruled by Darius the Great, a humane and intelligent dictator.

Darius had a triumphal monument carved high on a rock at Behistun, 500 feet above the highway which runs from Babylon to the Iranian plateau. The men of the caravans could see the monument and knew Darius to be the Great King. On it was a picture of him receiving homage and a powerful edict, which proclaimed: "I am Darius the Great King, the King of Kings . . ." The edict was written in three languages—Old Persian, Elamite, and Babylonian; in each case the wedge-shaped script known as cuneiform was used.

Cuneiform—it was a script that had baffled archaeologists for decades. Then, between 1835 and 1847 Colonel Henry Rawlinson, a British army officer and a scholar, made the perilous ascent to the inscriptions and took exact copies of the texts. From his knowledge of the ancient Pehlevi language he was able to solve the Old Persian inscription on the rock because the two languages belong to the same family. Having deciphered the Old Persian it was possible to solve the Babylonian, and finally to deal with the most difficult, the Elamite.

Rawlinson's work is particularly important because it provided the key to understanding all Asiatic languages written in cuneiform. The following is from an address Rawlinson gave to the Society of Antiquaries in which he describes how he copied the texts on the Behistun rock.

Excerpted from NOTES ON SOME PAPER CASTS OF CUNEIFORM
INSCRIPTIONS UPON THE SCULPTURED ROCK AT BEHISTUN,
(Society of Antiquaries of London, 1852) written by

SIR HENRY RAWLINSON

THE rock or, as it is usually called by the Arab geographers, the mountain of Behistun, is not an isolated hill, as has been sometimes imagined. It is merely the

Behistun Rock   Overall view of carvings.

King Darius the Great   Rifle bullets have slightly damaged the eye, the nose, and part of the beard of this skillfully carved head. The lower part of the beard was carved by the king's sculptors onto a deliberately inset piece of rock held in place by iron rods driven through solid rock.

terminal point of a long, narrow range which bounds the plain of Kermanshah to the eastward. This range is rocky and abrupt throughout, but at the extremity it rises in height, and becomes a sheer precipice. The altitude I found by careful triangulation to be 3,807 feet, and the height above the plain at which occur the tablets of Darius is perhaps 500 feet, or something more.

Notwithstanding that a French antiquarian commission in Persia described it a few years back to be impossible to copy the Behistun inscriptions, I certainly do not consider it any great feat in climbing to ascend to the spot where the inscriptions occur. When I was living at Kermanshah fifteen years ago, and was somewhat more active than I am at present, I used frequently to scale the rock three or four times a day without the aid of a rope or ladder; without any assistance, in fact, whatever. During my late visits I have found it more convenient to ascend and descend by the help of ropes where the track lies up a precipitate cleft, and to throw a plank over those chasms where a false step in leaping across would probably be fatal. On reaching the recess which contains the Persian text of the record, ladders are indispensable in order to examine the upper portion of the tablet; and even with ladders there is considerable risk, for the foot-ledge is so narrow, about eighteen inches or at most two feet in breadth, that with a ladder long enough to reach the sculptures sufficient slope cannot be given to enable a person to ascend, and, if the ladder be shortened in order to increase the slope, the upper inscription can only be copied by standing on the topmost step of the ladder, with no other support than steadying the body against the rock with the left arm, while the left hand holds the note-book, and the right hand' is employed with the pencil. In this position I copied all the upper inscriptions, and the interest of the occupation entirely did away with any sense of danger.

To reach the recess which contains the Scythic [Elamite] translation of the record of Darius is a matter of far greater difficulty. On the left-hand side of the recess alone is there any foot-ledge whatever; on the right-hand, where the recess, which is thrown a few feet further back, joins the Persian tablet, the face of the rock presents a sheer precipice, and it is necessary therefore to bridge this intervening space between the left-hand of the Persian tablet and the foot-ledge on the left-hand of the recess. With ladders of sufficient length, a bridge of this sort can be constructed without difficulty; but my first attempt to cross the chasm was unfortunate, and might have been fatal, for, having previously shortened my only ladder in order to obtain a slope for copying the Persian upper legends, I found, when I came to lay it across to the recess in order to get at the Scythic translation, that it was not sufficiently long to lie flat on the foot-ledge beyond. One side of the ladder would alone reach the nearest point of the ledge, and, as it would of course have tilted over if a person had attempted to cross in that position, I changed it from a horizontal to a vertical direction, the upper side resting firmly on the rock at its two ends, and the lower hanging over the precipice, and I prepared to cross, walking on the lower side, and holding to the upper side with my hands. If the ladder had been a compact article, this mode of crossing, although far from comfortable, would have been at any rate practicable; but the Persians merely fit in the bars of their ladders without pretending to clench them outside, and I had hardly accordingly begun to cross over when the vertical pressure forced the bars out of their sockets, and the lower and unsupported side of the ladder thus parted company from the upper, and went crashing down over the precipice. Hanging on to the upper side, which still remained firm in its place, and assisted by my friends, who were anxiously watching the trial, I regained the Persian recess, and did not again attempt to cross until I had made a bridge of comparative stability. Ultimately I took the casts of the Scythic writing by laying one long ladder, in the first instance, horizontally across the chasm, and by then placing another ladder, which rested on the bridge, perpendicularly against the rock.

The Babylonian transcript at Behistun is still more difficult to reach than either the Scythic or the Persian tablets. The writing can be copied by the aid of a good telescope from below, but I long despaired of obtaining a cast of the inscription; for I found it quite beyond my powers of climbing to reach the spot where it was engraved, and the cragsmen of the place, who were accustomed to track the mountain goats over the entire face of the mountain, declared the particular block inscribed with the Babylonian legend to be unapproachable. At length, however, a wild Kurdish boy, who had come from a distance, volunteered to make the attempt, and I promised him a considerable reward if he succeeded. The mass of rock in question is scarped, and it projects some feet over the Scythic recess, so that it cannot be approached by any of the ordinary means of climbing. The boy's first move was to squeeze himself up a cleft in the rock a short distance to the left of the projecting mass. When he had ascended some distance above it, he drove a wooden peg firmly into the cleft, fastened a rope to

Eight Captive Kings These figures are portrayed as standing in front of the Great Darius and below the winged symbol of the king's god, Ahuramazda.

Rawlinson's Mark The name of the great archaeologist and decipherer is carved below the relief and inscription, followed by the names of H. Jones and A. Hector.

this, and then endeavoured to swing himself across to another cleft at some distance on the other side; but in this he failed, owing to the projection of the rock. It then only remained for him to cross over to the cleft by hanging on with his toes and fingers to the slight inequalities on the bare face of the precipice, and in this he succeeded, passing over a distance of twenty feet of almost smooth perpendicular rock in a manner which to a looker-on appeared quite miraculous. When he had reached the second cleft the real difficulties were over. He had brought a rope with him attached to the first peg, and now, driving in a second, he was enabled to swing himself right over the projecting mass of rock. Here, with a short ladder, he formed a swinging seat, like a painter's cradle, and, fixed upon this seat, he took under my direction the paper cast of the Babylonian translation of the records of Darius which is now at the Royal Asiatic Society's rooms, and which is almost of equal value for the interpretation of the Assyrian inscriptions as was the Greek translation on the Rosetta Stone for the intelligence of the hieroglyphic texts of Egypt. I must add, too, that it is of the more importance that this invaluable Babylonian key should have been thus recovered, as the mass of rock on which the inscription is engraved bore every appearance, when I last visited the spot, of being doomed to a speedy destruction, water trickling from above having almost separated the overhanging mass from the rest of the rock, and its own enormous weight thus threatening very shortly to bring it thundering down into the plain, dashed into a thousand fragments.

The method of forming these paper casts is exceedingly simple, nothing more being required than to take a number of sheets of paper without size, spread them on the rock, moisten them, and then beat them into the crevices with a stout brush, adding as many layers of paper as it may be wished to give consistency to the cast. The paper is left there to dry, and on being taken off it exhibits a perfect reversed impression of the writing.

THE ELGIN MARBLES

The beautiful Greek Parthenon, rising high on the rocky Acropolis at Athens, was completed in the year 432 B.C. For centuries, it proudly withstood the ravages of time. Then, in A.D. 1687, during a petty war between Venetians and Turks, a shell exploded in the temple and reduced it to ruins. It was the last of the buildings of the Acropolis to collapse.

During the early 1800's, to preserve the memory of this and the other magnificent ancient buildings, the seventh Earl of Elgin determined to collect moulds, casts, and drawings of their sculptures to be shipped to England. He sent a team of experts to Athens. He did not intend to add to the spoliation of the monuments by removing the sculpture. But when his agents found that the contempt and carelessness of the authorities was leading to total destruction, he obtained permission from the Turkish authorities to remove the marbles themselves.

The work of collecting the marbles was carried out between 1801 and 1812. During this time Lord Elgin himself was taken prisoner by the French and held for three years; one of his ships containing a precious load was wrecked; and Turkish and French intrigue hampered his agents. But the marbles were brought safely to London, and eventually bought for the British nation. Today, this wonderful collection from classical Greece can be seen in the British Museum.

Excerpted from LORD ELGIN AND HIS COLLECTION, *(The Journal of Hellenic Studies, Vol. XXXVI, 1916) written by*

A. H. SMITH

THE present year, A.D. 1916, is the centenary of the acquisition by the public of the Elgin Collection of ancient sculptures, inscriptions, casts and drawings. It has therefore seemed a suitable moment to print a fuller account than has hitherto been attempted of the formation and purchase of that collection.

I should state that I have been engaged on this subject for some time past, by desire of the Earl of Elgin, who has put all his papers bearing on the subject into my hands.

Thomas Bruce, seventh Earl of Elgin, and eleventh Earl of Kincardine, was born on 20 July 1776, being the second son of Charles, fifth Earl of Elgin, who married Martha, the only child of Thomas White, a London banker. The fifth Earl died in May 1771, and was succeeded by his eldest son, William Robert, an infant who was born in 1764, held the title for two months, and died in 1771 at the age of seven. He was succeeded by his brother Thomas, a few days under the age of five.

Lord Elgin, the subject of this paper, was educated at Harrow (where he stayed for a short time only) and at Westminster. He also studied at St. Andrew's, and at Paris, where he acquired an excellent command of French. He entered the army in 1785, and without any active military service reached the rank of major-general in 1835. He was elected a Representative Peer of Scotland in 1790 and continued in that position till 1807. He was again elected in 1820, and held the post till his death (14 November 1841).

He entered on his diplomatic career in 1790, when he was sent on a special mission to the Emperor Leopold. He was made Envoy at Brussels in 1792; Envoy Extraordinary at Berlin in 1795; and Ambassador at the Porte in 1799.

By his appointment to the Constantinople Embassy and his tenure of that post during the Egyptian Expedition of Napoleon, the seventh Lord Elgin was made a leading actor in many great events. More particularly, however, his mind was turned from the outset towards those pursuits with which his name and reputation are associated. The source of the suggestion that he should connect his term of office with the study of antiquity was explained by himself in his evidence before the Select Committee which considered the purchase of his collection. He stated that it was in the year 1799, and on the occasion of his nomination to the Embassy at Constantinople, that the idea first occurred to him of making his term of office of service to the arts. Mr. Thomas Harrison, an architect (1744–1829), who was working for him in Scotland, and who had passed much of his life in Rome, represented that, though the public had a general knowledge of the remains of Athens, there was nothing that would serve as well as casts from the actual objects.

Upon that suggestion, I communicated very fully with my acquaintance in London. I mentioned it to Lord Grenville, Mr. Pitt, and Mr. Dundas, upon the idea that it was of such national importance as that the Government might be induced to take it up, not only to obtain the object, but also to obtain it by the means of the most able artists at that time in England. The answer of the Government, which was entirely negative, was, that the Government would not have been justified in undertaking any expense of an indefinite nature, particularly under the little probability that then existed of the success of the undertaking. Upon that understanding I applied to such artists here as were recommended to me as likely to answer the purpose, in particular to Mr. Turner, to go upon my own account. Mr. Turner's objection to my plan was, that as the object was of a general nature, and that the condition I insisted upon was, that the whole results of all the artists should be collected together and left with me, his objection was that he wished to retain a certain portion of his own labour for his own use; he moreover asked between seven and eight hundred pounds of salary, independently of his expenses being paid, which of course was out of my reach altogether; therefore nothing was done here preparatory to the undertaking at all.

J. M. W. Turner was twenty-four years old at the time in question. He was already well known as a topographical draughtsman, whose work was engraved by the topographical publishers. He had not yet visited the Continent, but in his tour to the North of England he had made many friends of influence. It was therefore quite natural that Lord Elgin, when in need of an artist, should think of Turner. Had he engaged him in place of Lusieri, it is probable that more drawings would have been completed, but it is certain that the Elgin collection of marbles would never have been made.

One of the friends who was consulted on the question of a draughtsman was a predecessor at the Constantinople Embassy, Sir Robert Ainslie, who during the years 1776–92 had employed an artist, Ludwig Mayer, for a very similar purpose. Mayer's *Views in Egypt, Palestine, and other parts of the Ottoman Empire* (1804), being a series of pleasing, coloured aquatint sketches in Egypt, Palestine, and Asia Minor, is still a frequent item in the lists of the second-hand booksellers.

Sir Robert Ainslie wrote to Lord Elgin to explain the terms of Mayer's engagement—namely, a salary of fifty guineas per annum, together with board and travelling expenses.

It was clearly understood that the whole of his works, drawings, pictures and sketches were to remain with me, as being my sole property. . . . I entirely agree with your Lordship in objecting to the conditions proposed by the artists who wish to accompany your Lordship to Turkey. To me it appears that the permission of Engraving any of the sketches, either in Turkey or elsewhere, ought to depend upon your Lordship's pleasure and ulterior determination.

217

The Parthenon The ruins of this ancient Greek temple stand on the Acropolis at Athens

Encouraged by such advice, Lord Elgin postponed the choice of a draughtsman until he had started from England. . . .

Lord Elgin started on his mission in 1799.

He had appointed William Richard Hamilton as his private secretary and, as will be seen hereafter, much of the success of his enterprise was to turn on Hamilton's zeal for the objects in view and his loyal friendship for his chief.

Arrived in Sicily, Lord Elgin opened communications, upon the recommendation of the then British Minister, Sir William Hamilton, with Giovanni Battista Lusieri, who was destined to be the agent to whose exertions the formation of the collection was, as we shall see, principally due. On 24 October 1799, Lusieri, then at Taormina, wrote to Lord Elgin explaining his position. He had found himself compelled, by the losses that he had suffered in the wars then in progress, to accept the position of King's Painter for the antiquities of Sicily, and was at present performing the duties of that post. It was therefore necessary that he should obtain superior permission, which, however, he thought would be granted without difficulty. He undertook to take steps to that end, and to go as quickly as possible to Messina to confer with Lord Elgin. The offer was cordially accepted by Lord Elgin, writing from Messina on the 15th. On October 18th, the meeting took place, and an agreement was speedily reached.

(Hamilton was busy engaging further members for the expedition and musicians and others to accompany Lord Elgin to Constantinople.)

Hamilton writes:

It was singular that all Rome could not afford a single *designateur de figures* among its Natives, that was even of ordinary Ability. We have selected one who is on all hands acknowledged to be the best in this line, of excellent character and good Manners. Perhaps he is the only man of taste his Nation ever produced; he is a Tartar and Native of Astracan, educated in Germany, and having studied eight years in Rome. His salary £100 per annum.

With regard to the Architect we have also a Roman who has universally the character of being the most scientific, and of drawing with the greatest Elegance and taste of any of his profession in Rome. If the countenance of our Tartar is extraordinary from the characteristic features of his Nation, our Architect is no less a singular Object, being an extremely deformed Humpback: the head however and hand were the objects of our Search. As on talking over the Subject with him and others we found it impossible that *one* man could engage in the Undertaking, we have agreed that he shall take with him a young Man accustomed to study under him as a Scholar, and we have fixed his salary at 500 Roman Piastres, or £125 per ann.

The Elgin Marbles   This fine collection of ancient Greek marble sculpture is now on display in the British Museum in London.

We have fortunately found an armed English Merchantman that is going in a few days to Messina. In this we shall take our passage, and there I hope to meet with the English convoy which is not yet come into the Sicilian or Italian Ports. The weather is now too unsettled to venture to cross to Sicily in the small Vessels of the country which indeed are all laid up for the Season.

I have also procured at Naples a *Maître de Chapelle*, with all the Qualities your Lordship had desired to find in him except the Inclination to appear occasionally as Groom of the Chamber, and as he is a very well-mannered young Man I did not think it proper to press it on him, particularly as I learned from every Quarter, that Persons of his Profession would with the natural Vanity of this people rather starve thro' Want, than stoop to such an imaginary Degradation. With regard to the two French-horns, the Clarionet, and the Violincello, it will I believe be feasible tho' difficult to prevail on them to wear a Livery, or at least a separate Uniform, which would, I suppose, answer fully as well. . . .

I am surprised not to have already heard of your Lordship's Arrival at Constantinople—but in this Corner of Europe we are almost completely excluded from communication with the rest, and what little we have is extremely slow and uncertain.

And so, at length, about 9 April 1800, after nearly six months of preparatory work in Italy and Sicily, Hamilton, Lusieri, and the other members of the expedition were able to set sail from Syracuse, for Constantinople, or for Athens. Careful instructions in twenty-two paragraphs were drawn up by Hamilton for the guidance of the *Signori Artisti* who were going direct to Athens. They were to start as arranged from Sicily for the Dardanelles; to proceed from the Dardanelles to Zea, and from Zea as soon as possible to Athens, where they would put themselves under the guidance of the British Consul, Logotheti. After visiting the antiquities, all would begin to work at their respective occupations. Balestra and Ittar, the two architects, would take measurements of the best preserved buildings, and would work out their drawings in case of bad weather; when the chief drawings were finished they would search for the ground-plans of buried ruins. They would also make careful drawings of all sorts of architectural details, and would write a description of what they had observed. If in their searches they found any pieces of ancient sculpture, they would consign them to Logotheti. Feodor meanwhile would make drawings on the scale that he thought most appropriate of all the better sculpture—also sketches of mediocre sculpture, to illustrate the progress or decadence of the art. Occasionally in bad weather the artists would draw costumes. The *formatori* would mould the sculpture that Feodor and Bernardino, the draughtsmen, thought the best. Rosati, the second *formatore,* would be under the orders of Bernardino. All the company would give their best attention to the acquisition of sculpture deserving transportation. The *formatori* would also mould small details chosen by Balestra; the moulds, carefully packed, would be put in the charge of the Consul, and no casts would be taken from them. Necessary money would be obtained from the Consul, who should also be consulted, if they were obliged to move on account of malaria. 'It is impossible to conclude these instructions without adding that all anxiously expect the worthy fruit of the expedition of such a company of chosen artists, who have already given such great proofs of their respective talents. . . .'

The Athens of 1800, the destined scene of Lusieri's activities, was a small and squalid town. It occupied an area immediately to the north and east of the Acropolis, whose boundaries can still be distinguished by the pedestrian tourist, or on inspection of a modern map, by the narrowness and intricacy of its streets and lanes. It was not yet pierced by the two chief thoroughfares, known by the names of Hermes and Aiolos respectively, which

Parthenon The east end of the ruins of the temple to the Goddess Athena, erected between 447 and 431 B.C.

Frieze of the Parthenon This is one slab of the great frieze depicting the Panathenaic procession which surrounded the central chamber.

were among the earliest works of the Bavarian engineers of the new kingdom. The present Constitution Square and the Palace Garden were an accidental clear space on the borders of the town. A Turkish wall, some ten feet high and having six gates, enclosed the whole of the town, the Temple of Theseus and the Acropolis. In its then form it dated from 1780, and its principal purpose had been to protect the inhabitants from the incursion of pirates and robbers. Between the houses and the town walls was a wide *pomoerium*, described by Hobhouse as an open space between the walls and the city, one hundred and fifty or two hundred yards in breadth, laid out in corn grounds, while other parts served as gardens, attached to some of the principal houses.

The number of houses in Athens was supposed to be between twelve and thirteen hundred; of these about four hundred were inhabited by Turks, the remainder by Greeks and Albanians, the latter of whom occupied about three hundred houses. There were also seven or eight Frank families, under the protection of the French Consul. None of the houses was well built or commodious, and the streets were all narrow and irregular. Hotels, of course, were as yet undreamt of. Even in 1810 Hobhouse writes of a scheme to provide Athens with a tavern, 'a novelty surely never before witnessed at Athens', as if it were a daring venture. The Frank traveller either hired a house, or enjoyed (for a consideration) the hospitality of some resident, such as Logotheti, or Theodora Macri, the daughter of his predecessor in office. Rooms could also be hired at the Capuchin Monastery which stood for western civilization. It possessed a pleasant garden, and incorporated in its buildings. the choragic Monument of Lysicrates, the interior of which served the superior as a book closet and library.

The chief buildings at Athens, about which Lusieri's operations turned, were not many in number.

On the Acropolis or citadel, the principal monument was the Parthenon, or temple of the Virgin Goddess Athena. It had been built at the crowning period of the glory of Athens (between 447 and 431 B.C.) during the administration of Pericles, and under the direction of Ictinos, the architect, and Pheidias, the sculptor. Its sculpture consisted firstly of groups in the round in the gables or pediments. In each case only a sorry remnant was left at the end of the eighteenth century in comparison with the original composition, yet such as they are they form the noblest group of ancient sculptures that time has left. Secondly, there were the square panels sculptured in high relief, the metopes, on the external order. Finally, there was the incomparable frieze, with the scene of the Panathenaic procession, which surrounded the central chamber. From the fall of Paganism to the Turkish conquest, the Parthenon had served as a church of the Virgin Mary. From the Turkish conquest onwards it had been a mosque. Its chief catastrophe had taken place in 1687 at the time of a Venetian siege, when the centre of the building was destroyed by a powder explosion. In Lord Elgin's time a small makeshift mosque was irregularly built on a part of the temple floor.

The other chief building on the Acropolis was the Erechtheum. This is a curiously complex group of sanctuaries incorporated in a single building of about 400 B.C. of great

225

refinement and beauty. In the eighteenth century it served as the house of the Disdar.

The Propylæa were the famous gateways and approaches to the Acropolis. On a projecting bastion of the Propylæa the temple of Wingless Victory (Athena Nike, or Nike Apteros) had once stood. It had been pulled down and its foundations had been incorporated in the Turkish works in the course of the preparations to resist the Venetian attack in 1687. Some of the slabs of its frieze were built into the walls of the Propylæa. The temple was reconstructed in its original position in 1835.

In the lower town the Theseum was a Doric temple, which had survived in excellent state as a church. Its sculptures consisted of metopes on and adjoining to the eastern end, and a frieze in high relief at each end of the temple.

The little monument dedicated by Lysicrates in honour of a musical victory has been already mentioned as incorporated with the buildings of the Capuchin Monastery. This list of course does not exhaust the monuments of Athens, but it includes those which appear most frequently in the course of the correspondence.

(The team under Lusieri worked away in Athens making casts and drawings and eventually gained possession of two noted marble monuments from the Church of St. George at Cape Sigeum. These two pieces formed the nucleus of the Elgin collection. They were working under difficulties however, as reported by Dr. Hunt, Chaplain to the Embassy at Constantinople.)

Of the Temples of Minerva, Theseus and Neptune, I can say nothing that would convey an idea of the effect they produce. They must be seen to know what the union of simplicity and beauty is capable of: and after having feasted the eyes with those exquisite specimens of Athenian Architecture, every deviation from them, even the edifices of Rome itself will almost disgust. Lusieri, tho' born on the banks of the Tiber, and attached as he was to the proud remains of the Mistress of the World, is now an enthusiastic Admirer of the Doric Buildings here, and turns with disgust from the works of Hadrian or Herodes Atticus, and everything on the Roman model.

He is employing his pencil on two general views of Athens, one from the Pnyx, the other from Mount Anchesmus (i.e. Lycabettos), which will embrace all the monuments and classic spots of the Citadel and the Town. He has also commenced near views of the Temples of Theseus, Minerva, and Pandrosos. Positive Firmans must, however, be obtained from the Porte, to enable the Architects and Modellers to proceed in their most interesting labours. Unfortunately the Temple of Minerva, called the Parthenon, and those of Neptune Arechtheus, of Minerva Polias, and Pandrosos, as well as the famous Propylæa, are all within the walls of the Acropolis, now a Turkish fortress, garrisoned by mercenary and insolent Janissaries, so that every obstacle which National jealousy and Mohometan bigotry, seconded by French intrigue, could produce, have been too successfully used to interrupt their labours. Till those Firmans are obtained, the bas-reliefs on the frieze, and the Groupes on the Metopes can neither be modelled nor drawn. The architects, therefore, in the meantime, are proceeding to make the elevations and ground plans, from the measures they had taken, and the Calmuc Theodore [Feodor, the draughtsman] employs his almost magic pencil in copying such remains of Sculpture as are beyond the walls of the citadel.

Up to this point, no ambitious designs of collecting the marbles had taken shape. Lord Elgin said before the Committee:

My whole plan was to measure and to draw everything that remained and could be traced of architecture, to model the peculiar features of architecture; I brought home a piece of each description of column for instance, and capitals and decorations of every description; friezes and moulds, and in some instances, original specimens; and the architects not only went over the measurements that had been before traced, but by removing the foundations were enabled to extend them and to open the way to further enquiries, which have been attended since with considerable success.

A nearer acquaintance, however, with the actual conditions soon began to influence Lord Elgin's mind.

From the period of Stewart's [an earlier traveller] visit to Athens till the time I went to Turkey, a very great destruction had taken place. There was an old temple on the Ilissus which had disappeared . . . every traveller coming, added to the general defacement of the statuary in his reach: there are now in London pieces broken off within our day. And the Turks have been continually defacing the heads; and in some instances they have actually acknowledged to me, that they have pounded down the statues to convert them into mortar. It was upon these suggestions and with these feelings, that I proceeded to remove as much of the sculpture as I conveniently could; it was no part of my original plan to bring away anything but my models.

(Eventually it was possible to negotiate with the Porte and a firman was issued.)

The terms of the new firman are published in the report of the Select Committee and elsewhere. It is in two parts, firstly reciting the prayer of the petitioner, and secondly granting it, point by point. The purport of the whole is sufficiently summarized in the evidence of Dr. Hunt.

It began by stating that it was well known to the Sublime Porte that foreigners of rank, particularly English noblemen and gentlemen, were very anxious to visit and examine the works of ancient art in Greece; particularly the Temples of the Idols; that the Porte had always gladly gratified that wish; and that in order to show their particular respect to the Ambassador of Great Britain, the august ally of the Porte, with whom they were now and had long been in the strictest alliance, they gave to his Excellency, and to his Secretary and the artists employed by him, the most extensive permission to view, draw and model the ancient temples of the idols and the sculpture upon them, and to make excavations, and to take away any stones that might appear interesting to them.

(With permission from the Porte—the work of salvaging and accumulating marbles began in earnest, Hunt reports.)

The inscriptions on the Acropolis were collected, including the treasure lists and other important Athenian documents now in the Elgin collection. The Caryatid porch of the Erechtheum was cleared of disfiguring accretions. 'The Cariatids that support it, and the rich ornaments of its cornice and ceiling, are now open to the day. If your Lordship,' Hunt continues, 'would come here in a large Man-of-War that beautiful little model of ancient art might be transported wholly to England. Nothing can exceed the exquisite beauty and delicacy of all its details.' A block of the Erechtheum cornice was taken down. On July 31st the Parthenon was first approached.

To-day the Ship-Carpenter and five of the Crew mounted the walls of the Temple of Minerva, and by the aid of Windlasses, Cordage and twenty Greeks, they succeeded in detaching and lowering down, without the slightest accident, one of the Statues or Groupes in the Metopes representing a combat between a youth (probably Theseus) and a Centaur; it has long been the admiration of the world; indeed nothing can equal it for beauty and grace. . . . A second which adjoins it, on the same subject, is to follow it to-morrow. . . . He (the son of the Disdar) tells me Choiseul gave his Father Eight Hundred Piastres for the Metope which adjoined these, but that it was taken down with so little skill, that the rope broke, and it was dashed into a thousand fragments.

The second Alto Rilievo [Hunt continues after a pause, presumably on the next day] is now lowered, and with equal success; they are to be brought as soon as possible to the Consul's; where the Calmuc is to design them, and then they are to be put on board. When I saw those beautiful statues hanging in the air, and depending on Ragusan Cordage, I was seized with a trembling and palpitation, which only ceased when they arrived safe to the Ground.

Hunt's letter of July 31st closed with a triumphant post-script: 'The most beautiful of the statues is now in the Consul's yard. We have been forced to get a gun-carriage and train of thirty men to bring it down. The other will follow to-night.'

At the same time that he reported these successes, Lusieri added that the garrison, and even the Disdar, were continually destroying some part of the Parthenon, in order to extract the lead with which its cramps were fastened. 'I am sure that in half a century there will not remain one stone on another. It would be well, my Lord, to ask for all that is left, or else to do all that is possible to prevent their going on in this fashion.'

At Athens, Hunt and Lusieri had arranged for the immediate shipping of a part of the collection, and particularly of the two

Metope of the Parthenon   This sculpture shows a contest between centaur and lapith.

metopes, but the work took longer than had been anticipated, and Hunt was thus able to prolong his tour. He learnt by letter that so many difficulties had occurred in casing the marbles, and transporting them to the Piræus, that it would be useless to return to Athens for some days. He employed the interval in excursions to Chæronea, Thermopylæ and Delphi.

(About this time, 28 March 1802, Lord and Lady Elgin set out from Constantinople to visit the scene of operations in person.)

From Lady Elgin's letters we learn that the party left Constantinople on Sunday evening, March 28th. It consisted of Lord and Lady Elgin, the children, and the doctor (Dr. Scott) in a Ragusan vessel; Colonel Murray and Hunt in the English brig which was to give protection from pirates; and

there was also 'a little ship filled with the Maltese that Elgin is sending to Malta'. The passage was rough—I believe Bruce was almost the only person on board who was neither sick nor frightened.' The Dardanelles were passed on the 31st. On April 1st it was still blowing hard, and Lady Elgin insisted on going ashore in the Bay of Mandria (i.e. Porto Mandri, or Thoricus, in the south-east of Attica). The children were left in the ship, and the night was passed in a tent pitched in a cave.

Three Fates These magnificent statues were once part of the Parthenon in Athens.

231

Some peasants told us that there were an amazing number of Pirates, and that the night before, eighteen of them had landed at *our cave* and carried away a Woman. However the Woman returned that morning, and said that if she had had another woman *like* herself, they two could have driven away the Robbers. We had plenty of Janissaries and lighted two large Fires close to our Tent to drive away the damps. We passed the night unmolested.

But the brig, which had stopped at Tenedos to take in wine, had been quite lost sight of, and it was therefore determined that the children should not remain in the Ragusan ship, unprotected from the pirates. With considerable difficulty, owing to the roughness of the sea, they also were brought ashore.

We had got from a neighbouring Village some Horses and Asses. You would have laughed had you seen the party. I was mounted upon an ass, Masterman *across* another, Mary's Paramana [i.e. wet-nurse] upon a third, and [there was also] a great fat washer-woman of mine who preferred walking to the horror of riding. . . . Thomas rode, and took Bruce up before him; Elgin and the Doctor walked. After six most tedious hours, scrambling over mountains, we arrived at the much wished for Village, where I expected to sleep *like a Queen!* But in this, Alas! I was sadly disappointed. We got to a *Han*, the people lighted a large fire in the middle, but not a crevise was left for the smoke to escape. I took possession of that Han for myself, Bratts, and Damsels; Elgin and the Doctor went into another. We expected to pass a most delightful night and arranged our Beds with great glee, but no sooner had we flung our weary limbs upon them than we were assailed in such a manner by flees not one of us could shut our eyes, it was quite dreadful for the poor Children. They were danced out of their beds every two minutes in order to catch the Flees. The next morning we all mounted as before, only we contrived two baskets, into which we put our Babs well bolstered up. The people told us we were nine hours' ride from Athens. We came to a village where we stopped and dined. Then we deposited our little treasures in the baskets and off we set. Lusieri and Monsieur Logothetté came to meet us, we were all sadly tired with this day's journey. I really thought of getting off my horse and laying down, for I never was so faged. It was between eight and nine o'clock when we arrived at Athens, and perfectly dark. Besides there was a great dew falling which made me very uncomfortable about Elgin. As for the children we wrapped them quite up and they arrived as fresh and lively as possible, I never saw them look so well as they do here.

On the 15th Lady Elgin wrote again. She had paid a sort of state visit to the Bath.

This morning I made myself as smart as possible, and having given some days notice that I intended *honoring* the Bath with my presence, I am sure there were three or four hundred Women, Greeks and Turks. Altho' I had formed a very pretty idea of the amusement, I must say it very far surpassed my expectation. Had you dancers, singers and Tambourine players in the Bath? The dancing was *too indecent* beyond anything. Mary shall not go to a Turkish Bath! We had a Ball here the other night. . . . We have all this house to ourselves. The Logothetties have gone into another, which makes it much more comfortable to us; I have made Hammerton's room the Nursery. Did you ever go up the outside flight of stairs? We have repaired the long room and put my Piano-forti into it, and we breakfast and sit reading, writing or arranging Medals in the Gallery. I have put a gate upon the top of the stairs, so there is a fine airy run for Bruce. We dine at two o'clock, and drive out in the *Curricle* every day after dinner. Tonight we dr[o]ve to the Monastery of Daphné, where you rode, [and] went all over it. I feel to know everything you *thought* and did here. But I have almost filled four pages without saying what I think of the Artist. I think the few things that remains, allmost all having been sent to England, far more beautiful than ever I dared imagine. But with Lusieri I own I am disappointed, not one single view finished —nothing but innumerable Sketches, but too much of a sketch for me. . . . We expect Hamilton every day from Egypt, he has been away many months. I shall be happy when he returns.

(Having arrived in Athens, Lady Elgin remained to expedite the loading of shipments to England.)

The letters from Lady Elgin to her husband are largely filled with the comings and goings of naval officers:

After dinner, as the Doctor, Lusieri and I were musing over the vicissitudes of human life, who should dash in at the door but Dicky Johnstone! dear fellow. How do [you] do, My Lady, How is My Lord?—I saw by his face there was no answer necessary to those *Queries*, so, *says I*, have you dined Mr. Johnstone? No My Lady, *says he*, moping a most profuse quantity of human Nature off his red face and still redder hair—But I have brought Mr. *Tinker* and Mr. *Blinker* with me, I thought my Lady you dined at three o'clock, but a bit of Bread & Cheese is all we want, My Lady—I am sorry, *Sir*, you have asked for the only thing I cannot give you *viz.* Cheese —(A notorious Lye by the bye for to Day we made the first incision into the last of the Conee's [?] cheeses) but I can give you Soup, fish, Beef stakes, Veal, Mutton, Lamb, Ducks, Turkeys &c. &c. &c. Upon which I got trusty Maraask & *really* produced dinner enough to *fill* the beasts. The Doctor you may be sure did not fail to do ye honors! I had to Overtalk him once or twice, *no* easy matter p'on honor!

In the morning I sent a *very civil* message to Capt. Hoste saying I was sorry to hear he was so ill & if there was anything I cd send him it wd give me great pleasure. I then coaxed over the Lieut. to prevale upon the Captain to take the Three, large Cases you saw in the Magazine. I told him they were seven feet long; he gave me little hopes, as it was impossible to put any thing above three feet long in the hold. I then found it necessary to use my persuasive powers, so I began by saying as the Capt. was going straight to Malta & there being no Enemies to encounter, I ventured to propose his taking them. It would be doing me a very great favor as you were extremely anxious to get them off, & *I* sh^d feel so proud to tell you how well I had succeeded during your absence— *Female* eloquence as *usual* succeeded, the Capt. sent me a very polite answer, & by peep of Day I send down the three Cases!

The Capt. is reading his Novel upon the Sopha and the Doctor is reading Herodote. . . . Nothing can be more obliging than he [the Captain] is, he saw the three cases at ye water side when he came up; having got them safely off my Hands, I next set to work to see if I could not contrive to get away something *more*. What say you to Dot? [her pet-name]. This is a Holliday, nobody will work, but I have offered *Backcheses*, Lusieri is all astonishment at me, he says he never saw anybody so keen as me.

I have made him set to work to pack up the Horse's head, the Urn and the stone that is in this house, a head, & the Capt. will take that also for me, he says he will stay to-morrow if it is any use—This is my grand Dinner day, the Count and his friend, the two Consuls, the Captain & Doctor, Lusierie & I—Dicky and three other officers came in this morning, but I took no notice of them & they are gone. . . . I have ordered the dinner & told Marco only to give *two Bottles* of Port, all the rest Zea; he told me with a long face that yesterday Dicky and his two friends drank three bottles of wine. They shall have as much Zea as they like, but no White wine, two Bottles of Port, no Porter, and not *a bit* of Cheese! Thomas, Piere & Marco wait at Table, three Boys run *to* and *fro* with the Dishes to the Kitchen, but are not to put their Noses in at the Door! I hear Dicky and his three Companions are above stairs, it is odd if they stay unasked by me, I have dinner enough— Have I not arranged all my affairs famously? . . . Capt. H. says he will take the packages he has got on board the Madras with him. He did not know he was really appointed till I send him word.

Eleven o'clock at night—

Now for some news that will please you. I have got another large case packed up this Day, a long piece of the Baso Relievo from ye Temple of Minerva, I forget the *proper term*, so I have by *my* management *got on board* four immense long heavy packages, & to-morrow the Horse's head &c. &c. is to be carefully packed up and sent on board; this is *all* that is ready for going. If there were twenty ships here nothing more could be sent for some time.—The *two* last Cases is *intirely* my doing, and I feel proud, Elgin!

And so, load by load, the marbles came to England.

SEA DIGGING

To anyone interested in ancient trade, the sea-bed of the Mediterranean is a veritable library of information. Through the centuries heavily laden merchant ships have foundered on the rocky coasts and have sunk with their precious cargoes.

Now, at last, the doors of that deep sea library are being opened by the techniques of sea digging. The following article vividly describes some famous ancient wrecks, and tells of great advances in underwater archaeology.

Excerpted from ARCHAEOLOGY, *Vol. 10, No. 4, Winter 1957, written by*

LIONEL CASSON

JUST before Easter in the year 1900 a group of Greek sponge-divers, returning from their season off Tunisia, ran into a storm and took refuge in a sheltered cove on Antikythera, a little island off the south coast of Greece. To pass the time, some of the crew slipped over the side. When, a few minutes later, one reappeared lugging the bronze arm of a Greek statue, underwater archæology was born.

Its infancy was spectacular. The divers had blundered on the wreck of an ancient ship loaded with works of art; it gave up a harvest of Greek statues that include some of Athens's National Museum's prize pieces. A second ship, discovered some years afterward off the coast of North Africa, also turned out to be loaded with objects of art. Then a long time went by without further reports of underwater finds. In the twenties deep-sea divers fished up some superb Greek bronzes and all the earlier expectations revived. But for various reasons no further efforts were made.

Shortly after the end of World War II a new type of diving apparatus became available. It was a simple affair, consisting of little more than a mouthpiece and a couple of oxygen bottles. A diver so equipped, with a mask to shield his eyes and flippers on his feet to give him drive, could wander about the sea floor for as long as twenty minutes. Underwater secrets were no longer open only to the sponge fisherman or to the professional deep-sea diver with his expensive and clumsy equipment; any interested amateur was in a position to go after them. A new period of sea digging opened.

The use of the new apparatus—called free-diving to distinguish it from that in which the diver is coupled by an air hose to the surface—found its most enthusiastic practitioners among the French. At first they concentrated their efforts along their own Riviera, and very soon startling reports began to come in of the discovery of numbers of Greek and Roman wrecks. Soon they and others moved farther afield, and wrecks began to turn up along the Italian Riviera, in the straits between Sardinia and Corsica, between Euboea's southern tip and the Greek mainland, and elsewhere. Unlike the first ships discovered, none of these, it turned out, were carrying works of art. They were all merchantmen loaded for the most part with those items that formed so large a part of the commerce of the Greeks and Romans—wine and oil.

We ship cargoes to-day in wooden tubs or barrels, paper cartons, metal drums or the like. In the world of the Greeks and Romans the standard shipping container was the amphora, a large clay jar. Long before any ancient wrecks were discovered we knew a good deal about these containers, since they turned up on land in quantities. We knew that they varied in size and shape from place to place and from century to century, and scholars had even made a good start on the difficult job of identifying which shape and size belonged to which place and time. These jars to-day form the key element in underwater archæology. The wrecks that the free-divers are now locating are not at all like the mental image we commonly have of a romantic hulk lying half-buried in sand; most often all that is left of them is the containers which held their cargoes—a mound of amphoræ jutting up from the sea floor, or an expanse of them strewn over it. When such objects, encrusted with marine growth, are brought to a museum curator, he can hardly be blamed for not displaying them among his treasured pieces. But these prosaic jars have a vital importance of their own.

For years scholars have studied the overseas commerce of the ancient world: what ships went where and with what sort of cargoes. What could be gleaned from the writings of ancient authors and other sources they had long ago collated and studied. Their findings led them to picture a trade that, although far-flung and brisk, was carried on (except for certain major routes) by smallish vessels which coasted along picking up cargo at dozens of points along the way.

The discoveries of art treasures which I mentioned at the outset and, even more, a haphazard dribble of jars from the

Byzantine Merchant Ship This wreck of a Byzantine merchant ship, lying at a depth of 120-140 feet was excavated jointly by the University Museum of the University of Pennsylvania and the National Geographic Society in the years 1961-1964 at Yassi Ada, Turkey. Here the diver is using a grid to plot the location of each piece before it is removed.

237

nets of Mediterranean fishermen were a steady reminder that valuable clues to the story of ancient commerce were to be found on the sea floor. About 1950 a new epoch opened. Nino Lamboglia, the enterprising Director of Antiquities for the area along the Italian Riviera, talked a salvage expert into a hurried but intensive investigation of a wreck a fisherman had found off Albenga in 1929. About the same time the amateur free-divers began reporting their finds. And then in 1952 Commandant Jacques-Yves Cousteau, the famous explorer of the world under the sea, started a full-scale scientific excavation of a ship that had gone down off the tiny island of Grand Congloué, just outside the harbour of Marseilles. The very first reports were revealing: neither the ship off Albenga nor that off the Grand Congloué was small or loaded with the miscellaneous merchandise that a tramp working the coasts would pick up. Both were big merchantmen, over one hundred feet long, and both were loaded with thousands of wine jars. I had long been studying the history of ancient commerce and I was convinced that these excavations demanded on-the-spot investigation. In 1953 I visited both sites and reported on what I had found. But after that, more and more enticing reports of new finds kept filtering through. This summer I decided to return for another look at the whole field.

'Anything new? Plenty—and not all of it from the Grand Congloué.' Fernand Benoit was speaking—curator of the Musée Borély, the archæological museum at Marseilles, and a key figure in underwater archæology to-day. As the Director of Antiquities for Provence and Corsica, all that the sea diggers find falls under his jurisdiction. No museum has a better display of amphoræ and the other objects that turn up in ancient wrecks than the Musée Borély, and no person knows more about them than M. Benoit.

'Here, look at this,' he said, and tossed me a photograph of a rather insignificant-looking jar. 'It's an Etruscan amphora,' he added with satisfaction. 'It's from a wreck found off the Cap d'Antibes; there are fragments of over forty jars. Sixth-century B.C.—the earliest wreck identified yet. There's no doubt that the Etruscans were trading in this area at that time; we've found their pottery in many places in southern Gaul. But come with me; I've got more to show you.'

He led me to a room where, in a fine new display, were objects chiefly from the Grand Congloué wreck: bits of bronze ship's fittings; a box made of lead; masses of Campanian pottery. On the wall was a sketch showing the exact position of the wreck and how the divers worked on it. In the same display case was a unique find—a hoard of bronze coins that, through the action of water, had fused into one solid mass; it was fished up in the bay off Ciotat (east of Marseilles) and may have come from a wreck or may merely have been lost overboard. From there he led me to the museum's 'maritime history room'. One wall was covered with examples of the various types of jars from the Grand Congloué wreck; there are upwards of two thousand more in storage and perhaps several thousand more still on the sea bottom. On the other walls were specimens from other wrecks found along the Riviera. For some reason the first century B.C. is especially well represented and there were many tall slender amphoræ of this period. But there were also plenty of others: wide-necked jars and narrow-necked ones, tubby jars and tall ones—almost an inventory of the many shapes we know.

All this material Benoit has arranged, analysed and given preliminary publication. The prize, of course, is the wreck off the Grand Congloué, and a good deal more is known about it now than when I made my first visit four years ago. The chief items in her cargo were, first, a consignment of tubby Græco-Italic amphoræ which, along with a shipment of Campanian pottery, were stored in the hold and, second, a swinging load of Italic wine jars stowed upright on the deck, precisely as we see them in pictures of ancient merchantmen. Over seventeen hundred of these last have been recovered. Their insides had been smeared with resin to prevent seepage and many still retained their plugs, a piece of cork topped by a clay stopper. On the outside of the lip they bore the name of the man who had shipped them: SES (an abbreviation for Sestius) followed by his company's device, a trident or an anchor. The Sestius family apparently had a long career in the shipping business, for amphoræ bearing their name have turned up in many places dating over a considerable span of years. Almost certainly, to judge by the fabric of the jars and by the presence of Campanian pottery, the wine was shipped from South Italy and was probably intended for distribution to the interior from Marseilles. In some instances we know from whom Sestius bought the wine: the wine-seller stamped his name on the stoppers, and on a few of them can still be read L. TITI. C.F. (Lucius Titius, son of Caius).

Though the wreck off the Grand Congloué is the greatest single contributor to the Musée Borély, it is not the only one. To date Benoit has been able to confirm the existence of at least seventeen wrecks lying between Marseilles and the Italian border, ranging in time from the sixth century B.C. to the fourth century of our era. But miscellaneous finds which keep coming

Amphorae   These containers in which goods—primarily wine and olive oil—were transported by ship during the 6th century B.C. are shown as they were found lying on the bottom of the Mediterranean Sea.

in indicate that this figure will soon have to be raised.

On still another score Benoit had interesting progress to report. Every ancient ship carried several anchors. Divers have recovered a good many, and the museum has a rich collection. The part the divers usually find is the stock—a long heavy bar either completely of lead or a wooden core sheathed in lead, fitted to receive the shank. The shank itself and the flukes were usually of wood and are only rarely recovered. Not all the stocks are alike and one particular form has led Benoit to conclude that it was the ancients who first invented the anchor with a movable stock, a convenient feature which enables sailors to lay the whole contraption flat on the deck and out of the way when not in use. In medieval times it apparently went out of existence and was unknown until the British re-invented it a century ago.

'We haven't found anything startlingly new since you were here last, but we've turned up a good many interesting things.' The speaker this time was Henri Broussard, Secretary of the *Club Alpin Sous-Marin* at Cannes. The club is the most important organization of its kind in France. All serious divers are members, and it is they who have investigated most of the wrecks along the French Riviera, as well as a good many elsewhere. M. Broussard, a skilled diver and expert underwater photographer, after a few preliminary remarks launched into one of his favourite topics: the wrecks of the Balise de la Chrétienne.

A little west of Cannes, at the point where the village of Agay rubs shoulders with Anthéor, a buoy called the Balise de la Chrétienne marks a particularly dangerous spot along this rocky coast. Diving here in 1948, Broussard came across what appeared to be a field of amphoræ. After a great many dives and careful investigation it was determined that there were three distinct wrecks in the vicinity.

For lack of better names the wrecks were dubbed A, B, and C. Not much could be gleaned from the last two: C was carrying tubby jars which may have been used for olive oil and are probably of the second century B.C., while B held wine jars of the first century A.D. Wreck A had a good deal more to offer. Its amphoræ were of the tall, slender, first-century B.C. type that turns up so frequently along the Riviera. Lying on the sea floor, they outlined the shape of the vessel, and Broussard estimates that it was about a hundred feet long. In 1954 the divers came upon a unique find, the stock of the ship's anchor with a piece of the wooden shank still fixed in it. This established beyond question that the vessel was a big fellow. The stock is one of the largest ever recovered, a massive piece of lead over six feet long and weighing nearly seven hundred pounds.

The remnant of its shank was $8\frac{1}{2}$ inches wide, 7 inches thick, and $33\frac{1}{2}$ inches long; originally it was at least twice as long.

The vessel had been carrying a cargo of wine (although a few oil jars were also found). Their stoppers had been stamped with the name of the wine seller: M. C. LASS—probably M(arcus et) C(aius) Lass(ius). Lassius is a name that was common in the area about Naples in the first century B.C. The ship, then, like that off the Grand Congloué, had very likely been transporting a big load of South Italian wine to southern France when it came to grief. Some of the wood from the hull was recovered, notably a rib which revealed the craftsmanship of the ancient shipwright in pinning planks to frame. Pegs held the two together, and to make sure the pegs fitted snugly, copper nails had been driven through them, forcing them to expand in their holes. Some tools from the ship's carpenter's chest were preserved in a curious way. Two formless chunks of corroded iron discovered in the wreck, when broken open, were found to contain perfect moulds of what they had been originally: one of a hatchet, the other of an adze. Even the piece of the wooden helve of one was preserved.

When sea digging is mentioned one almost automatically thinks of the French Riviera, but this region is far from having a monopoly of ancient wrecks. At least two have been identified along the Italian Riviera, the one off Albenga and another, of the second century B.C., off Pegli near Genoa. Divers have discovered that the floor of the straits between Corsica and Sardinia is strewn with jars. And of course there are wrecks in the eastern Mediterranean as well. But in this area I discovered a paradox: a good deal of the investigating must be done on land.

In 1955 a report was published that a wreck of the fifth century B.C. had been located off the island of Chios. So I stretched my itinerary to include this island. I quickly discovered that there was little more to add to the published notice. The wreck was in bad shape; only some fragments of jars had been recovered, just enough to prove that they were definitely of the fifth century.

This, however, was not the end of the trail on Chios. Before going there I had a long conversation in Athens with Virginia Grace, the acknowledged expert on Greek amphoræ. She informed me that the wreck reported off Chios was only one of many, assured me that there was a harvest of jars to be found on the island, and gave me clues as to where to do my searching. In the little museum at Chios I came upon a helter-skelter collection of amphoræ encrusted with marine growth. But outside the museum the finds were richer. The local fishermen use the dragnet, the type pulled in such a way that it brushes the bottom. It's hard on the fish—the grounds are gradually becoming exhausted—but it's wonderful for bringing up jars. The Chians prize these relics of their past: they set them out in their gardens, or use them as ornaments in their houses. Finding them is simply a matter of looking over garden walls and knocking on the doors of fishermen's houses. In one fishing village I got the impression that there was at least one jar in every home, and one house I visited had four, one adorning each room.

The varied shapes of these amphoræ show that they span the centuries from the fifth century B.C. to the late Roman Empire; the waters about the island must literally teem with wrecks. But Miss Grace assures me that Chios is not unique; She has been over most of the islands of the Ægean and the Eastern Mediterranean and has come across jars on practically all of them. There are clearly many, many wrecks to be found; merely to pinpoint them and explore only the most promising would require time, energy, organization, and money on a staggering scale.

Thus underwater archæology has one job before it which doesn't involve sea digging at all, namely the collating and study of all these amphoræ that turn up so haphazardly. Miss Grace is doing this for the east, Benoit and Lamboglia for parts of the west. This work is, of course, far less expensive and time-consuming than sea digging itself. Yet in a way it is almost as important, for it can help establish the date, the use, and the provenience of the various shapes. Once such problems are solved, divers will be in a position to identify quickly and precisely what they discover.

The immediate future of actual underwater exploration unquestionably lies along the French and Italian Rivieras. Here the sea diggers have already accomplished enough to give a vivid picture of the nature of ancient commerce and of the ships used in it. The coastal area from Italy to Marseilles was a waterway for international commerce as early as the sixth century B.C., and by the second B.C. it was clearly the scene of traffic on a large scale. In this and the subsequent century ships one hundred feet in length and more, capable of carrying upwars of two hundred tons of cargo, travelled this route, transporting huge quantities of Italian wine—the wreck off Grand Congloué carried perhaps fifteen thousand or twenty thousand gallons—and much Italian olive oil and pottery to the south coast of France.

We know less about succeeding centuries, but there is every

chance that the sea diggers will soon fill in this gap. Although work on the Grand Congloué wreck has virtually stopped, there is an exciting new prospect to take its place. At the northeast tip of the Île du Levant (in the Hyères group) is a beacon called 'the Titan' which warns ships away from a dangerous reef. Here was found a well-preserved wreck loaded with amphoræ from the age of Augustus. Many were still plugged with clay stoppers, and in some of the jars were found remains of tunny bones and of molluscs which had been preserved in fish sauce. Within the near future Phillip Tailliez, commanding officer of the *Groupe d'Études de Recherches Sous-Marines* attached to the naval base at Toulon, will start a full-scale investigation. His chances are bright indeed, for he has at his disposal the *Élie-Monnier*, a ship specially equipped for underwater research. There is some urgency because the wreck is easily reached and enthusiastic amateur diggers have been helping themselves to the jars.

Some of the high hopes raised earlier for underwater archæology are probably not to be realized. When Cousteau started to investigate the Grand Congloué wreck, he talked optimistically of raising the hull itself and giving the world its first look at a Roman merchantman. This is probably not to be. One of the serious problems connected with sea-digging is the preservation of the pieces of wood that are brought up, for they deteriorate rapidly on exposure to air. At an international congress (1955) devoted to underwater archæology a good part of one session was devoted to this topic, but no satisfactory conclusions were reached.

The technical side of underwater archæology has made tremendous strides in the past years. Divers now have powerful lamps to illumine the work, effective suction cleaners to remove the marine growth and much that cling to wrecks, devices to raise heavy finds to the surface. They have worked out techniques to plot the exact location of the various parts of a wreck and to set out markers so that a wreck, once found, will not have to be searched for all over again.

Underwater photography has made remarkable progress. Movies and still shots in black and white or colour record with dramatic clarity what lies on the floor of the sea. I was lucky enough to be present at a demonstration of how far the art of taking pictures under water had advanced—a live television of sea diggers at work on the Grand Congloué, arranged by Commandant Cousteau.

When I visited the Grand Congloué in 1953 it was the epitome of barrenness and loneliness, just an oversized naked white rock projecting above the surface of the sea. This time,

Byzantine Amphorae These jars lay untouched on the floor of the Aegean Sea on a shipwreck of the early 7th Century A.D.

as the launch rounded a point and the island came into sight, the changes were almost unbelievable. Over the spot where the wreck lay were anchored the two famous French underwater research ships, Cousteau's *Calypso* and Tailliez's *Élie-Monnier*. On one end of the island a veritable Eiffel Tower had been built; the rest was swarming with people and covered with a clutter of cables, generators, cameras, and the other paraphernalia needed for a television broadcast. The broadcast was a triple-barrelled affair: Cousteau had arranged to do it first in English, then in Italian, and finally in French. While the technicians, the director, and other personnel did their part ashore and on deck, down on the sea-floor diving-excavators worked on the wreck. Around them swam men carrying powerful lamps, and behind were the cameramen, tracking the work with their lenses. I watched the first broadcast on the spot, then raced to a set on shore to see the third on the screen. It went off without a hitch; Cousteau had attempted a daring experiment and carried it off brilliantly.

A copy of the English broadcast was made on film, and it may be shown in America. I hope it will. Its short minutes give, as no words can, a fascinating glimpse of the promise of underwater archæology—and a sobering realization of its expense and limitations.

THE·ROSETTA STONE

The rich and exciting history of ancient Egypt was hidden from
the world until the discovery of the Rosetta Stone in 1799 and
its translation in the early 1800's. How tantalizing it must have
been for earlier scholars to be able to see innumerable Egyptian inscriptions on temple walls, in tombs, and on papyri, and
not to be able to read the hieroglyphics. And then the discovery of the stone, with its bilingual inscription in Greek and
Egyptian, changed everything. The ancient Egyptians emerged
as personalities; they stepped boldly into time, so that we can
now read of their exploits, their poetry, and their intrigues.

The following account of the Rosetta Stone is written by
E. A. Wallis Budge of the British Museum. He tells how the
stone was discovered, brought to England, and eventually deciphered by the French scholar Jean François Champollion.
The stone can be seen today at the British Museum.

Excerpted from THE ROSETTA STONE, *(Trustees of the British Museum,
Revised 1950) written by*

E. A. WALLIS BUDGE

THE DISCOVERY OF THE STONE

THE famous slab of black basalt which stands at the
southern end of the Egyptian Sculpture Gallery in the
British Museum, and which has for more than a century
been universally known as the 'Rosetta Stone', was found in
July 1799, at a spot near the mouth of the great arm of the
Nile that flows through the Western Delta to the sea, not far
from the town of Rashîd, or as Europeans call it 'Rosetta'.
According to one account it was found lying on the ground, and
according to another it was built into a very old wall, which a
company of French soldiers had been ordered to remove in
order to make way for the foundations of an addition to the
fort, afterwards known as 'Fort Julien'.* The finder of the
Stone, a French Officer of Engineers named Bouchard, and his

* This fort is marked on Napoleon's Map of Egypt, and it stood on the left or
west bank of the Rosetta arm of the Nile.

companions observed that it bore inscriptions in three different scripts, and rightly supposed that they represented three versions of the same text. Since the last of these inscriptions was written in Greek and could therefore be read, they realized the possible importance of the Stone for the decipherment of the hieroglyphics in the first inscription. News of the discovery soon reached Cairo, whither the Stone was removed and placed in the Institut National which had recently been founded in that city. On its arrival in Cairo it became at once an object of the deepest interest to the body of learned men whom Napoleon had taken with him on his expedition to Egypt, and the General himself exhibited the greatest curiosity in respect of the contents of the inscriptions cut upon it. The inscription placed between the hieroglyphic and Greek versions was soon identified by Jean-Joseph Marcel and Remi Raige as a cursive form of hieroglyphic writing, but no progress was made in the decipherment of either of the Egyptian versions. Napoleon subsequently ordered a number of copies of the Stone to be made for distribution among the scholars of Europe, and two skilled lithographers, 'citizens Marcel and Galland', were specially brought to Cairo from Paris to make them. The plan which they followed was to cover the surface of the Stone with printer's ink, and then to lay upon it a sheet of paper which they rolled with india-rubber rollers until a good impression had been taken. Several of these ink impressions were sent to scholars of great repute in many parts of Europe, and in the autumn of 1800 General Dugua took two to Paris, where he committed them to the care of 'citizen Du Theil' of the Institut National of Paris.

THE ARRIVAL OF THE STONE IN ENGLAND

After the successful operations of Sir Ralph Abercromby in Egypt in the spring of 1801, a Treaty of Capitulation was drawn up, and by Article XVI the Rosetta Stone and several other large and important Egyptian antiquities were surrendered to General Hutchinson at the end of August in that year. Some of these he despatched at once to England in H.M.S. *Admiral* and others in H.M.S. *Madras*, but the Rosetta Stone did not leave Egypt until later in the year. After the ink impressions had been taken from it, the Stone was transferred from Cairo to General Menou's house in Alexandria, where it was kept covered with cloth and under a double matting. In September 1801, Major-General Turner claimed the Stone by virtue of the Treaty mentioned above, but as it was generally regarded as the French General's private property, the surrender of it was accompanied by some difficulty. In the following month Major-General Turner obtained possession of the Stone, and embarked with it on H.M.S. *L'Egyptienne*, and arrived at Portsmouth in February 1802. On March 11th it was deposited at the Rooms of the Society of Antiquaries of London, where it remained for a few months, and the writings upon it were submitted to a very careful examination by many Oriental and Greek scholars. In July the President of the Society caused four plaster casts of the Stone to be made for the Universities of Oxford, Cambridge, Edinburgh, and Dublin, and had good copies of the Greek text engraved, and despatched to all the great Universities, Libraries, Academies, and Societies in Europe. Towards the close of the year the Stone was removed from the Rooms of the Society of Antiquaries to the British Museum, where it was mounted and at once exhibited to the general public.

DESCRIPTION OF THE STONE

The Rosetta Stone in its present state is an irregularly-shaped slab of compact black basalt, which measures about 3 feet 9 inches in length, 2 feet $4\frac{1}{2}$ inches in width, and 11 inches in thickness. The top right and left hand corners, and the right hand bottom corner, are wanting. It is not possible to say how much of the Stone is missing, but judging by the proportion which exists between the lengths of the inscriptions that are now upon it, we may assume that when it was complete it was at least 12 inches longer than it is now. The upper end of the Stone was probably rounded, and, if we may judge from the reliefs found on stelæ of this class of the Ptolemaïc Period, the front of the rounded part was sculptured with a figure of the Winged Disk of Horus of Edfû, having pendent uræi, one wearing the Crown of the South, and the other the Crown of the North. Below the Winged Disk there may have been a relief, in which the king was seen standing, with his queen, in the presence of a series of gods, similar to that found on one of the copies mentioned below of the inscriptions on the Rosetta Stone. Whatever the sculptured decoration may have been, it is tolerably certain that, when the Stone was in a complete state, it must have been between five and six feet in height, and that when mounted upon a suitable plinth, and placed near the statue of the king in whose honour it was engraved, it formed a prominent monument in the temple in which it was set up.

The inscription on the Rosetta Stone is written in two languages, that is to say, in Egyptian and in Greek. The

Egyptian portion of it is cut upon it in: I. the Hieroglyphic Character, that is to say, in the old picture writing which was employed, from the earliest dynasties, for nearly all state and ceremonial documents that were intended to be seen by the public; and II. the Demotic Character, that is to say, the conventional, abbreviated and modified form of the Hieratic character, or cursive form of hieroglyphic writing, which was in use in the Ptolemaïc Period. The Greek portion of the inscription is cut in ordinary uncials. The hieroglyphic text consists of 14 lines only, and these correspond to the last 28 lines of the Greek text. The Demotic text consists of 32 lines, the first 14 being imperfect at the beginnings, and the Greek test consists of 54 lines, the last 26 being imperfect at the ends. A large portion of the missing lines of the hieroglyphic text can be restored from a stele discovered in 1898 at Damanhûr in the Delta (Hermopolis Parva), and now in the Egyptian Museum in Cairo (No. 5576), and from the copy of a text of the Decree cut on the walls of a temple at Philæ.

THE EARLIEST DECIPHERERS OF THE ROSETTA STONE

An English translation of the Greek text was made by the Rev. Stephen Weston, and was read by him before the Society of Antiquaries of London in April 1802, and a French translation was made by 'citizen Du Theil', who declared that the Stone was 'a monument of the gratitude of some priests of Alexandria, or some neighbouring place, towards Ptolemy Epiphanes'; a Latin translation by 'citizen Ameilhon' appeared in Paris at about the same time. The first studies of the Demotic text were those of Sylvestre de Sacy and Åkerblad, a Swedish diplomat, in 1802. The latter succeeded in identifying in the Demotic version the equivalents of all the proper names which occurred in the Greek text, and he also recognized the words for 'temples', 'Greeks', and the third person masculine pronoun. In all probability Åkerblad's contribution to the decipherment of the Demotic text would have been even more substantial if he had not assumed that the script was exclusively

The Rosetta Stone   This slab of black basalt found by a French Officer of Engineers named Bouchard in July of 1799 became the key to ancient Egyptian hieroglyphics. The inscription on the stone is written in two languages, Egyptian and Greek, and in three scripts. At the top of the stone is the Hieroglyphic character, in the middle is the Demotic character, and at the bottom is the Greek. The translation of the Greek led eventually to the deciphering of the hieroglyphics.

alphabetic. The credit for being the first to recognize that Egyptian writing consisted mainly of phonetic signs belongs to Thomas Young, the author of *The Undulatory Theory of Light*, who obtained a copy of the Rosetta Stone in 1814; he also demonstrated a fact which had previously been suspected by Zoëga, de Guignes and others, that the ovals, or cartouches, in the hieroglyphic version contained royal names. Thomas Young's discoveries were not, however, limited to the Rosetta Stone, but included among many other achievements the decipherment of the names of Berenice and Cleopatra, the latter on a granite obelisk with a bilingual text in Greek and hieroglyphics which had been excavated at Philæ in 1815 by W. J. Bankes of Kingston Lacy. It is difficult to estimate the extent to which Young's discoveries assisted the French scholar Jean François Champollion (1790–1832), but it is likely that in many cases both these pioneers reached similar conclusions independently. In 1822 the list of alphabetic Egyptian characters that had been drawn up by Young was corrected and greatly enlarged by Champollion, who, between that date and the year of his death, correctly deciphered the hieroglyphic forms of the names and titles of most of the Roman Emperors, and drew up a classified list of Egyptian hieroglyphs, and formulated a system of grammar and general decipherment which is the foundation whereon all later Egyptologists have worked.

The decipherment of proper names, although providing the key to the system of writing, could not have led to an understanding of the Egyptian language without the assistance of Coptic. Christian descendants of the ancient Egyptians are called Copts, a name which is only a corruption of the Greek 'Aiguptos', 'Egypt'; the translations of the Holy Scriptures, liturgies and other sacred writings which they made from Greek into their native tongue are written in the Greek script supplemented by seven characters derived from Demotic. The knowledge of Coptic has never been lost, and its literature has always been available in manuscripts for study by scholars. Champollion, whilst still a youth in the early years of the nineteenth century, realized the great importance of Coptic for the purpose of Egyptian decipherment, and he studied it to such good purpose that he was able to identify very many of the Egyptian words which he could read with their Coptic equivalents. In his studies of the inscription on the Rosetta Stone, his knowledge of Coptic enabled him to deduce the phonetic values of many syllabic signs, and to assign correct readings to many pictorial characters, the meanings of which were made known to him by the Greek text on the Stone.

METHOD OF DECIPHERMENT

The method by which the greater part of the Egyptian alphabet was recovered is this: It was assumed correctly that the oval ( ), or 'cartouche' as it is called, always contained a royal name. There is only one cartouche (repeated six times with slight modifications) on the Rosetta Stone, and this was assumed to contain the name of Ptolemy, because it was certain from the Greek text that the inscription concerned a Ptolemy. It was also assumed that if the cartouche did contain the name of Ptolemy, the characters in it would have the sounds of the Greek letters, and that all together they would represent the Greek form of the name of Ptolemy. Now on the obelisk which Mr. Bankes had brought from Philæ there is an inscription in two languages, Egyptian and Greek. In the Greek portion of it two royal names are mentioned, that is to say, Ptolemy and Cleopatra, and on the second face of the obelisk there are two cartouches, which occur close together, and are filled with hieroglyphs which, it was assumed, formed the Egyptian equivalents of these names. When these cartouches were compared with the cartouche on the Rosetta Stone it was found that one of them contained hieroglyphic characters that were almost identical with those which filled the cartouche on the Rosetta Stone. Thus there was good reason to believe that the cartouche on the Rosetta Stone contained the name of Ptolemy written in hieroglyphic characters. The forms of the cartouches are as follows:

On the Rosetta Stone

On the Obelisk from Philæ

In the second of these cartouches the single sign ▭ takes the place of the three signs ⚷ ⏐⏐ at the end of the first cartouche. Now it has already been said that the name of Cleopatra was found in Greek on the Philæ Obelisk, and the cartouche which was assumed to contain the Egyptian equivalent of this name appears in this form:

Taking the cartouches which were supposed to contain the names of Ptolemy and Cleopatra from the Philæ Obelisk, and numbering the signs we have:

Ptolemy, A.

Cleopatra, B.

Now we see at a glance that No. 1 in A and No. 5 in B are
identical, and judging by their position only in the names they
must represent the letter P. No. 4 in A and No. 2 in B are
identical, and arguing as before from their position they must
represent the letter L. As L is the second letter in the name of
Cleopatra, the sign No. 1 ◿ must represent K. Now in the
cartouche of Cleopatra we know the values of Signs Nos.
1, 2 and 5, so we may write them down thus:

In the Greek form of the name of Cleopatra there are two
vowels between the L and the P, and in the hieroglyphic
form there are two hieroglyphs, ╒ and ⟨, so we may assume
that ╒ = E and ⟨ = O. In some forms of the cartouche of
Cleopatra No. 7 ⊂⊃ is replaced by ◠, which is identical with
No. 2 in A and No. 10 in B. As T follows P in the name
Ptolemy, and as there is a T in the Greek form of the name of
Cleopatra, we may assume that ◠ and ⊂⊃ have substantially
the same sound, and that that sound is T. In the Greek form
of the name Cleopatra there are two A's, the positions of
which agree with No. 6 and No. 9, and we may assume that

has the value of A. Substituting these values for the
hieroglyphs in B we may write it thus:

Thomas Young noticed that the two signs always followed
the name of a goddess, or queen, or princess, and the other
early decipherers regarded the two signs as a mere feminine
termination. The only sign for which we have no phonetic
equivalent is No. 8 ⊂⊃ and it is obvious that this must represent
R. Inserting this value in the cartouche we have the name of
Cleopatra deciphered. Applying now the values which we
have learned from the cartouche of Cleopatra to the cartouche
of Ptolemy we may write it thus:

We now see that the cartouche must be that of Ptolemy, but it is also clear that there must be contained in it many other hieroglyphs which do not form part of his name. Other forms of the cartouche of Ptolemy are found, even on the Stone, the simplest of them written thus: ⟨cartouche⟩. It was therefore evident that the other signs ⟨hieroglyphs⟩ were royal titles corresponding to those found in the Greek text on the Rosetta Stone meaning 'ever-living, beloved of Ptah'. Now the Greek form of the name Ptolemy, i.e. Ptolemaios, ends with S. We may assume therefore that the last sign in the simplest form of the cartouche given above has the phonetic value of S. The only hieroglyphs now doubtful are ⟨sign⟩ and ⟨sign⟩, and their position in the name of Ptolemy suggests that their phonetic values must be M and some vowel sound in which the I sound predominates. These values, which were arrived at by guessing and deduction, were applied by the early decipherers to other cartouches, e.g.:

1. ⟨cartouche⟩   2. ⟨cartouche⟩

Now, in No. 1, we can at once write down the values of all the signs, viz., P. I. L. A. T. R. A, which is obviously the Greek name Philotera. In No. 2 we know only some of the hieroglyphs, and we write the cartouche thus: ⟨A L ⟨sign⟩ S ⟨sign⟩ ᴡᴡᴡ T R ⟨sign⟩⟩

It was known that ᴡᴡᴡ occurs in the name Berenice, and that it represents ⟨sign⟩, and that ⟨sign⟩ is the last word of the transcript of the Greek title 'Kaisaros', and that it therefore represents some S sound. Some of the forms of the cartouche of Cleopatra begin with ⟨sign⟩, and it is clear that its phonetic value must be K. Inserting these values in the above cartouche we have:

⟨A L K S ⟨sign⟩ N T R S⟩

which is clearly meant to represent the name 'Alexandros', or Alexander. The position of the sign ⟨sign⟩ shows that it represented some sound of E or A.

Returning to the signs ⟨hieroglyphs⟩ which we have assumed to represent the royal titles 'ever-living, beloved of Ptah', we have to decide whether this assumption be correct or not. It was known by tradition and from Coptic that the old Egyptian word for 'life' or 'living', was 'ānkh', or 'ōnkh', and that it was represented by the symbol ⟨ankh⟩ which occurs several times in the inscriptions. It was therefore guessed that the next signs ⌐⌐| meant 'ever'. Coptic again showed that one of the old Egyptian words for 'ever, age, eternity', was 'djet', and as we already know that the phonetic value of the second sign in the word is T, we may assume that the value of ⌐ is DJ. The third sign ▬ is a 'determinative', and was not pronounced. Thus the first title ♀ ⌐⌐| means 'living ever', or 'ever-living'. Of the remaining signs ▫⌐ ︙ ▬ we know that the first two are P and T, i.e. the first two letters of the name of Ptah; the third sign ︙ must then have the value of H or something like it. If the signs ▫⌐ ︙ form the name of Ptah, then the sign which follows them must mean 'loving', or 'loved'. Here again the Coptic helped the early decipherers in assigning a phonetic value to ▬, for the Coptic word for 'to love' is 'mere', ⲙⲉⲣⲉ, and they assumed that the value of the sign was 'mer'. Now in the cartouche of Ptolemy on the Rosetta Stone after the name Ptah ▫⌐ ︙, we have the signs ⅄ ⎜⎜, and these are, clearly, a variant of ▬. We already know that ⎜⎜ = I, and therefore ⅄ must be the equivalent of ▬

and have the value of 'mer'. By the comparison of texts containing variant forms, and by the skilful use of his knowledge of Coptic, Champollion succeeded in formulating the system of decipherment of Egyptian hieroglyphs that is, substantially, that in use at the present day.

THE CONTENTS OF THE INSCRIPTION ON THE ROSETTA STONE

The inscription on the Rosetta Stone is a copy of the Decree passed by the General Council of Egyptian priests assembled at Memphis to celebrate the first commemoration of the coronation of Ptolemy V, Epiphanes, King of all Egypt. The young king had been crowned in the eighth year of his reign, therefore the first commemoration took place in the ninth year, in the spring of the year 196 B.C. The original form of the Decree is given by the Greek section, and the Hieroglyphic and Demotic versions were made from it.

The inscription is dated on the fourth day of the Greek month Xandikos (April), corresponding to the eighteenth

day of the Egyptian month Meshir, or Mekhir, of the ninth
year of the reign of Ptolemy V, Epiphanes, the year in which
Aetus, the son of Aetus, was chief priest and Pyrrha, the
daughter of Philinus, and Areia, the daughter of Diogenes,
and Irene, the daughter of Ptolemy, were chief priestesses.
The opening lines are filled with a list of the titles of Ptolemy
V, and a series of epithets which proclaim the king's piety
towards the gods, and his love for the Egyptians and his
country. In the second section of the inscription the priests
enumerate the benefits which he had conferred upon Egypt,
which may be thus summarized:

1. Gifts of money and corn to the temples.
2. Gifts of endowments to temples.
3. Remission of taxes due to the Crown.
4. Forgiveness of debts owed by the people to the Crown.
5. Release of the prisoners who had been languishing in
   gaol for years.
6. Abolition of the press-gang for sailors.
7. Reduction of fees payable by candidates for the
   priesthood.
8. Reduction of the dues payable by the temples to the
   Crown.
9. Restoration of the services in the temples.
10. Forgiveness of rebels, who were permitted to return to
    Egypt and live there.
11. Despatch of troops by sea and land against the enemies
    of Egypt.
12. The siege and conquest of the town of Shekan
    (Lycopolis).
13. Forgiveness of the debts owed by the priests to the
    Crown.
14. Reduction of the tax on byssus.
15. Reduction of the tax on corn lands.
16. Restoration of the temples of the Apis and Mnevis
    Bulls, and of the other sacred animals.
17. Rebuilding of ruined shrines and sacred buildings,
    and providing them with endowments.

As a mark of the gratitude of the priesthood to the king for
all these gracious acts of Ptolemy V, it was decided by the
General Council of the priests of Egypt to 'increase the ceremonial observances of honour which are paid to Ptolemy, the
ever-living, in the temples'. With this object in view it was
decided:

257

1. To make statues of Ptolemy in his character of 'Saviour of Egypt', and to set up one in every temple of Egypt for the priests and people to worship.
2. To make figures of Ptolemy (in gold), and to place them in gold shrines, which are to be set side by side with the shrines of the gods, and carried about in procession with them.
3. To distinguish the shrine of Ptolemy by means of ten double-crowns of gold which are to be placed upon it.
4. To make the anniversaries of the birthday and coronation days of Ptolemy, viz., the XXXth day of the month Mesore and the XVIIth day of Paophi, festival days for ever.
5. To make the first five days of the month of Thoth days of festival for ever; offerings shall be made in the temples, and all the people shall wear garlands.
6. To add a new title to the titles of the priests, viz., 'Priests of the beneficent god Ptolemy Epiphanes, who appeareth on earth', which is to be cut upon the ring of every priest of Ptolemy, and inserted in every formal document.
7. That private individuals may borrow the shrines with figures of Ptolemy inside them from the temples, and may take them to their houses, and carry them about in procession.
8. That copies of this Decree shall be cut upon slabs of basalt in the 'writing of the speech of the god', i.e. hieroglyphs, and in the writing of the books, i.e. demotic, and in the writing of the Ueienin, i.e. Greek. 'And a basalt slab on which a copy of this Decree is cut shall be set up in the temples of the first, second and third orders, side by side with the statue of Ptolemy, the ever-living god.'

THE MAHDIA WRECK

One of the first underwater excavations was made in 1907, its purpose: to recover the treasure of the Mahdia Wreck.

Monsieur Merlin, who was then Head of the Department of Antiquities at Tunis, has related the hopes, fears and difficulties of the team who salvaged the many works of art from the wreck. About two thousand years earlier, the ship had foundered. Since then it lay undisturbed in deep, dangerous water off the African coast until the exciting marine excavation of 1907.

Many of the beautiful things that were brought to the surface can be seen today in the Bardo Museum in Tunis.

Excerpted from LES FOUILLES SOUS-MARINES DE MAHDIA,
(Tunis, 1911) written by

A. MERLIN

Ladies and Gentlemen,

YOU have all surely heard of the underwater excavations at Mahdia; you know that to the east of Tunis, between Sousse and Sfax, the remains of an ancient wreck have been found. But perhaps you do not know the way in which the exploration was carried out at the bottom of the sea, and the nature and interest of the objects that were salvaged. Where was the ship coming from and where was it going to when disaster overtook it? I propose to tell you something of the story of this richly laden vessel which was carrying works of art, furniture, and building materials, all snatched from Athens and bound for Italy; how the ship foundered on the inhospitable coast by Syrtes at the beginning of the first century B.C.; and how we, two thousand years later, have been able to retrieve this treasure.

The discovery was made by sponge-fishers. In June 1907, some Greek divers were working in the vicinity of Mahdia, and one of them returned to the surface with a strange tale. He declared that he had seen a 'row of big cannons' lying in the mud. There was great speculation among the crew and the captain decided to spend a little time investigating the area. It was then that the wreck was found. Since then the Antiquities Department has taken charge and has carried out the excavations which have produced outstanding and important results. The objects that have been found are of high artistic quality, but an added interest comes from the fact that they were salvaged from the sea, and that is why, before I give you an account of the works of art themselves, I will tell you something of the manner in which the exploration was carried out. I will tell you of the difficulties and attempt to make you share the hopes and fears of those concerned in this deep-sea catch.

We are now at Mahdia. It is early morning of a summer's day, and we board one of the Greek sponge-fishers' boats which unfurls its huge sail. Leaving the port, we pass the Arab quarter and the lighthouse as we round the headland along which the small town has sprawled. With a good wind we shall have yet an hour's sailing, but without it we must put out the great oars and toil for three long hours for we must make our way some five kilometres to the NE. of the Point. We cannot guarantee a calm sea for there is always the chance of rough weather and the Mediterranean hereabouts justifies Sallust's comment—a 'terrible' sea. The trip is hard on those who are not good sailors because these boats toss and pitch in any water. But when there is a high wind blowing it is unsafe to venture past the protecting arm of the promontory and we cannot work on such a day.

Little by little we approach the spot; and we can see the marking buoy. Sometimes during the night gales have torn it away and we have had to begin again to locate the wreck by using fixed points from the shore. It is a laborious business—but happily such tiresome time-wasters occur rarely. We throw the anchor overboard and the day's work begins.

Our boat carries a team of divers. Some of them leisurely await their turn in the stern of the ship; others prepare themselves in the bow for the descent, and the leader holds the line to which each diver in his turn is attached. Amidships is the airpump which is worked by hand. Already one diver has come up and another puts on his helmet and climbs overboard. Now we can only follow him in imagination.

Weighted with small packets of lead strapped to his back and chest he sinks for a long time, because here the depth is about 120 feet, the height of two six-storey houses, one on top of the other.

When at last he gets to the bottom he is confronted with a great mass of columns (there are sixty in all) and they lie side

Vase This beautifully sculptured vase depicting the Satyr, the Maenad with Cithara, and Dionysus was found in the Mahdia wreck.

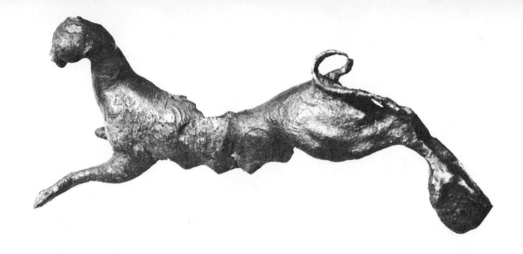

Panther One of the many pieces of bronze sculpture removed from the Mahdia wreck.

Chimera A bronze statuette of a she-monster usually represented as having a lion's head, a goat's body, and a dragon's tail. Occasionally, the chimera has a lion's body.

Bronze Sculpture A beautifully wrought Satyr.

Grotesque Dwarf   A statuette recovered from the Mahdia wreck.

by side in six rows. The shafts of the columns are not all of equal length but they have been placed in continuous lines that stretch from north to south for 96 feet. Pieces of marble are scattered about in profusion, as well as capitals and bases of columns, carefully squared blocks and architectural fragments. Among all this material, especially at the northern end of the ship, there are innumerable broken pots, all that remains of earthenware vessels that had been stacked aboard: cracked and broken amphorae, jars of all kinds that had contained oil, wine, water, foodstuffs, and other things needed

Architrave   Bronze head of Dionysus.

Candelabrum This bronze statuette of Eros Androgyne was designed to hold one candle.

by the crew during the voyage. At the southern end of the ship are enormous masses of lead—one piece we were able to haul up weighed as much as 600 kilos. These leaden bars constituted the remains of the anchors which had been in the bow. But all that I have told you so precisely appeared far less distinctly as originally found. At first it seemed just to be a *mélange* of columns, blocks of marble, amphorae and anchors, all buried in the mud.

In order to get our results it was necessary to remove all obstructions and to dig away the cloak of covering mud. There was no easy way of lifting the columns, for the shafts were, on an average, twelve feet long and twenty-five inches in diameter. To dig them out the diver has to stir up the mud which constantly permeates the water and envelops everything in an opaque gloom. He kneels there on the sea-bed working with his hands, in the faint glimmer of light which penetrates to this depth. Slowly he makes a tunnel under some object through which he can pass a rope to haul it aside, or if it is a good piece to drag it into position for raising. At certain times his task is very gruelling, and even dangerous, because not only is he subject to the severe pressure of the water above him but there is often an icy current, against which he must battle all the time in order to retain his place.

When the men manage to dig under or between certain of the columns, they come across an eighteen-inch layer of partially decomposed wood. This had once been the deck, and below this they find the delicate objects which had been stowed away in the holds. Here, there are fine statuettes in bronze and pieces of furniture with graceful inlay. It seems clear that the ship, when she foundered, must have gone straight to the bottom without turning turtle or breaking up, and that for the two thousand years which followed not only has she been supported by mud, but many of the objects have been protected from damage and corrosion in this firm bed of slime.

Each diver trained to work at such depths is able to stay below for thirty or forty minutes, after which he comes to the surface bringing with him anything that he has been able to retrieve from the wreck. It is an exciting moment for those waiting above, where time seems endless while the diver is at his work below. You must not think that each time a diver returns he is able to bring a masterpiece to the surface—sometimes he only clutches a fragment from the ship, oxidized nails, wood, bits of lead. And often whole days pass and we find nothing worthwhile. But there are the occasions when the chief diver, hauling a comrade upwards, feels a heavier weight on the rope and we all wonder what it can be. Perhaps it is a bronze statuette. Should this be so, no matter how formless it may appear, covered with slime and marine deposit, we all feel that our labours have been rewarded and we forget our exhaustion and continue with renewed enthusiasm.

Once the objects have been extracted they are cleaned—we remove the dense crust of shellfish and marine deposit that envelops them and makes them almost unrecognizable. We piece together the fragments: arms and legs have sometimes been found months later, bits of furniture must be joined together and it is sometimes possible to identify the decorative inlay from the pattern that has been left on metal. Thus, thanks to minute and complicated work, we are able to restore many of the objects to their original shape and, in spite of the damage caused by twenty centuries at the bottom of the sea, we can appreciate their artistic value and obtain an important and documentary picture of those far-off times. . . .

But I hasten to come to the question that you must be asking yourselves: whence did this cargo come and where was it going when disaster overtook the ship?

All these works of art in marble and bronze, all these building materials and pieces of furniture, came from Athens. We have found inscribed Greek slabs, one of which is a decree issued by the Paroloi, the citizens of Athens who formed the crew of the trireme Parolos which was one of the two Sacred Ships; others are dedication stones from the shrines of Piræus. Without doubt it was from the arsenal at Piræus that two huge bronze cornices, adorned with the heads of Dionysos and Ariadne, were wrenched away. It is from the temple of Asklepios at Piræus, too, that the ex-voto offering must come which shows the figure of the god reclining on a couch in front of a table laden with food, with his daughter Hygieia seated by him. They are attended by a serving-man and a number of worshippers.

Some of the capitals, decorated on either face with gryphons' heads and two curled wings, take us back again to Athens. The type is very rare, not only on our ship, where most of the capitals are Ionic, but in the ancient world, types such as these appear in two buildings only: a tomb at Pompeii where most probably they are imports, and the theatre of Dionysos at Athens. The white heavily veined marble from which the columns, capitals and statues are cut could have come only from Hymettus.

Our ship then, set out from Athens, but in order to know where she was going let us first establish the date.

The earliest date that we have so far is given by the Hermes of Boëthos, which cannot be earlier than the beginning of the

Hermes of Dionysus   A bronze cornice
adorned with a sculptured head of Dionysus.

second century B.C., but we have another object of fixed date which is a terracotta lamp, salvaged with its charred wick *in situ* and obviously part of the ship's furniture. This lamp is characteristic of the end of the second century B.C. and could have still been in use in the early years of the first. For the rest, if our ship carried inscribed stones from the sanctuaries of the Piræus, the journey must have been made after the taking of Piræus by Sulla in 86 B.C. It was then that the arsenal and storehouses were sacked and burnt and the temples desecrated.

Nike Bronze sculpture of the goddess of victory.

Since there are no objects of a later date it appears that the voyage and wreck took place shortly after the capture of the town by Sulla.

But where was the cargo being taken to? There was no person or town of sufficient importance in Africa at this time to have been in a position to have commanded such treasures. If the ship sank off the coast of Syrtes it was not because it was about to put in there but because it had been driven there by storms. The ship was probably going to Italy, to the Campagna, or more likely, to Rome. This is a suggestion which cannot be

Minerva   Bronze sculpture of the head of the Roman goddess of war and wisdom.

substantiated but it is in accordance with all that we know of the tastes of the Romans at that time. Sulla himself ordered Athenian columns to be re-used when the Capitol was rebuilt after the great fires of the Civil War in 83 B.C., and Lucian reminds us of a ship, loaded with works of art, sent to Rome by Sulla from Athens which sank after rounding Cape Malea. This example is significant and curiously like our own. Typical too of those times are these extracts from Cicero's letters to his friend Atticus, who was in Athens in 67-66 B.C. (a date near the time of our wreck). Cicero writes: 'I was glad to learn that you had bought me some statues of Hermes in Pentelic marble. Send them to me as quickly as possible. I want to have them at once.' Or: 'I have received the statue in Megara marble that you sent me. It is beautiful and I will have it in my villa at Tusculum. If you find any other suitable statuary, do not hesitate to buy it for me.' And some years later he went to considerable trouble to procure columns for his daughter Tullia's tomb.

In fact, during the next few years, ships were constantly leaving Athens bound for Italy, bearing away works of art and columns for public buildings, private houses and villas, for the adornment of porticos and gardens, and for the furnishing of staterooms and banqueting halls.

Could we want better comparisons? The columns from our wreck would adorn any building, as would the statues and candelabra. Our statuettes would please the eye with their elegance or bring a smile to the lips with their lively caricature. We have found furniture to grace salons and inscriptions to please the man of letters.

Is it not legitimate then to suppose that ours was one of those ships carrying loot to Rome, and that the cargo was composed of the spoil of Athens and Piræus.

But those who awaited the arrival of our ship carrying their treasures had not thought of the hazards of the crossing or the dangers of the sea by Syrtes. Battered by gales, the ship was driven towards the African coast, and, being too heavily loaded to ride out the storm, sank, taking with her the precious cargo.

It is possible that the ship sailed under bad auspices, that it had been cursed by the gods whose altars had been despoiled. And if, after more than nineteen hundred years we, here in Africa, have inherited the works of art intended by Rome for the glorification of the Republic, perhaps it is those same gods, in a moment of anger, who wish still to be revenged on Rome by enriching Carthage and the soil of Africa at Rome's expense.

THE MYSTERY OF TOLLUND MAN

One afternoon in May, 1950, Professor P. V. Glob was phoned by the police during a lecture at Aarhus University in Denmark. They had found the corpse of a man lying in a peat bog in nearby Tollund and suspected a murder.

Here Professor Glob describes his investigation of the "murder" and his discovery that the victim had been dead for 2,000 years!

Excerpted from ILLUSTRATED LONDON NEWS,
(24th November, 1951) written by

P. V. GLOB

PEAT-CUTTING in the Danish bogs frequently brings objects to light which have lain hidden since before the written history of the country began. Many of the treasures of Danish antiquity, such as the 'lurs', the widely-known Bronze Age trumpets, and many ornaments of gold, silver and bronze, were found by this process, all of them objects which would hardly have found their way by chance into the peat-bogs, but must rather have been deposited there as offerings to some divine power. A similar interpretation must be made in the case of the twenty or so ploughs, dating to the middle of the first millennium B.C., and again of the human bodies, about forty in all, dating from before the introduction of Christianity, all found in the peat-bogs. Almost all these objects are characteristically found in quite small 'saucer' bogs, or in small branches of the larger fen areas.

One of the best preserved and most thoroughly investigated bodies was brought to light in May 1950, in the course of peat-cutting in Tollund Bog in Central Jutland. While lecturing at Aarhus University, I received a telephone call from the police, who informed me of the discovery of a well-preserved corpse and requested me to investigate the matter, as they suspected an unsolved murder. A visit to the finding-place, however, a little elongated peat-bog surrounded by high, steep hills in a desolate heather-clad area, established that the crime, if crime it was, had taken place perhaps 2,000 years ago. It was an amazing sight to see this prehistoric man, his face so well preserved and as expressive as though he had but a moment ago fallen asleep. He lay in a contracted position as though sleeping, with wrinkled brow, closed eyes and mouth fast shut, with all the appearance of a strong personality. Only the dark, brown-leather colour showed his age. But this man of a bygone age had not of his own free will laid himself to sleep on this spot and been covered in the course of centuries by successive layers of peat. A rope formed of two smooth plaited leather thongs lay in a noose round his neck, pulled tight and choking, with the long, free end lying along his back. And he was naked. On his head he bore a skin cap, sewn together from eight pieces of leather with the fur inwards, and fitted with a chin-strap. But the only body clothing was a leather belt knotted in a noose over the stomach. It is obvious that this man, clothed only in cap and belt, had been hanged and then deposited in the bog. But why? It is improbable that a common criminal would have been treated in this way, while many people would regard the fine lines of the Tollund man's countenance as telling against such a theory.

About a hundred bodies of men, women and children have, in the course of the last two centuries, been recovered from peat-bogs in the area covering Jutland, north-west Germany and Holland. Of these only a few can have come there accidentally, drowned in the treacherous bogs, while the lack of burial furnishings shows that there can be no question of normal burial. A characteristic of the majority of the bodies discovered is their scanty attire. Many, like the Tollund man, are practically naked, and many have only a leather cape over their shoulders. Very many have a noose of rope or leather round their necks, while others have crushed heads, broken limbs, or mortal wounds in their body. Some are bound hand and foot, and others are pinned down in the bogs by a wooden stake or a hook, this last being a precaution against haunting. A medieval tradition in this connection relates that King Abel could not, on account of a fratricide, rest in his grave in Schleswig Cathedral, and was therefore exhumed and laid in a near-by bog, held fast by a stake through the body. Ancient writings tell how criminals ended their days staked down in peat-bogs; Tacitus, for example, describing this as a custom of the Germani about A.D. 100, while other early authors tell us that human sacrifices were offered to the gods in Scandinavia right up to the introduction of Christianity about A.D. 1000.

274

Sacrifice to the Gods   This body was found in a peat bog, curled as though in sleep, naked except for a leather cap and belt. There was a leather rope drawn tight around the neck. On the basis of previous finds, it has been concluded that this man must have been used as an offering to the Gods.

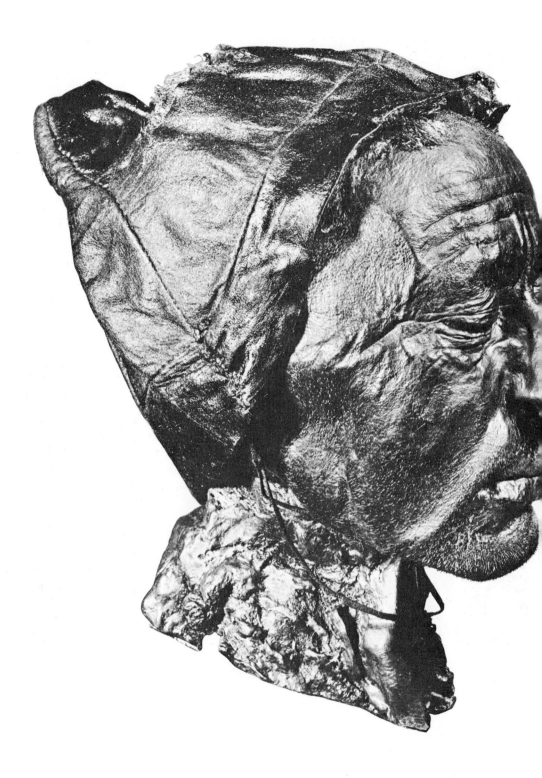

Tollund Man The Tollund Man's head was perfectly preserved by the chemicals of the peat bog. Here is an unprecedented example of a man who lived 2,000 years ago.

Hanging was, moreover, in ancient times not considered a dishonourable death, this viewpoint only coming in with Christianity, based on the fact that hanged men were sacred to Odin, the wise, one-eyed god, one of the chief gods of the close of the heathen period.

There is perhaps reason to emphasize two points in connection with the Tollund man; that he was hanged and that he was naked. Many of the other bodies from the peat bogs are naked, and many still have the rope with which they were hanged around their necks. *And the general belief is that such naked hangings were ritual sacrifices in connection with the great spring fertility festivals of antiquity.* An investigation of the stomach contents of the Tollund man throws an interesting sidelight on the question of the food of prehistoric man. This investigation showed that he had eaten no animal food recently, but only a porridge of vegetables and seeds. This porridge consisted mainly of barley, linseed, 'gold of pleasure' (*Camelina linicola*) and pale persicaria (*Polygonum lapathifolium*), all of which were cultivated during the Iron Age; but, in addition, it contained a number of wild plants such as sheep's sorrel (*Rumex acetosella*), white goosefoot (*Chenopodium album*), brassica, corn spurrey and many others which would scarcely come to be accidentally mixed with the cultivated plants. Thus we may conclude that the seeds of wild plants formed an important part of the diet of prehistoric peoples.

In many ways the Tollund man causes prehistory to live before our eyes. His handsome countenance, fantastically well-preserved, makes a stronger and more real impression than the work of the best sculptor could give. The strange circumstances in which he was found give us a glimpse of a remarkable religion. Well may he have been an offering to the gods to bring fertility and fortune to his fellow-men. The old gods did at least not relinquish him to the scientists of today without exacting their price. They took man for man. While the Tollund man was being lifted from his desolate resting-place to be taken for investigation to the National Museum in Copenhagen, one of the helpers dropped dead, struck down by heart failure. . . .

MAIDEN CASTLE

Maiden Castle is perhaps the most famous earthwork in Great Britain. It has been vividly described by Thomas Hardy who could see it from the windows of his house at Dorchester.

From 1934 onwards, a series of excavations was carried out there. Perhaps the most vivid episode which these revealed was the manner in which, in A.D. 44, the Roman invaders overwhelmed the place.

Excerpted from MAIDEN CASTLE, DORSET *(Society of Antiquaries of London, 1943) written by*

SIR MORTIMER WHEELER

AND so we reach the Roman invasion of A.D. 43. That part of the army of conquest wherewith we are concerned in Dorset had as its nucleus the Second Augustan Legion, whose commander, at any rate in the earlier campaigns, was the future Emperor Vespasian. Precisely how soon the invaders arrived at Maiden Castle can only be conjectured, but by A.D. 47 the Roman arms had reached the Severn, and Dorset must already have been overrun. Suetonius affirms that Vespasian reduced 'two very formidable tribes and over twenty towns (*oppida*), together with the Isle of Wight', and it cannot be doubted that, whether or no the Durotriges (as is likely enough) were one of the tribes in question, the conquest of the Wessex hill-fort system is implied in the general statement. Nor is it improbable that, with the hints provided by the mention of the Isle of Wight and by the archæological evidence for the subsequent presence of the Second Legion near Seaton in eastern Devon, a main line of advance lay through Dorset roughly along the route subsequently followed by the Roman road to Exeter. From that road today the traveller regards the terraced ramparts of the western entrance of Maiden Castle; and it requires no great effort of the imagination to conjure up the ghost of Vespasian himself, here confronted with the greatest of his 'twenty towns'. Indeed, something less than imagination is now required to reconstruct the main sequence of events at the storming of Maiden Castle, for the excavation

281

Maiden Castle Here are the defenses as seen from the air.

of the eastern entrance has yielded tangible evidence of it. With only a little amplification it may be reconstructed as follows.

Approaching from the direction of the Isle of Wight, Vespasian's legion may be supposed to have crossed the River Frome at the only easy crossing hereabouts—where Roman and modern Dorchester were subsequently to come into being. Before the advancing troops, some two miles away, the sevenfold ramparts of the western gates of Dunium towered above the cornfields which probably swept, like their modern successors, up to the fringe of the defences. Whether any sort of assault was attempted upon these gates we do not at present know; their excessive strength makes it more likely that, leaving a guard upon them, Vespasian moved his main attack to the somewhat less formidable eastern end. What happened there is plain to read. First, the regiment of artillery, which normally accompanied a legion on campaign, was ordered into action, and put down a barrage of iron-shod ballista (catapult) arrows over the eastern part of the site. Following this barrage, the infantry advanced up the slope, cutting its way from rampart to rampart, tower to tower. In the innermost bay of the entrance, close outside the actual gates, a number of huts had recently been built; these were now set alight, and under the rising clouds of smoke the gates were stormed and the position carried. But resistance had been obstinate and the fury of the attackers was roused. For a space, confusion and massacre dominated the scene. Men and women, young and old, were savagely cut down before the legionaries were called to heel and the work of systematic destruction began. That work included the uprooting of some at least of the timbers which revetted the fighting-platform on the summit of the main rampart; but above all it consisted in the demolition of the gates and the overthrow of the high stone walls which flanked the two portals. The walls were now reduced to the lowly and ruinous state in which they were discovered by the excavator nearly nineteen centuries later.

That night, when the fires of the legion shone out (we may imagine) in orderly lines across the valley, the survivors crept forth from their broken stronghold and, in the darkness, buried their dead as nearly as might be outside their tumbled gates, in that place where the ashes of their burned huts lay warm and thick upon the ground. The task was carried out anxiously and hastily and without order, but, even so, from few graves were omitted those tributes of food and drink which were the proper and traditional perquisites of the dead. At daylight on the morrow, the legion moved westward to fresh conquest,

Skeleton of One of the Slain

doubtless taking with it the usual levy of hostages from the vanquished.

Thereafter, salving what they could of their crops and herds, the disarmed townsfolk made shift to put their house in order. Forbidden to refortify their gates, they built new roadways across the sprawling ruins, between gateless ramparts that were already fast assuming the blunted ramparts that are there today. And so, for some two decades, a demilitarized Maiden Castle retained its inhabitants, or at least a nucleus of them. Just so long did it take the Roman authorities to adjust the old order to the new, to prepare new towns for old. And then finally, on some day towards the close of the sixties of the century, the town was ceremonially abandoned, its remaining walls were formally 'slighted', and Maiden Castle lapsed into the landscape amongst the farm-lands of Roman Dorchester.

So much for the story; now for its basis. First, scattered over the eastern end of Maiden Castle, mostly in and about the eastern entrance and always at the same high level, were found upwards of a dozen iron arrow-heads of two types: a type with a pyramidal point, and the simple flat-bladed type with turn-over socket. Arrow-heads occurred at no other Iron Age level, but both types are common to Roman military sites where *ballistae* but not hand-bows are to be inferred. There, then, in the relatively small area uncovered, are the vestiges of the bombardment.

Roman Arrowhead   This weapon was found in the vertebra of one of the defenders' skeletons.

Secondly, the half-moon bay, close outside the portals of the eastern entrance, was covered with a thick layer of ash associated with the post-holes of three or more circular or roundish huts. In and immediately below this ash were quantities of late prehistoric (Belgic) pottery. In the surface of the ash was similar pottery with scraps of early Roman red-glazed pottery. There are the burnt Belgic huts, covered by the trodden vestiges of the continued post-conquest occupation for which more tangible evidence will be offered shortly.

Thirdly, into this ash a series of graves had been roughly cut, with no regularity either of outline or of orientation, and into them had been thrown, in all manner of attitudes—crouched, extended, on the back, on the side, on the face, even sitting up—thirty-eight skeletons of men and women, young and old; sometimes two persons were huddled together in the same grave. In ten cases extensive cuts were present on the skull, some on the top, some on the front, some on the back. In another case, one of the arrow-heads already described was found actually embedded in a vertebra, having penetrated the body from the front below the heart. The victim had been finished off with a cut on the head. Yet another skull had been pierced by an implement of square section, probably a ballista-bolt. The last two and some of the sword-cuts were doubtless battle-wounds; but one skull, which had received no less than nine savage cuts, suggests the fury of massacre rather than the tumult of battle—a man does not stay to kill his enemy eight or nine times in the mêlée; and the neck of another skeleton had been dislocated, probably by hanging. Nevertheless, the dead had been buried by their friends, for most of them were accompanied by bowls or, in one case, a mug for the traditional food and drink. More notable, in two cases the dead held joints of lamb in their hands—joints chosen carefully as young and succulent. Many of the dead still wore their gear: armlets of iron or shale, an iron finger-ring, and in three cases bronze toe-rings, representing a custom not previously, it seems, observed in prehistoric Britain but reminiscent of the Moslem habit of wearing toe-rings as ornaments or as preventives or cures of disease. One man lay in a double grave with an iron battle-axe, a knife and, strangely, a bronze ear-pick across his chest. The whole war cemetery as it lay exposed before us was eloquent of mingled piety and distraction; of weariness, of dread, of darkness, but yet not of complete forgetfulness. Surely no poor relic in the soil of Britain was ever more eloquent of high tragedy, more worthy of brooding comment from the presiding Spirits of Hardy's own *Dynasts*.

THE DEAD SEA SCROLLS

"Muhammad Adh-Dhib has lost a goat." So begins the story of the discovery of the Dead Sea Scrolls—one of the most exciting tales that can be told.

What were these scrolls that have cost so much in intrigue and money? They were the treasured manuscripts of a sect of Jews who had retired into the wilderness and had built themselves a monastery beside the Dead Sea. For 150 years these Sectarians flourished under their strict religious discipline. Then, in A.D. 68, Roman armies swept across the land and the monastery was abandoned.

But the sect's valued library was saved, carefully hidden away in caves in the wild adjacent hills. There the manuscripts lay until 1947, when they were discovered by chance by a Bedouin lad. Today scholars of many nations are poring over these old texts, which include books of the Old Testament written in Hebrew that are nearly a thousand years older than any previously known.

Excerpted from THE DEAD SEA SCROLLS, *(Penguin Books, 1956) written by*

J. M. ALLEGRO

MUHAMMAD ADH-DHIB had lost a goat. The lad was a member of the Ta'amireh tribe of semi-Bedouin who range the wilderness between Bethlehem and the Dead Sea, and he had been out all this summer's day tending the animals entrusted to his care. Now one of them had wandered, skipping into the craggy rocks above. Muhammad pulled himself wearily up the limestone cliffs, calling the animal as it went higher and higher in search of food. The sun became hotter, and finally the lad threw himself into the shade of an overhanging crag to rest awhile. His eye wandered listlessly over the glaring rocks and was suddenly arrested by a rather queerly placed hole in the cliff face, hardly larger than a man's head. It appeared to lead inwards to a cave, and yet was too high for an ordinary cave entrance, of which there were hundreds round about. Muhammad picked up a stone

Essene Monastery The largest room at the settlement, used by the Essene's for their ceremonial meals and services.

and threw it through the hole, listening for the sound as it struck home. What he heard brought him sharply to his feet. Instead of the expected thud against solid rock, his sharp ears had detected the metallic ring of pottery. He listened a moment, and then tried again, and again there could be no doubt that his stone had crashed among potsherds. A little fearfully the Bedouin youth pulled himself up to the hole, and peered in. His eyes were hardly becoming used to the gloom when he had to let himself drop to the ground. But what he had seen in those few moments made him catch his breath in amazement. On the floor of the cave, which curved back in a natural fault in the rock, there were several large cylindrical objects standing in rows. The boy then pulled himself up again to the hole and, holding on until his arms and fingers were numb, saw, more clearly this time, that they were large, wide-necked jars, with broken pieces strewn all about them. He waited no longer, but dropped to the ground and was off like a hare, his goat and flock forgotten in a frantic desire to put as much distance between himself and this jinn-ridden cave as possible. For who else but a desert spirit could be living in such a place with an entrance too small for a man?

That night Muhammad discussed his discovery with a friend who, being the elder, was entitled to scoff at the superstitions of his junior. He urged Muhammad to take him to the spot, and the next day the two of them went to the cave, and this time squeezed through the hole and dropped inside. It was just as the younger lad had described. The jars stood in rows on each side of the narrow cave, and, in the middle, broken sherds lay amidst debris fallen from the roof. There were seven or eight of the jars all told, and some had large, bowl-like lids. They lifted one and peered in, but found it empty. And so with another, and another, until in the third they saw a bundle of rags and under it two more. If they had hoped for the glitter of gold and precious stones they were sorely disappointed, for the bundles crumbled at a touch, and, pulling away some of the folds, they could see only some black tarry substance and, below that, folds of smooth brown leather. When, later, the boys had taken this booty back to their camp, they took off all the wrappings from the large bundle, and unrolled the scroll it contained, until, as they later recounted wonderingly, it stretched from one end of the tent to the other. It seems certain that this must have been the larger of the two manuscripts of Isaiah, the news of which was to set the biblical world astir. However, at the time it evoked little interest among its new owners who could neither read the strange writing inscribed on it, nor think of anything useful to which

Cave Treasures This hoard of Tyrian silver coins of the 1st Century B.C., a bronze pot, oil lamps, and pottery jars and bowls were found in the area where the Dead Sea Scrolls were located.

they could put the leather, fragile as it was. So for a time the Bedouin carried the scrolls about with them as they pastured their flocks and made what trade they could with their neighbours. These Bedouin have no real home. The world is their prey and usually their enemy. This tribe has been in the vicinity since the seventeenth century, and they have managed to eke out a sparse enough living with their few animals, now and again putting their detailed knowledge of the territory to better gain in smuggling. Until the area became effectively policed by the Arab Legion, they practised highway robbery when they could, and always found a ready market for their trading, legal or illegal, in Bethlehem. It was to this town that they made regular visits to sell their milk and cheese, and there, one market day, they took the three scrolls. Their general dealer happened to be an Assyrian Christian, by name Khalil Iskander Shahin, known locally as Kando, who, besides the small general store patronized by the Ta'amireh, owned a cobbler's shop next door. When the Bedouin showed him the scrolls, he evinced little interest, but thought they might

Kh. Qumran   The kiln in the potter's workshop.

serve as raw material for his cobbler's business. Later, after they had been kicking about the floor of his shop for some days, he picked one up and looked more closely at the surface. The writing was as meaningless to him as to the Bedouin, but it occurred to him that his spiritual guardians in Jerusalem might know more about it, and accordingly, one day when he was going up to the city, he took the scrolls along with him to the Syrian Convent of St. Mark in the Old City. This much is certain, but it must be confessed that from here on the story begins to disintegrate, as love of truth on the parts of the chief actors in the drama gives way before fear and cupidity. One thing is certain, however; Kando began to realize that the scrolls had some monetary value and found out that the Bedouin had by no means cleared the cave. He and his accomplice George accordingly launched a minor archæ-ological expedition to the cave indicated by the Bedouin and collected at least a number of large fragments and probably at this time the remainder of the scrolls, making seven in all. After they had taken all they could find, they seem to have let the Syrian authorities of St. Mark's into the secret. In any case the Metropolitan organized his own expedition to the cave, which proceeded to ransack the place, making a large opening near the ground, and pulling out everything they could lay their hands on. Of course, it will be realized that all such excavations were and are completely illegal under the laws of the country, whether of the Mandate or of the succeed-ing Jordan Government. All such archæological material remains the property of the country in which it is found, until the Government directs otherwise. So complete secrecy shrouded all these operations, and much harm was done as a result. It is certain that the Syrians found some more fragments, but valuable archæological data like linen wrappings and sherds from the broken jars they threw on to a rubbish dump outside. Kando had meanwhile deposited the scrolls in his possession with the Metropolitan, on a security, he now says, of £24; and these and some fragments the Church leader began to hawk round the various scholastic institutions of Jerusalem to get an idea of their worth. It seems that one of the scrolls was shown to the late Professor E. L. Sudenik of the Hebrew University, who kept it for some time and then set about finding the rest of the scrolls, which he had realized were very old and of considerable value. He made a perilous journey to Bethlehem, for by now the Jewish-Arab hostilities had become open warfare following on the withdrawal of the Mandate. There he seems to have contacted Kando and brought away three more scrolls. This gentleman now began to get scared since he was afraid that the news of the illegal excavations would leak out, and he would rightly be held responsible by the authorities. He therefore took the precaution of burying some of the largest fragments from the cave in his garden at Bethlehem! Unfortunately, the soil of Kando's back garden is somewhat different from the parched dust of the Qumran caves, and when later he went to retrieve them he found only several lumps of sticky glue.

Meanwhile, in Jerusalem, the Syrian Metropolitan was continuing his rounds, trying to discover if the scrolls were really old. Finally, on 18th February, 1948, he called up the American School of Oriental Research and spoke to Dr. John C. Trever, who had been left in temporary charge of the establishment during the absence of the Director. He told Trever that during a clear-out of his library at the Convent, he had found some old Hebrew manuscripts on which he would like his advice. An appointment was made for the next day, and the Metropolitan sent round the scrolls packed in an old suitcase, by the hand of a Father Butros Sowmy and his brother. After some hasty comparing of pictures of other ancient Hebrew manuscripts, and complicated research into dictionaries and concordances, Trever discovered that he was looking at a scroll of Isaiah, and that as far as he was able to tell, it was genuinely very old. He asked permission to make photographs of the scroll, and after some negotiations did so. As he worked he became more and more excited, for if it was as old as a favourable comparison with a photograph of a pre-Christian Hebrew papyrus fragment would seem to indicate, then he was handling the oldest manuscript of the Bible ever known. It was only with great difficulty that Trever could restrain his impatience when, half-way through the work of photography, he had to fulfil a long-standing engagement with the Curator of the Palestine Museum, then Mr. Harry Iliffe, to go to Jericho and take photographs of a local excavation. However, he seems to have restrained both his impatience and his tongue, for neither then nor at any other time was any mention of the discovery made to the authorities responsible for the control of antiquities in Palestine, who alone could have taken adequate and immediate steps to safeguard the treasures and seal the cave until a properly organized expedition could learn its secrets. Rather did Trever urge the Metropolitan to take the documents out of the country, since the situation was fast deteriorating, and war was beginning to stalk the streets and hills of that unhappy land. It was not until November of 1948, when the April copies of the *Bulletin of the American Schools of Oriental Research* reached Jerusalem,

Scroll Jars Receptacles for storing scrolls which were found in the vicinity of Kh. Qumran.

that Mr. G. Lankester Harding, newly responsible for the archæological interests of Arab Palestine as well as Trans-Jordan, learnt that eighteen months before, a fabulous discovery had been made by the Dead Sea. By now photographs of the scrolls had been examined by competent palæographers like Professor W. F. Albright and pronounced definitely pre-Christian, probably dating to the first or second centuries before our era. Excitement ran high all over the scholarly world, and in Jordan, Harding was now faced with an extremely difficult and urgent problem. The source of these scrolls had to be found, and if any related archæological material remained, it had to be expertly examined at the first opportunity, not only to confirm the palæographical dating but to determine the community from whose library they had come. Furthermore, it seemed not improbable that there might be more scrolls, and certainly fragments, since apparently some of the documents found were in a fragile condition with pieces missing from the outside and edges. But the original discovery had taken place so long ago that the chances of finding the source relatively free from tampering were very slight. The Metropolitan had succeeded in smuggling the scrolls in his possession out of the country, and had taken them to America. The Jordan Government, of course, demanded their immediate return, but by now the monetary values being accorded them in the popular Press were so astronomical as to persuade the Syrian Church leader that the chances of his returning were well worth sacrificing for the sake of the money he could expect to raise in their sale. The one bright light in the whole miserable affair at this stage was that he had agreed with Trever and the American Schools to allow them to photograph and publish the scrolls immediately whilst their sale was being negotiated. The Americans had told him, apparently, that if they were published quickly their value would be much enhanced. In fact, it declined, since once they were readily available in printed form the need for the originals became less urgent. The American scholars did, in fact, publish them extraordinarily well and quickly, putting the scholarly world greatly in their debt.

Back in Jordan, Harding had gone immediately to the Palestine Archæological Museum in Jerusalem, and in his capacity as Acting Curator instructed Joseph Saad, the new Secretary, to spare no effort in discovering the whereabouts of the fabulous cave and any other information he could about the find and the personalities involved. Saad's first call was to the American School, and there Dr. O. R. Sellers, that year's Director, immediately offered all the help in his power.

Together they went to St. Mark's Monastery, despite the
extremely dangerous nature of the journey through the Old
City, where Jewish shells and sniping were making it near
suicide to be out of doors during daylight. Slipping from
shelter to shelter they finally arrived at the building which
backs on to the dividing wall between Arab and Jewish
Jerusalem, and there interviewed a person by the name of
George Isaiah. It became clear from the beginning that he
was not going to be very helpful, and, although he did not
deny that the Monastery had organized an excavation of the
cave, refused point-blank to disclose its whereabouts. Saad
argued, cajoled, and bullied, but all to no effect, and he was
just about to give up hope of gaining any useful information
at all when, out of the corner of his eye, he saw one of the
Syrian fathers approaching, a venerable saint called Father
Yusif. When the old man had drawn quite near, Saad suddenly
turned from George and asked Yusif what he knew about the
cave. Before George could stop him, the old man began to
describe the excavations and their whereabouts. George turned
on him fiercely, but could not silence him before he had given
at least a general idea of the cave's position. It seemed that it
was somewhere south of the junction of the roads to Jericho
and the Dead Sea, amongst the cliffs which border the Sea
to the west. Now those limestone cliffs are honeycombed with
caves and clefts in the rock, and the mountains rise nearly a
thousand feet from the marly plateau, so that with a southern
limit at Ras Feshkha about six miles to the south, a good deal
more detailed pin-pointing was going to be necessary for the
cave to be discovered. As Saad and his companion retraced
their steps through the Old City, they discussed the next move.
It seemed obvious that they would have to try the great
stand-by of the East, bribery. Most things out there have their
price, and it only remained to find out how high it was going
to be. So on their return, negotiations with George Isaiah
were opened, on the general principle that, if he would lead
a party to the cave, he would receive a cash payment, and
the custody of any further scrolls found would be equally
shared between them. These negotiations took a considerable
time, involving many trips to the Monastery through gun-fire.
Finally, when it seemed that arrangements were sufficiently
far advanced, Saad arranged for the mayor of Jerusalem and
his dignitaries to accompany them to St. Mark's to witness
the formal agreement. The party arrived on the day appointed
and took their seats. Everybody asked after everybody else's
health, and were asked in return, and Allah duly thanked.
Coffee was passed round, and after that, the customary small

talk ensued, without which no Arab meeting is considered opened. Sellers was beginning to get restless, but Saad, raised in the traditions of the East, played the game in all its formality and was patient. At last, after the seventh round of thanking Allah for their individual good health, the main subject was broached, the terms stated, and nothing but the clasping of hands remained to seal the bargain. And George Isaiah would have nothing to do with it.

Sellers and Joseph parted gloomily at the gates of the American School, and Saad carried on to the Museum. Weeks of negotiation had produced practically nothing and, apart from its general locality, they knew little more about the

Kh. Qumran   A general panoramic view of Kh. Qumran.

Copper Scrolls   Two metal scrolls as they were found within the cave.

cave than what had been learnt from the American *Bulletin*. Now it happened that the Museum at this time was in the hands of the Arab Legion, and Saad had to pass a ring of sentries to reach his quarters. He made a perfunctory greeting to the man on duty at the gate and then something prompted him to hesitate and look at the soldier more closely. He was a lean, dark-skinned Arab of the desert, of the type Glubb always chose for his picked troops, and Saad studied his face for a moment, noticing his long, straight Semitic nose, his short curly beard, and black smouldering eyes. He was a true son of the desert from the sandy wastes of the Hijaz, trained from his boyhood in desert lore and with eyes as keen as an eagle's. It occurred to Saad that if anybody could find that cave, given general directions as to its whereabouts, men like this soldier could. They would be able to perceive from an amazing distance any disturbance of the ground round the illicit excavations, and so detect the cave perhaps even from ground level. The idea crystallized into a plan of campaign, and waiting only to collect Sellers from the American School, Saad went in search of the officer in charge of the troops in the Jerusalem area, a Major-General Lash. He found this officer well prepared, for only a night or two before he had been discussing the problem with a Belgian United Nations observer, Captain Lippens, and had that day telephoned to Harding in Amman, asking if he would like him to send a few of his desert troops down to the area and search for the caves. Harding had agreed, and now, with the added information Saad was able to provide, no further time was lost and a detachment of troops under the direction of an English officer, Brigadier Ashton, and a Jordanian Captain (now Major) Akkash el Zebn, was sent down to the road junction by the Dead Sea. Deploying from this point, in such a way that as far as possible no section of the cliffs at all visible from the littoral plain would miss their scrutiny, they set off slowly, working their way south. Within seventy-two hours, Akkash was on the phone reporting that they had found the cave, and asking for further instructions. Whilst waiting for Harding's arrival, Ashton plotted the cave and started collecting the pottery which lay round about, making accurate notes and drawings which were of the greatest help to the excavators later. Then Harding arrived, and together they made the first preliminary excavation. Harding confesses that when he first saw the cave he was dubious of its being the source of the scrolls, but the presence of undoubtedly ancient pottery made it worth investigating further. He asked Ashton to mount a guard on the cave until such time as a properly equipped archæological party could be assembled. This was done, but the expedition was dogged by bad luck for days. Every time they gathered at the road junction it rained, which made the tracks completely impassable to their transport, and once it even snowed! Ashton could not leave his men standing about outside a cave by the Dead Sea for long, however, and it became urgent to mount the expedition, which finally started work on 15th February, 1949, a fortnight after the rediscovery of the cave. Father De Vaux of the French School of Archæology, Joseph Saad, and two others joined the excavation, and the early finding of scores of small inscribed fragments of leather, together with pieces of the linen wrappings, and the sherds of dozens of the characteristic large scroll jars, in which it was said that the original scrolls had been found, soon made it plain that this was certainly a scroll cave, if not the original one. The damage caused by illegal excavations was all too plain; no hope could now be entertained of any stratification of the remains, and some of the most valuable of the pottery and wrappings had been tossed outside onto a dump. The number of jars originally placed in the cave was now seen to have been between forty and fifty, and if, as it was then thought, each of those jars had held several scrolls, then it became a matter of extreme urgency to find the rest, which might still be in the country and perhaps suffering damage. In any case, there must clearly have been hundreds of fragments and these had also to be found and studied together, if they were to be of any use at all.

Another detective inquiry was instituted, and Saad given *carte blanche* to find and, if necessary, buy those pieces regardless of cost. It was clear now, as more and more reports came in from scholars studying the first scrolls, that every word of these documents was going to be worth its weight in gold and, indeed, that was just about what they were going to cost before they were all finally in safe hands.

Saad went again to the Monastery of St. Mark's, this time accompanied by Harding himself. The object of this inquiry was to find out the name of the dealer in Bethlehem who had continually cropped up in reports, but had never been named. If there were more scrolls and fragments about, he was the most likely person to know about them, and he would also know the names and tribe of the Bedouin who had found the cave. George Isaiah was a little more informative this time, but could not or would not describe the cave in sufficient detail to make its identification with the Legion's discovery certain, and refused to disclose the name of the dealer. Saad knew better this time than to waste much time over him. After the inevitable coffee, and inquiries after each other's health, with no more useful information forthcoming, they rose to leave, keeping their eyes open all the time for Father Yusif. It was as they were leaving the gate of the Monastery that they saw the frail figure approaching, and immediately engaged him in conversation on the cave. Unfortunately, they now seemed to know more than he, and still they lacked the name of the Bethlehem dealer. Then they had an amazing piece of luck. Harding had noticed that as they had been speaking to Father Yusif, a woman across the road had been showing keen interest in their conversation. Finally, she came across to them and spoke. Were they talking about the excavations of the Dead Sea cave which George Isaiah had organized about a year ago? Her husband had taken part in the 'dig', and had even been rewarded for his pains with a leather fragment, which the priests had told him was most valuable,

Scroll of Thanksgiving   A fragmentary parchment.

חזי אבת בגל

ומשמיעו שמחה לאבל יד

ויזקום לעש לבבו ומאזיו

ואתו פיעדה לשוון יד שגיעו ותסתר עשו בחוזק איתנם

ואמרו מנעמר נעפו בגבול רשעה ואחיה טו לנישיעם ופרעא לטל

שבע נשע ערמה לטעוים ויעד סמך לטל נמחרו לב ותשיעמו חרפה

וקיש לבנעדים טוד אמן ובוטה לישוה ומך ואחיה על עצן רשעום

רבה בשעת עריעוט יעם יחריקו שטם ואנו חייתו טוטה לטטיעום

ועלו קהלת רשעוט תתרגע וחמי טחשולי ונים בהדגש גלוהם רגש

ותואכט וגרישו ותשומט נם לבחורי עדק ומלין ריעת טרו עלא לבחא

אמת וילנסות אוחט מסד ואחיה איש רוב לבליע תשו

חוו עוחות ואחיה לריח קושה לעד כל ויושו

רפיה עלו וחמ צקול חמן מים רבוט ומוט בלוע

עטבטו לשוחח חוו גבר אשר חטעוות טו ותלמד טן

שבטה כ שטו לטוטח בקור ריעת לטל מטוינט ויטריום בערול שטח

ולשוון אחרת יעם עא בטעת להיונו במשגאט

אורכט לו כי ישטוע עשיו בשניר החוס

ותשווך בשעיו מטל מקשו שחת עריעוט בקשו עשו בתובבו

בבריותרח וחמד סור שוא ועית טל יא ורשו עא פאתבד פיומרי

ובחשירונט תישוע עשו טא מאטה בינעריו וחמך ף אתטך ןרו

על לעשו בעטבו לטטריט בבשעבט רשעוט והגבורונה טו עני בן

איטם טא בחטטרוט עבריו ואנו אפטו חו עלו גבורים טבבוים בבל

ולחמוטם ויטרו חיעם לאין טרטא לחוב חות פאש טמבלת עעום

שמון מים רטוט שאוו קולם נטץ ורטס לה שוחית רטוט לטוורות ובקיעו

וישוא בחטריום גלוהם יאט בגוס לב נעט אתחוק עשו בטריוני

רשת טרשו לו תלטור רעוה וחוק כלעו לעשו נעלו בטם

אברטח שטטה

אריוני טא עולטו עשו ותעולט ישואת בליעו טב

דורשו חלקות נרום אשור חישבו יחוטו רפו

על עבוף יכנה אנס טו פאטך בינעשי וישומטו

עטו טל ויורשיו רעוה שוחעות נעש עטו

חוק מטט ותטו עשו פלר עייום ובריוטך לא החוטתו

עבריוחטנה פאחח חנות רם בחו לו ויעד טייך

נתע וריות

although he had not yet discovered a way of converting it into hard cash. However, if they would like to wait a moment she would see if she could find him; he could not be far away. Saad and Harding looked at each other, and then to heaven. They finally ran the man, Jabra by name, to earth in a nearby coffee shop, and induced him to come along to the Museum. In the basement, the spoils of the official excavation of the cave were arranged on large trestle tables, and, bringing him near, Harding asked Jabra if he could see anything there that he recognized. The man looked long and earnestly over the table, and then a broad smile lit his face. Yes, this. Amidst the broken pottery and linen wrappings, the Roman lamp and the cooking pot, he had spied his own dear, long-lost but never forgotten cigarette roller. So another link in the chain was forged, the cave was now definitely identified, and it now remained to find out how much more Jabra knew. An Arab who realizes that he has partaken, however unwittingly, in an illegal act, is a wary creature. Harding and Saad had somehow to win his confidence, if they were to obtain the information they so desperately wanted. Bribery was of course inevitable, and a generous tip went far towards loosening Jabra's tongue. He admitted that they had found some scroll fragments, and the Metropolitan had taken most of them away with him when he left. They tackled him about the name of the Bethlehem dealer; but at once he shut up like a clam, and for a long time would say nothing on the subject. Harding saw the fear of death in his eyes, and the man confessed that he was literally scared for his life. It took a great deal of threatening and reassuring before they finally forced the truth from him, and when they had let him scurry off home, Saad and Harding sat down and faced one another. Events now had taken a sinister turn. If Jabra's fears were justified, it meant that this dealer and his confederates were willing to go to any length to avoid interference in their territory. It was clear that from now on the game would be played to very high stakes, perhaps to higher values than mere money.

The journey to Bethlehem was an adventure in itself. Today it takes only half an hour of smooth driving on a new tarmac road to go from Jerusalem to Bethlehem, and before the troubles a more direct road took only half that time. In 1949, with this in Jewish hands, as it still is, the make-shift route was long and dangerous, a dirt track which snaked far out into the Judæan hills by the monastery of Mar Saba. Transport was by donkey, and the journey took half a day. The morning following the interview with Jabra, Saad set out, taking with him two of the Museum guards, and reached

Bethlehem shortly after midday. Leaving the guards and the animals on the outskirts of the town, he walked into the centre, feeling suddenly lonely and unprotected. From now on he would be working alone; any sign of official support, and every way would be blocked; the dealer, scrolls, and everything else would go underground and nothing ever recovered.

But Bethlehem in those days, cut off from a central government by the fighting, was no place for an unprotected man to face a gang of desperate brigands, and Joseph hesitated a moment outside the shop which had been pointed out to him as Kando's. It opened, like all such eastern shops, straight on to the street, and behind the piles of vegetables and hanging kuffiyas, the bright sunlight did not penetrate. Joseph peered into the shadows but could see nothing from outside. Then he entered.

His eyes took a little time to accustom themselves to the gloom, so he did not at first see the men standing at the back of the room, watching him. One of them was rather portly, heavy-jowled, and dressed in the long Arab night-shirt type of garment, with a red tarbush on his head. His companion was an older man who stared at Joseph suspiciously from beneath heavy eyebrows, and glanced from time to time at his companion and the door standing ajar behind him. Saad realized from their manner that news of his arrival had preceded him and came straight to the point. He had heard that Kando knew something about the scrolls which had been found in a cave, and furthermore, had some of the illegally excavated fragments in his possession. There was a moment's heavy silence, and then the old man flew at him, calling him a Government spy and worse, pushing Saad against the wall as he hurled abuse at him. Joseph raised his arms to fend off his assailant, but, even as he did so, saw the other man slip out of the open door and shut it behind him. Almost immediately the old man calmed down, glancing behind him to ensure that Kando had got clear, but Saad knew now that there was nothing to be gained by waiting longer and left the shop to return to his friends. Now the fat was really in the fire. Kando knew what he was after and suspected him of being in league with the Government. The chances were that either he would try and silence Saad, or smuggle the incriminating evidence out of the country and make off, until things had quietened down. The safest thing for Saad to do would have been to make tracks for Jerusalem and his well-guarded Museum. Instead he sent his men away, and took lodgings in Bethlehem, determined to try and win his way into Kando's confidence. It was the act of a brave man.

Day after day Joseph returned to the little shop, engaging Kando in conversation at first on anything but the scrolls. He made the acquaintance of George, who appeared to be Kando's right-hand man, and had certainly co-operated with him in the illicit digging. Slowly he won their confidence, and one day brought up the subject of the scrolls again. He hastened to reassure them that no ill would come to them from working with him; indeed, if they would trust him he would find them a market for their fragments which would pay well and be perfectly safe. After all, if they tried to smuggle them out of the country they might lose everything, including their freedom. They would lose nothing doing things Saad's way. The logic of Joseph's reasoning gradually had its effect, and the first suspicion gave way to a wary, but nevertheless, genuine friendship. When he finally left Bethlehem, it was with a promise from Kando that he would come and visit him at the

Letter of Warning   Letter to Yoshua Ben Gilgula, chief of the Jewish Insurgents at Murabba'at, containing a hint of the approach of the Roman Army. (132-135 A.D.)

Museum. On the journey back, Joseph reflected rather rue-fully that he had not seen a single fragment during all those days in Bethlehem; yet, on balance, he was not displeased with progress.

Kando kept his word and soon after appeared at Jerusalem, and Saad in due course paid a return visit. This went on for some weeks without further mention being made of the frag-ments, and Joseph was almost beginning to wonder if Kando had already sold them or, indeed, had ever possessed any. Then one day, in the gardens of the Museum, Kando took Saad over to a shady corner, looked at him hard, and then thrust his hand into the grimy 'night-shirt' and brought out a wallet. Inside, as he slowly opened it, there lay a piece of inscribed parchment, about the size of three or four fingers. Saad took the piece in his hand and studied it. There could be no doubt that the writing was very similar to that on the fragments he had already seen and the leather on which it was written was genuinely old. He replaced it carefully in the folds of Kando's wallet, knowing that one false move now could forfeit in a moment all the confidence he had built up over these trying weeks. Nevertheless, as he watched the wallet go back into its home, he wondered if he would ever see that precious fragment again. However, the game had to be played out the hard way; if Kando had that piece he would probably have a lot more, and Harding had told him to get the lot. Saad showed his interest in buying the piece and any more that Kando might have, and on this they parted, Joseph reporting the new development to Harding. In a few days Kando returned, ready to take negotiations further. Who was Saad acting for? Joseph answered that an English Professor visiting the country was anxious to buy these fragments, but wanted more than this one piece; how much had he to offer? Kando rather warily replied that he had 'quite a lot', and arranged a rendezvous at which Saad would bring the 'English Professor' and where Kando would have all the pieces in his possession. The place appointed was to be in Jericho, and, when the date and time had been arranged, Saad went off to find the mythical financier. It so happened that, working with Harding at this time as a non-technical assistant, was an Englishman, Mr. Richmond Brown, who willingly agreed to take the part. At a preliminary meeting Harding handed over a thousand pounds in one dinar notes (1 Jordan dinar = the pound sterling), but told Saad to try and obtain all the frag-ments in Kando's possession for eight hundred pounds. The absolute maximum was fixed at a pound per square centimetre of fragment, but to try and ascribe any monetary value at all to this priceless material was extremely difficult. If this price seems outrageously high, it must be remembered that, at that time, the Syrian Metropolitan was asking something like a million dollars for the scrolls in his possession, and reports to this effect were being heard all over Jordan on the radio. The Bedouin and Kando were now well aware that these scrolls were considered beyond price by the outside world, and that their recovery was worth almost any amount of money. It should be also recognized that behind all these negotiations there lay the shadow of irresponsible people who were willing to buy illegally smuggled pieces for their collections or as souvenirs, or in order to make a profit on a further transaction. The danger of such loss was ever present, forcing the pace, and thus raising the price. It was bad enough that the complete scrolls should be taken from the country, but at least they could be published as a unity, as the American scholars were doing so admirably. But with fragments, it was different. They could only be made of use to scholarship if they were kept together, and as far as possible reunited with their parent documents. A small piece of Dead Sea Scroll may look very nice framed and hung over the mantelpiece, but it may well ruin the value of other larger pieces, depending for their sense on the inscription on the 'souvenir'. Furthermore, irresponsibility is not the sole prerogative of tourists and dealers. At a later stage, one world-famous museum was willing to consider buying fragments smuggled from Jordan in order to have them in their cases, even though to have taken them would have delayed the publication of thousands of others, or, at least, reduced their value for want of the additional evidence. Happily the possibility was then foiled by the more responsible attitude of an Eastern University who procured the fragments and returned them immediately to Jordan. Thus at this stage there was little quibbling about price; the main thing was to rescue the fragments and give them to the world in as complete a form and as soon as possible.

Kando's choice in hotels ran pretty low. This was a dirty, fifth-rate hovel, and, as the two drew near, Saad could see that Kando was fearing a trap and taking no chances. Lounging on both sides of the street and round the entrance were some of the grimmest, toughest-looking characters one could wish not to meet anywhere, and they watched Saad and his companion through every move and gesture as they approached. Joseph felt the thick wad of notes bulging in his pocket, and thought they could not have been more conspicuous if he had carried them in his hand. The hairs on their necks bristled as they walked in through the porch, trying to look unconcerned.

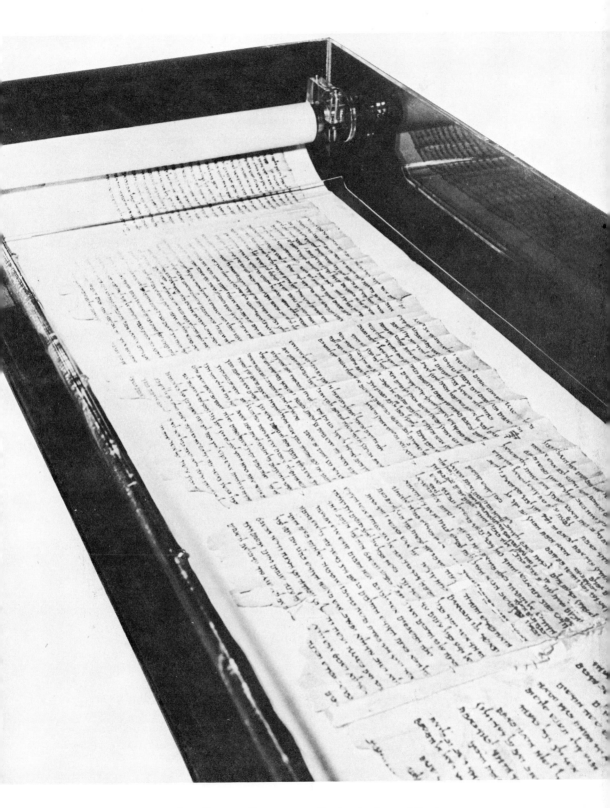

Dead Sea Scrolls The scrolls, now on display to the public, have
been on tour through many countries.

Casually they asked a shifty-looking proprietor if Kando was there, and he motioned them to a room leading off the main entrance hall. Saad put his hands on the notes in his pocket, squared his shoulders, and the two of them walked in.

Kando was standing with George at the far side of the room. A table covered with a greasy cloth stood in the centre, and Saad noticed that, as usual, Kando had prepared for a quick exit with a window standing wide open behind him. It idly crossed Joseph's mind to wonder if they were as well prepared. A brief greeting did nothing to relieve the tension, and Saad asked abruptly if Kando had got the fragments. The man nodded and raised his eyebrows questioningly in return. In answer, with studied carelessness, Joseph brought out the bundle of notes, stripped off the band, and fanned them out on to the table. It was a magnificent gesture and Kando hesitated no longer but laid on to the table beside the notes a pile of decrepit-looking pieces of skin, torn and rotted at the edges, and covered with a fine white dust through which the ancient writing could just be seen. Saad passed them over to the 'English Professor' who at once began measuring them with a pocket rule. The tension had now decreased considerably, and whilst Richmond Brown was at work, Saad engaged Kando in conversation. Brown's calculations actually brought the figure to 1,250 sq. cm., but following his instructions he said, 'I can only give eight hundred pounds for this lot.' Saad looked at Kando expectantly, but the latter jerked his head and gave the click of the tongue which is the Arabic refusal. Then he began to collect the fragments together, and Saad after a while did the same with the notes. Each delayed the process as long as possible, hoping for the other to give way, but when they both had finished the silence remained unbroken. Saad walked to the door, followed by Brown, both wondering if Kando would let them go through that grim circle of henchmen with a thousand pounds in their pockets. However, they passed unmolested and started to walk towards the Winter Palace Hotel where Harding awaited them. Certainly they were alive, and had handled the precious fragments, but were they to lose them all for the sake of two hundred pounds? Harding, however, having heard their story supported their action, and was sure that the next day would see Kando at the Museum with his pieces, more than willing to sell them for eight hundred pounds.

The next day sure enough, Kando appeared. But he seemed curiously certain of his ground, and would not go below a thousand pounds. Saad said he would go and ask the 'Professor' and stepped next door to where Harding sat in the Board

Room, awaiting developments. Harding agreed to the price and Saad returned and gave Kando the money. Then part of the cause of his confidence became apparent, for as Kando handed him the fragments, he looked at Joseph and said, 'And give my greetings to Mr. Harding.' Saad remembered then that, when the three of them had left the Winter Palace in Jericho that day, a bystander had stared curiously into the windows of the car. Of course, Kando now knew the secret of Saad's relationship with the Director of Antiquities, and probably realized that the 'English Professor' had been a fake. He knew too that the Government meant to deal leniently with him so long as he played their game. Indeed, Harding still had much to learn about the finding of that cave, and wanted badly to know the names of the Bedouin lads who had climbed through the hole. It was by no means certain that with Kando's collection all the fragment material from the cave had been exhausted, and there was always the possibility that new caves in the vicinity might be found any day, now that the Bedouin were on the look-out.

Eventually, Kando told Saad the names of the Bedouin and their tribe, and in due course they were persuaded to leave their desert camps and come to Amman. There Harding learned the full story of the discovery, and the Bedouin found a new friend in the Director of Antiquities. Well dined and liberally tipped, the lads returned to their shepherding to enliven the camp fires of their tribe with marvellous tales of the great city across the Jordan, and of an English official of their Government who spoke their tongue as well as they, and knew their customs and their lore better than any foreigner they had ever met. The wise administrator knows when to put the letter of the law into second place, and to the fact that Harding is such a person, the world owed much of the light which further discoveries in the Judæan desert were to throw upon this important Jewish sect by the Dead Sea.

POMPEII: A CITY BURIED ALIVE

Towards the end of August in A.D. 79 the town of Pompeii on the west coast of Italy was obliterated.

The following extracts are accounts of how a whole city was buried and lost, and thereby preserved for archaeologists. Excavations at Pompeii have proceeded intermittently through the centuries. But since 1860, a systematic plan has been followed, and slowly the town is emerging from the pall of volcanic ash which smothered it.

Included here are two contemporary letters written by the Younger Pliny to Tacitus, which bring home to us the unspeakable horror of the disaster.

Excerpted from POMPEII: ITS LIFE AND ART, *(Macmillan, 1899) written by*

AUGUST MAU

PREVIOUS to the terrible eruption of 79, Vesuvius was considered an extinct volcano. 'Above these places,' says Strabo, writing in the time of Augustus, 'lies Vesuvius, the sides of which are well cultivated, even to the summit. This is level, but quite unproductive. It has a cindery appearance; for the rock is porous and of a sooty colour, the appearance suggesting that the whole summit may once have been on fire and have contained craters, the fires of which died out when there was no longer anything left to burn.'

Earthquakes, however, were of common occurrence in Campania. An especially violent shock on 5th February, A.D. 63, gave warning of the reawakening of Vesuvius. Great damage was done throughout the region lying between Naples and Nuceria, but the shock was most severe at Pompeii, a large part of the buildings of the city being thrown down. The prosperous and enterprising inhabitants at once set about rebuilding. When the final catastrophe came, on 24th August, A.D. 79, most of the houses were in a good state of repair, and the rebuilding of at least two temples, those of Apollo and of Isis, had been completed. This renewing of the city, caused by the earthquake, may be looked upon as a fortunate circumstance for our studies.

313

Our chief source of information for the events of 24th-26th August, 79, is a couple of letters of the Younger Pliny to Tacitus, who purposed to make use of them in writing his history. Pliny was staying at Misenum with his uncle, the Elder Pliny, who was in command of the Roman fleet. In the first letter he tells of his uncle's fate. On the afternoon of the twenty-fourth, the Admiral Pliny set out with ships to rescue from impending danger the people at the foot of Vesuvius, particularly in the vicinity of Herculaneum. He came too late; it was no longer possible to effect a landing. So he directed his course to Stabiæ, where he spent the night; and there on the following morning he died, suffocated by the fumes that were exhaled from the earth. The second letter gives an account of the writer's own experiences at Misenum.

To this testimony little is added by the narrative of Dion Cassius, which was written a century and a half later and is known to us only in abstract; Dion dwells at greater length on the powerful impression which the terrible convulsion of nature left upon those who were living at that time. With the help of the letters of Pliny, in connection with the facts established by the excavations, it is possible to picture to ourselves the progress of the eruption with a fair degree of clearness.

The subterranean fires of Vesuvius pressed upward to find an outlet. The accumulations of volcanic ash and pumice-stone that had been heaped up on the mountain by former eruptions were again hurled to a great height, and came down upon the surrounding country. On the west side of Vesuvius they mingled with torrents of rain, and flowed as a vast stream of mud down over Herculaneum. On the south side, driven by a north-west wind as they descended from the upper air, they spread out into a thick cloud, which covered Pompeii and the plain of Sarno. Out of this cloud, first broken fragments of pumice-stone—the average size not larger than a walnut—rained down to the depth of eight to ten feet; then followed volcanic ash, wet as it fell by a downpour of water, to the depth of six or seven feet. With the storm of ashes came successive shocks of earthquake.

Such was, in outline, the course of the eruption. It must have begun early in the morning of the 24th, and the stream of mud must have commenced immediately to move in the direction of Herculaneum; for shortly after one o'clock on that day the Admiral Pliny at Misenum received letters from the region threatened, saying that the danger was imminent, and that escape was possible only by sea. Even then the Younger Pliny saw, high above Vesuvius, the cloud, shaped like an umbrella pine, which was to rain down destruction on Pompeii.

Amphitheatre   An aerial view of the ruins.

Toward evening, the ships off Herculaneum ran into the hail
of pumice-stone, which, during the night, reached Stabiæ and
so increased in violence that the Admiral Pliny was obliged to
leave his sleeping-room from fear that the door would be
blocked up by the falling masses.

Early in the morning of the 25th there was a severe shock
of earthquake, which was felt as far as Misenum. Then the
ashes began to fall, and a cloud of fearful blackness, pierced
through and through with flashes of lightning, settled down
over land and sea. At Misenum, even, it became dark; 'not,'
says Pliny, 'as on a cloudy night when there is no moon, but
as in a room which has been completely closed.'

How long the storm of ashes lasted we can only infer from
this, but when it ceased the sun had not yet set. In Misenum,
which the shower of pumice-stone had not reached, everything

Via Dell'Abbondanza This stone street is lined on either side by wide sidewalks. The houses were built of brick or stone.

was covered with a thick layer of ashes. Although the earth-quake shocks continued, the inhabitants went back into their houses. But Pompeii and Stabiæ had been covered so deep that only the roofs of the houses, where these had not fallen in, projected above the surface; and Herculaneum had wholly disappeared.

All the plain of the Sarno was buried, as were also the slopes of the mountains of the south. Stabiæ, as we have seen, lay at the foot of the mountains, on the coast. It had been destroyed by Sulla in the Social War; its inhabitants, forced to scatter, settled in the surrounding country. In the years 1749-82 numerous buildings were excavated in the vicinity, in part luxurious country seats, in part plain farm buildings; but the excavations were afterwards filled up again. The covering of Stabiæ was like that of Pompeii, only not so deep.

Herculaneum was covered with the same materials; they were not, however, deposited in regular strata, but were mixed together, and being drenched with water, hardened into a kind of tufa which in places reached a depth of sixty-five feet. Excavation at Herculaneum is in consequence extremely difficult; and the difficulty is further increased by the fact that a modern city, Resina, extends over the greater part of the ancient site. The excavations thus far attempted have in most cases been conducted by means of underground passageways. The statement that Herculaneum was overflowed by a stream of lava, though frequently repeated, is erroneous.

The woodwork of buildings in Pompeii has in many cases been preserved, but in a completely charred condition. Fre-quently where walls were painted with yellow ochre it has turned red, especially when brought immediately into contact with the stratum of ashes—a change which this colour under-goes when it is exposed to heat. Nevertheless, the inference would be unwarranted that the products of the eruption fell upon the city red-hot and caused a general conflagration. The fragments of pumice-stone could scarcely have retained a great degree of heat after having been so long in the air; it is evident from Pliny's narrative that they were not hot.

With the ashes a copious rain must have fallen; for the bodies of those who perished in the storm of ashes left perfect moulds, into a number of which soft plaster of Paris has been poured, making those casts of human figures which lend a melancholy interest to the collections in the little Museum at Pompeii. The extraordinary freshness of these figures, without any suggestion of the wasting away after death, is explicable only on the supposition that the enveloping ashes were damp, and so commenced immediately to harden into a permanent shape.

If the ashes had been dry and had packed down and hardened afterwards, we should be able to trace at least the beginnings of decay.

Neither the pumice-stone nor the ashes, then, could have set wood on fire. The woodwork must have become charred gradually from the effect of moisture, as in the case of coal, and the change in the colour of the yellow ochre must be due to some other cause than the presence of heat. This is all the more evident from the fact that vestiges of local conflagrations, confined within narrow limits, can here and there be traced, kindled by the masses of glowing slag which fell at the same time with the pumice-stone, or by the fires left burning in the houses.

From the number of skeletons discovered in the past few decades, since an accurate record has been kept, it has been estimated that in Pompeii itself, about two thousand persons perished. As the city contained a population of twenty thousand or more, it is evident that the majority of the inhabitants fled; since the eruption commenced in the morning, while the hail of pumice-stone did not begin till afternoon, those who appreciated the greatness of the danger had time to escape. It is, however, impossible to say how many fled when it was already too late, and lost their lives outside the city. Mention has already been made of some who perished at the harbour; others who went out earlier to the Sarno may have made good their escape. Of those who remained in the city part were buried in the houses—so with twenty persons whose skeletons were found in the cellar of the villa of Diomedes; others, as the hail of pumice-stone ceased, ventured out into the streets, where they soon succumbed to the shower of ashes that immediately followed. As the bodies wasted away little except the bones was left in the hollows formed by the ashes that hardened around them, and the casts already referred to, which have been made from time to time since 1863, give in some cases a remarkably clear and sharp representation of the victims.

The Emperor Titus sent a commission of senators into Campania to report in what way help could best be rendered. A plan was formed to rebuild the cities that had been destroyed, and the property of those who died without heirs was set aside for this purpose. Nothing came of it, however, so far as our knowledge goes. Pompeii is indeed mentioned in the Peutinger Table, a map for travellers made in the third century, but the name was apparently given to a post station in memory of the former city. Conclusive evidence against the existence of a new city is the absence of any inscriptions referring to it.

LETTERS FROM THE YOUNGER PLINY TO TACITUS
(From PLINY. LETTERS. *Heinemann*, 1915)

Your request that I would send you an account of my
uncle's end, so that you may transmit a more exact relation
of it to posterity, deserves my acknowledgements; for if his
death shall be celebrated by your pen, the glory of it, I am
aware, will be rendered for ever deathless. For notwithstanding
he perished, as did whole peoples and cities, in the destruction
of a most beautiful region, and by a misfortune memorable
enough to promise him a kind of immortality; notwithstanding
he has himself composed many and lasting works: yet I am
persuaded, the mentioning of him in your immortal writings,
will greatly contribute to eternize his name. Happy I esteem
those whom Providence has gifted with the ability either to do
things worthy of being written, or to write in a manner worthy
of being read; but most happy they, who are blessed with both
talents: in which latter class my uncle will be placed both by
his own writings and by yours. The more willingly do I undertake, nay, solicit, the task you set me.

He was at that time with the fleet under his command at
Misenum. On the 24th of August, about one in the afternoon,
my mother desired him to observe a cloud of very unusual size
and appearance. He had sunned himself, then taken a cold
bath, and after a leisurely luncheon was engaged in study. He
immediately called for his shoes and went up an eminence from
whence he might best view this very uncommon appearance.
It was not at that distance discernible from what mountain
this cloud issued, but it was found afterwards to be Vesuvius.
I cannot give you a more exact description of its figure, than
by resembling it to that of a pine-tree, for it shot up a great
height in the form of a trunk, which extended itself at the top
into several branches; because, I imagine, a momentary gust of
air blew it aloft, and then failing, forsook it; thus causing the
cloud to expand laterally as it dissolved or possibly the downward pressure of its own weight produced this effect. It was
at one moment white, at another dark and spotted, as if it had
carried up earth or cinders.

My uncle, true savant that he was, deemed the phenomenon
important and worth a nearer view. He ordered a light vessel
to be got ready, and gave me the liberty, if I thought proper,
to attend him. I replied I would rather study; and, as it
happened, he had himself given me a theme for composition.
As he was coming out of the house he received a note from
Rectina, the wife of Bassus, who was in the utmost alarm at the
imminent danger (his villa stood just below us, and there was

The Forum   Here was once the life center of the city of Pompeii.

no way to escape but by sea); she earnestly entreated him to save her from such deadly peril. He changed his first design and what he began with a philosophical, he pursued with an heroical turn of mind. He ordered large galleys to be launched, and went himself on board one, with the intention of assisting not only Rectina, but many others; for the villas stand extremely thick upon that beautiful coast. Hastening to the place from whence others were flying, he steered his direct course to the point of danger, and with such freedom from fear, as to be able to make and dictate his observations upon the successive motions and figures of that terrific object.

And now cinders, which grew thicker and hotter the nearer he approached, fell into the ships, then pumice-stones too with stones blackened, scorched and cracked by fire, then the sea ebbed suddenly from under them, while the shore was blocked up by landslips from the mountains. After considering a moment whether he should retreat, he said to the captain who was urging that course, 'Fortune befriends the brave; carry me to Pomponianus.' Pomponianus was then at Stabiæ*, distant by half the width of the bay (for, as you know, the shore, insensibly curving in its sweep, forms here a receptacle for the sea). He had already embarked his baggage; for though at Stabiæ the danger was not yet near, it was full in view, and certain to be extremely near, as soon as it spread; and he resolved to fly as soon as the contrary wind should cease. It was full favourable, however, for carrying my uncle to Pomponianus. He embraces, comforts, and encourages, his alarmed friend, and in order to soothe the other's fears by his own unconcern, desires to be conducted to a bathroom; and after having bathed, he sat down to supper with great cheerfulness, or at least (what is equally heroic) with all the appearance of it.

In the meanwhile Mount Vesuvius was blazing in several places with spreading and towering flames, whose refulgent brightness the darkness of the night set in high relief. But my uncle, in order to soothe apprehensions, kept saying that some fires had been left alight by the terrified country people, and what they saw were only deserted villas on fire in the abandoned district. After this he retired to rest, and it is most certain that his rest was a most genuine slumber; for his breathing, which, as he was pretty fat, was somewhat heavy and sonorous, was heard by those who attended at his chamber-door. But the court which led to his apartment now lay so deep under a mixture of pumice-stones and ashes, that if he had continued longer in his bedroom, egress would have been impossible. On

* Now called Castel è Mar di Stabia in the gulf of Naples.

being aroused, he came out, and returned to Pomponianus and the others, who had sat up all night. They consulted together as to whether they should hold out in the house, or wander about in the open. For the house now tottered under repeated and violent concussions, and seemed to rock to and fro as if torn from its foundations. In the open air, on the other hand, they dreaded the falling pumice-stones, light and porous though they were; yet this, by comparison, seemed the lesser danger of the two, a conclusion which my uncle arrived at by balancing reasons, and the others by balancing fears. They tied pillows upon their heads with napkins; and this was their whole defence against the showers that fell around them.

It was now day everywhere else, but there a deeper darkness prevailed than in the most obscure night; relieved, however, by many torches and divers illuminations. They thought proper to go down upon the shore to observe from close at hand if they could possibly put out to sea, but they found the waves still ran extremely high and contrary. There my uncle having thrown himself down upon a disused sail, repeatedly called for, and drank, a draught of cold water; soon after, flames and a strong smell of sulphur, which was the forerunner of them, dispersed the rest of the company in flight; him they only aroused. He raised himself up with the assistance of two of his slaves, but instantly fell; some unusually gross vapour, as I conjecture, having obstructed his breathing and blocked his windpipe, which was not only naturally weak and constricted, but chronically inflamed. When day dawned again (the third from that he last beheld) his body was found entire and un-injured, and still fully clothed as in life; its posture was that of a sleeping, rather than a dead man.

Meanwhile my mother and I were at Misenum. But this has no connection with history, and your inquiry went no farther than concerning my uncle's death. I will therefore put an end to my letter. Suffer me only to add, that I have faithfully related to you what I was either an eye-witness of myself, or heard at the time, when report speaks most truly. You will select what is most suitable to your purpose; for there is a great difference between a letter, and an history; between writing to a friend and writing for the public. Farewell.

.   .   .

The letter which, in compliance with your request, I wrote to you concerning the death of my uncle, has raised, you say, your curiosity to know not only what terrors, but what calamities I endured when left behind at Misenum (for there I broke off my narrative).

The Vetii House   This family house built in a rectangle around an open garden is one of the loveliest unearthed by the excavations of Pompeii. Many of the garden sculptures were intact.

'Though my shock'd soul recoils, my tongue shall tell.'

My uncle having set out, I gave the rest of the day to study —the object which had kept me at home. After which I bathed, dined, and retired for short and broken slumbers. There had been for several days before some shocks of earthquake, which the less alarmed us as they are frequent in Campania; but that night they became so violent that one might think that the world was not being merely shaken but turned topsy-turvy. My mother flew to my chamber; I was just rising, meaning on my part to awaken her, if she was asleep. We sat down in the forecourt of the house, which separated it by a short space from the sea. I know not whether I should call it courage or inexperience—I was not quite eighteen—but I called for a volume of Livy, and began to read, and even went on with the extracts I was making from it, as if nothing were the matter. Lo and behold, a friend of my uncle's, who was just come to him from Spain, appears on the scene; observing my mother and me seated, and that I have actually a book in my hand, he sharply censures her patience and my indifference; nevertheless I still went on intently with my author.

It was now six o'clock in the morning, the light still ambiguous and faint. The buildings around us already tottered, and though we stood upon open ground, yet as the place was narrow and confined, there was certain and formidable danger from their collapsing. It was not till then we resolved to quit the town. The common people follow us in the utmost consternation, preferring the judgement of others to their own (wherein the extreme of fear resembles prudence), and impel us onwards by pressing in a crowd upon our rear. Being got outside the houses we halt in the midst of a most strange and dreadful scene. The coaches which we had ordered out, though upon the most level ground, were sliding to and fro, and could not be kept steady even when stones were put against the wheels. Then we beheld the sea sucked back, and as it were repulsed by the convulsive motion of the earth; it is certain at least the shore was considerably enlarged, and now held many sea animals captive on the dry sand. On the other side, a black and dreadful cloud bursting out in gusts of igneous serpentine vapour now and again yawned open to reveal long fantastic flames, resembling flashes of lightning but much larger.

Our Spanish friend already mentioned now spoke with more warmth and instancy: 'If your brother—if your uncle,' said he, 'is yet alive, he wishes you both may be saved; if he has perished, it was his desire that you might survive him. Why therefore do you delay your escape?' We could never think of our own safety, we said, while we were uncertain of his. Without more ado our friend hurried off, and took himself out of danger at the top of his speed.

Soon afterwards, the cloud I have described began to descend upon the earth, and cover the sea. It had already begirt the hidden Capreæ, and blotted from sight the promontory of Misenum. My mother now began to beseech, exhort and command me to escape as best I might; a young man could do it; she, burdened with age and corpulency, would die easy if only she had not caused my death. I replied, I would not be saved without her, and taking her by the hand, I hurried her on. She complies reluctantly and not without reproaching herself for retarding me. Ashes now fall upon us, though as yet in no great quantity. I looked behind me; gross darkness pressed upon our rear, and came rolling over the land after us like a torrent. I proposed while we yet could see, to turn aside, lest we should be knocked down in the road by a crowd that followed us and trampled to death in the dark. We had scarce sat down, when darkness overspread us, not like that of a moonless or cloudy night, but of a room when it is shut up, and the lamp put out. You could hear the shrieks of women and crying children, and the shouts of men; some were seeking their children, others their parents, other their wives or husbands, and only distinguishing them by their voices; one lamenting his own fate, another that of his family; some praying to die, from the very fear of dying; many lifting their hands to the gods; but the greater part imagining that there were no gods left anywhere, and that the last and eternal night was come upon the world.

There were even some who augmented the real perils by imaginary terrors. Newcomers reported that such or such a building at Misenum had collapsed or taken fire—falsely, but they were credited. By degrees it grew lighter; which we imagined to be rather the warning of approaching fire (as in truth it was) than the return of day: however, the fire stayed at a distance from us: then again came darkness, and a heavy shower of ashes; we were obliged every now and then to rise and shake them off, otherwise we should have been buried and even crushed under their weight. I might have boasted that amidst dangers so appalling, not a sigh or expression of fear escaped from me, had not my support been founded in that miserable, though strong consolation, that all mankind were involved in the same calamity, and that I was perishing with the world itself.

At last this dreadful darkness was attenuated by degrees to a kind of cloud or smoke, and passed away; presently the real day returned, and even the sun appeared, though lurid as when an eclipse is in progress. Every object that presented itself to our yet affrighted gaze was changed, cover'd over with a drift of ashes, as with snow. We returned to Misenum, where we refreshed ourselves as well as we could, and passed an anxious night between hope and fear; though indeed with a much larger share of the latter, for the earthquake still continued, and several enthusiastic people were giving a grotesque turn to their own and their neighbours' calamities by terrible predictions. Even then, however, my mother and I, notwithstanding the danger we had passed, and that which still threatened us, had no thoughts of leaving the place, till we should receive some tidings of my uncle.

And now, you will read this narrative, so far beneath the dignity of a history, without any view of transferring it to your own; and indeed you must impute it to your own request, if it shall appear scarce worthy of a letter. Farewell.

MANUSCRIPTS IN A BUDDHIST SHRINE

Ever since the travels of Marco Polo, Europeans have had an insatiable curiosity about the far-off and mysterious Orient. During the late 1800's and early 1900's, adventurers and archaeologists turned their attention to the vast Tarim Basin. In ancient times this arid wasteland had been a busy highway, along which stately caravans carried silks and spices from China to trade in the rich markets of India and Persia. Also along this route, monks and holy men, pilgrims and envoys had moved back and forth bearing messages and visiting holy places. Later, water travel replaced this slow land route, and the desert highway was neglected and eventually forgotten.

Between 1900 and 1914, Aurel Stein, a Hungarian Jew who worked for the Education Department of the government of India, became caught up with the idea of tracing the old Chinese highway and of finding the remains of the people who had used the remote route. He led three expeditions into Central Asia, and wrote fascinating accounts of his travels.

On one of Stein's trips, he made a remarkable discovery. At Tun-huang, where the old road enters China, he found a small chapel filled with manuscripts, silk banners, and embroideries. His findings were part of the treasures of a Buddhist monastery. They had been stowed away during the early years of the 11th century to protect them against marauders. Drift sand had blocked the entrance to the shrine and the hoard had been lost until Stein's discovery. The manuscripts and objects he found represent a collection of accumulated Buddhist treasures from the fifth to the tenth centuries.

Excerpted from SERINDIA, *Vol. II, (Clarendon Press, Oxford, 1921) written by*

SIR AUREL STEIN

THE hurried preliminary visit I had paid, soon after my first arrival in March, to the Caves of the Thousand Buddhas sufficed to impress me with the abundance of interesting materials which their fully accessible remains offered for the study of Buddhist art. Yet there was even then in view for me another and more pressing task which was bound to engross my attention at the outset.

It was at Tun-huang and through Zahīd Beg, the intelligent Turkī trader of Urumchi who had established himself there at the head of a small colony of Mohammedan exiles from Hsinchiang, that the first vague rumour had reached me of a great mass of ancient manuscripts, which had been discovered by chance several years before, hidden away in one of the cave-temples. There these treasures were said to have been locked up again by official order in charge of the Taoist priest who had come upon them. Zahīd Beg's assertion that some of these manuscripts were not in Chinese writing had naturally made me still keener to ascertain exact details. The result of Chiang Ssŭ-yeh's cautious inquiries seemed to support the rumour, and in close council with him I had carefully considered the question how best to gain access to the find.

On my first visit to the site the Taoist priest was away, engaged apparently with his two acolytes on a begging tour in the oasis. Nor would it, perhaps, have been wise to attempt starting operations then at once. But fortunately the young 'Ho-shang' of Tangutan extraction, then the only dweller at the site, proved to be possessed of useful local knowledge, and it did not take Chiang Ssŭ-yeh long to extract from him some interesting details.

The place of discovery of the manuscript hoard was a large shrine near the northern end of the main group of caves. Its gaily painted outer structures bore evidence of extensive recent restoration, the result of pious labours started and maintained by Wang, the 'Tao-shih', or Taoist priest, who had established himself here some seven years before. The entrance to the cave-temple had been formerly blocked by fallen rock debris and drift-sand, as was still partially the case at several of the caves situated at the foot of the cliff further south. While restorations were slowly being carried on in the temple *cella* and the place now occupied by its antechapel, the labourers engaged had noticed a crack in the frescoed wall of the passage connecting the two. An opening was thus discovered that led to a recess or small chamber excavated from the rock behind the stuccoed north wall of the passage.

Manuscript rolls, written in Chinese characters but in a non-Chinese language, were said to have filled the recess completely. Their total quantity was supposed to be so great as to make up several cart-loads. News of the discovery having reached distant Lan-chou, specimens of the manuscripts were asked for from provincial headquarters. Ultimately orders were supposed to have come from the Viceroy of Kan-su to restore the whole of the find to its original place of deposit. So now this strange hoard of undeciphered manuscripts was declared to be kept by the Tao-shih behind the carefully locked door with which the hidden recess had been provided since its first discovery.

In the absence of the priest it was impossible to pursue these preliminary inquiries further. But I lost no time in visiting the alleged place of discovery. Fortunately, the young Ho-shang's spiritual guide, a Tibetan monk then also away on a begging tour, had borrowed one of the manuscripts in order to give lustre to a little private chapel of his own that he had improvised as his temporary abode in the tumble-down pilgrims' rest-house. The young monk was persuaded by Chiang Ssŭ-yeh to bring us this specimen. It was a beautifully preserved roll of paper about ten inches high, and, when we unfolded it, in front of the original hiding-place, proved to be about fifteen yards long. The paper, yellowish in tint, looked remarkably strong and fresh. But in a climate so dry and in a carefully sheltered hiding-place it was impossible to judge age from mere outward appearance, and with its fine texture and carefully smoothed surface it looked to me decidedly old. . . .

Thus the rapid inspection of this single specimen suggested that the reported great manuscript deposit might prove to be largely of Buddhist character. At the same time the fact that the text was written on a roll, and not in the 'concertina' or book form which has prevailed in China ever since block printing became common about the beginning of the Sung period (A.D. 960), seemed to raise a strong presumption as to the early date of the deposit. All further speculation had to be put off until I should secure access to the whole of the hidden library. It was enough encouragement at the time to find its existence confirmed.

The thought of the great store of old manuscripts awaiting exploration drew me back to the Caves of the Thousand Buddhas with the strength of a hidden magnet. But by the time at which my return to the site became possible I had learned enough of the local conditions of Tun-huang to realize that there were good reasons for caution in my first endeavours to secure access to the Tao-shih's jealously guarded treasures. The fact alone that the cave-temples, notwithstanding all apparent decay, were still real places of worship 'in being' would, by every consideration of prudence, impose obvious limitations upon my archæological activity there. But what my sagacious secretary had meanwhile gathered about the character and ways of the monk holding charge of that ancient hidden store was a further warning to me to feel my way with discretion and studied slowness. Chiang Ssŭ-yeh, however, had succeeded in inducing Wang Tao-shih to await my arrival at the caves instead of starting at once, when the great annual fête there had concluded, on one of his usual tours in the district to collect temple subscriptions, etc. It was encouraging, too, to feel that, apart from the genuine interest which Wang Ta-lao-yeh, the learned sub-prefect of Tun-huang, had, from the first shown in my antiquarian labours, I could to some extent rely also on the favourable impression which gradually had spread among the people of Tun-huang about my scholarly aims and methods.

When by May 21st I returned to the caves for the eagerly planned operations, it was satisfactory to find the site completely deserted but for Wang Tao-shih with his two acolyte-servitors and a humble Tibetan Lāma, knowing no Chinese and obviously harmless. The Tao-shih had come to welcome me at what for most of the year he might well claim as sacred ground entrusted to his own exclusive care. He looked a very curious figure, extremely shy and nervous, with a face bearing an occasional furtive expression of cunning which was far from encouraging. It was clear from the first that he would be a difficult person to handle. Purposely avoiding any long interview with him, I started next morning what was to be ostensibly the main object of my stay at the site, a survey of the principal shrines and the photographing of the more notable frescoes. While thus engaged at the northernmost caves near the great shrine restored by Wang Tao-shih, I cast a glance at the entrance passage, behind the wall of which the manuscript hoard was declared to have been discovered and to be still kept. To my dismay I now found the narrow opening of the recess, about five feet above the floor of the passage, completely walled up with brick-work. It seemed like a special precaution taken against my inquisitive eyes. Necessarily the sight recalled to my mind the similar device by which the Jain monks at Jesalmīr had endeavoured to keep the store of ancient palm-leaf manuscripts in their temple vault hidden from Professor Bühler.

The chief task at the beginning was to make sure that I should be allowed to see the whole of the manuscripts in their original place of deposit. With a view to sounding the priest in a confidential fashion about the facilities to be given for this purpose, I had dispatched Chiang Ssŭ-yeh to another cave-temple which Wang had partially restored and annexed as his living quarters. In spite of the Ssŭ-yeh's tactful diplomacy, the negotiations proceeded very slowly. The promise of a liberal donation for his work of pious restoration had, indeed, the initial effect of inducing the priest to explain that the walling-up of the door was a precaution primarily taken against the curiosity of the pilgrims who had recently flocked to the site in their thousands. But, being wary and of a suspicious mind, he was careful to evade any promise about showing the collection to us as a whole. All that he would agree to, and that with manifold reservations, was to let me eventually see some manuscript specimens within convenient reach of his hands. A hint cautiously put forward by my zealous secretary about the possibility of my wishing, perhaps, to acquire one or other of these specimens had caused such manifestly genuine perturbation to the Tao-shih that the subject had promptly to be dropped.

Lotus Sutra   Colophon dates this piece at 674 A.D.

However, in one direction at least some reassuring information emerged from these hours of diplomatic converse. From statements heard by us at Tun-huang it had appeared likely that, when the great find of manuscripts had been officially reported through the Tao-t'ai at Su-chou to the Viceroy of Kan-su, orders had been issued from the latter's Ya-mên for the transmission of specimens, and subsequently for the safe keeping of the whole collection. Fortunately, Chiang's apprehension about an official inventory having been taken on that occasion was dispelled by what the Tao-shih in a talkative mood let drop in conversation. Some rolls of Chinese texts, apparently Buddhist, had indeed been taken from him and sent to the Viceregal Ya-mên at Lan-chou. But they had failed to attract any interest there, and to Wang's undisguised chagrin no further notice had been taken of his treasured old manuscripts or, indeed, of his pious labours which had led to their discovery. Officialdom had been content with a rough statement that the manuscripts would make up seven cart-loads, and, evidently grudging the cost of transport or the trouble of close examination, had left the whole undisturbed in charge of the Tao-shih as self-constituted guardian of the temple.

Chiang's report, nevertheless, gave reason to fear that the priest's peculiar disposition would prove a serious obstacle to the realization of my hopes. The temptation of money would manifestly not offer an adequate means for overcoming his scruples, whether prompted by religious feeling or fear of popular resentment—or, as seemed likely, by both. It seemed best for me to study his case in person. So, accompanied by the Ssŭ-yeh, I proceeded to pay my formal visit to the Tao-shih and asked to be shown over his restored cave-temple. Ever since he had first come to the sacred site, some eight years earlier, it had been the chief care as well as the mainstay of his Tun-huang existence. Hence my request was met with alacrity.

As he took me through the airy front loggia of the shrine and the lofty antechapel, substantially built of timber and brickwork, I expressed due admiration for the lavish gilding and painting. As we proceeded through the high passage or porch giving access and light to the *cella*, it seemed difficult not to fix my attention on the spot where, close to the outer end on the right, an ugly patch of brickwork then still masked the door of the hidden chapel. But instead of asking questions of my pious guide as to its contents, I thought it more useful to display my interest in what his zeal had accomplished in the clearing of the *cella* and in its sacred adornment. . . . Within the *cella*, measuring about fifty-six by forty-six feet, a horseshoe-shaped dais, old but replastered, displayed a collection of new clay images, all over life-size and more ungainly than any, I thought, to be seen in these caves.

The fresco decoration of the *cella*, consisting chiefly of large diapers of seated Buddhas on the walls, and of floral patterns on the ceiling, had fared better and remained well preserved for the most part. Though obviously not as old and artistic as in some of the other large temples, this pictorial work of the *cella* caused the gaudy coarseness of the statuary and the other modern additions to stand out in painful contrast. But this could not prevent me from being impressed with all that the humble monk's zeal had accomplished. His devotion to this shrine and to the task of religious merit which he had set himself in restoring it was unmistakably genuine.

Having come to the sacred site as a poor friendless mendicant from Shan-hsi, some eight years before my visit, he had devoted himself to restoring this great and badly decayed temple to what he conceived to have been its original glory. Masses of fallen conglomerate then covered the floor of the ante-chapel and almost completely blocked the mouth of the passage. Heavy drift-sand filled the rest and a considerable portion of the *cella*. I could not help being touched by the thought of the enthusiasm, perseverance, and efforts which it must have cost the quaint, frail-looking priest by my side to beg all the money needed for the labour of clearing out the sand from the temple and for the substantial reconstructions, as besides the ante-chapel there were several stories of temple-halls solidly built above of hard brick and timber, right to the top of the cliff. His list of charitable subscriptions and his accounts, proudly produced later on to Chiang Ssŭ-yeh, showed in fact quite a respectable total, laboriously collected during years and all spent upon these labours of piety. That he spent next to nothing on his person or private concerns was clear from the way in which he lived with his two devoted acolytes and from all that Chiang heard about him at Tun-huang.

Wang Tao-shih's ignorance of all that constitutes traditional Chinese scholarship had soon been correctly diagnosed by Chiang Ssŭ-yeh. So I knew that no useful purpose could be served by talking to him about my archæological interests, about the value of first-hand materials for historical and antiquarian research, and the like, however helpful I had always found such topics for securing the friendly interest and good will of educated Chinese officials. But there was another source of aid to fall back upon—the memory of Hsüan-tsang (a Chinese Buddhist monk who made the arduous pilgrimage from China to India between the years A.D. 630–645), an appeal to which had never failed to secure me a sympathetic

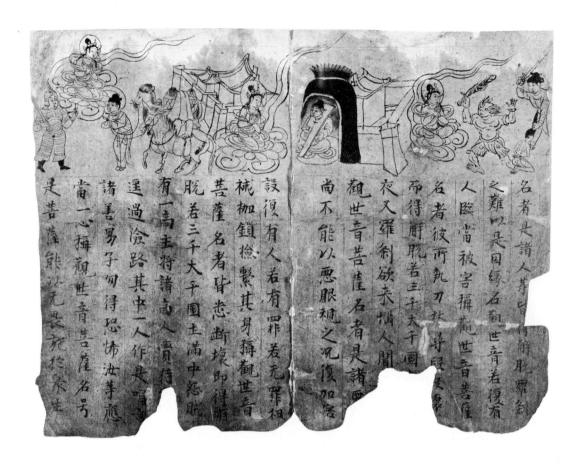

Old Chinese Manuscript This apocryphal work on filial piety was written
in the 10th century A.D.

hearing alike among the learned and the simple. The very
presence of this quaint priest, embodying in his person a
compound as it were of pious zeal, naïve ignorance, and astute
tenacity of purpose, was bound to recall those early Buddhist
pilgrims from China who, simple in mind but strong in faith
and in superstition, had made their way to India, braving all
difficulties and risks. Wang Tao-shih, too, was likely to have
heard of my attachment to the saintly traveller whom I was
accustomed to claim as my Chinese patron saint.

So, amidst the tokens of lingering Buddhist worship surrounding us in the temple *cella*, I proceeded to tell the Taoist
priest of my devotion to Hsüan-tsang: how I had followed his
footsteps from India across inhospitable mountains and deserts;

336

how I had traced the ruined sites of many sanctuaries he had visited and described; and so on. However poor my Chinese, it was a familiar theme for me to expatiate upon, and, as always, I found my efforts eagerly seconded by Chiang Ssŭ-yeh, elaborating details and making the most of my knowledge of Hsüan-tsang's authentic records and of the distant scenes of his travels. There was encouragement in the gleam of lively interest which I caught in the Tao-shih's eyes, otherwise shy and fitful, and soon the impression made upon him was plainly readable in his generally puzzling countenance.

The priest, though poorly versed in, and indifferent to, things Buddhist, proved in fact quite as ardent an admirer in his own way of T'ang-sêng, 'the great monk of the T'ang', as I am in another. Of this fortunate link between us I had ocular evidence to assure me when he took me outside into the spacious loggia he had built in front of the temple, and proudly showed the series of quaint but spirited paintings representing scenes from the great pilgrim's marvellous adventures with which he had caused its walls to be decorated by a local artist. The fantastic legends there depicted were just those which have transformed Hsüan-tsang in modern popular belief throughout China into a sort of saintly Münchausen. The fact that they are not to be found in the pilgrim's genuine *Memoirs of the Western Regions* and biography could in no way detract from the satisfaction with which I listened to my credulous cicerone expounding in voluble talk the wonderful stories of travel illustrated in the successive panels.

There was one picture in particular in which I saw good reason to display a marked interest, though it was not till later that I appealed again and again to the moral it pointed. It showed a scene which I thought at the time curiously adapted to my own case. There was T'ang-sêng standing on the bank of a violent torrent, and beside him his faithful steed laden with big bundles of manuscripts. A large turtle was to be seen swimming towards him to help in ferrying across such a precious burden. Here was clearly a reference to the twenty pony-loads of sacred Buddhist texts which the historical pilgrim managed to bring safely with him from India to China, and also to the great risks to which they had necessarily been exposed in crossing the many rivers and mountain torrents on the long journey—all facts duly related in his authentic *Life*. But the question remained whether the Tao-shih would read aright the obvious lesson here illustrated and be willing to acquire spiritual merit by letting me take back to India some of the ancient manuscripts which chance had placed in his keeping. . . .

I left Chiang Ssŭ-yeh behind to make the most of the favourable impression produced, and to urge an early loan of the promised manuscript specimens. But the priest had again become timorous and reserved, and vaguely postponed their delivery until later. So I remained in suspense until late that night Chiang, in silent elation, came to my tent with a small bundle of Chinese manuscript rolls which the Tao-shih had just brought him in secret, carefully hidden beneath his flowing black robe, as the first of the promised 'specimens'. The rolls, as regards writing and paper, looked as old as the one which the young Ho-shang had shown us on my first visit in March, and probably contained Buddhist canonical texts; but my zealous secretary, ever cautious in scholarly matters, asked for time to make sure of their character.

By daybreak next morning Chiang came to inform me, with an expression of mingled amazement and triumph, that these fine rolls contained Chinese versions of Buddhist Sūtras (*ching*) which the colophons distinctly declared to have been first brought from India and translated by Hsüan-tsang. He was much impressed by the strange chance which had thus at the very outset placed in our hands texts bearing the name of Hsüan-tsang and undoubtedly early copies of his labours as a sacred translator. I, too, was struck by this auspicious omen—especially when I realized how useful an argument with the timorous Tao-shih was supplied by the interpretation which Chiang Ssŭ-yeh unhesitatingly put upon it. Surely it was T'ang-sêng himself, so he declared with a tone which had a sound of genuine superstitious faith, very different from his usual scepticism, who at the opportune moment had revealed the hiding-place of all those manuscripts to an ignorant priest in order that I, his admirer and disciple from distant India, might find a fitting antiquarian reward awaiting me on the westernmost confines of China.

Wang Tao-shih in his ignorance could have had no inkling, when he picked up those specimens, of their connexion with Hsüan-tsang's sacred memory. Chiang Ssŭ-yeh realized at once that this discovery was bound to impress the credulous priest, as a special interposition of the Arhat, my 'patron saint', on my behalf. So he hastened away to carry the news to the Tao-shih, and on the strength of this manifest proof of T'ang-sêng's support, to urge afresh the plea for free access to the hoard of hidden manuscripts. The effect was such as we both hoped for, and shortly Chiang came back convinced that the portent would work its spell. When after a few hours he returned to the Tao-shih's temple, he found the wall blocking the entrance to the recess in the passage removed, and, on its door being opened by the priest, he caught a glimpse of a small room crammed full to the roof with bundles of manuscript.

All through the morning I had purposely kept away from the Tao-shih's quarters and temple. But on getting this news I could no longer restrain my impatience to see the great hoard myself. It was a hot day, and no one stirring abroad, when accompanied by Chiang I went to the temple. There I found Wang Tao-shih evidently not yet quite relieved of his scruples and nervous apprehensions. But under the influence of that quasi-divine hint he now summoned up courage to open before me the rough door closing the narrow entrance which led from the north side of the passage or porch into the rock-carved recess. The sight disclosed within made my eyes open wide. Heaped up in closely packed layers, but without any order, there appeared in the dim light of the priest's flickering lamp a solid mass of manuscript bundles rising to a height of nearly ten feet. They filled, as subsequent measurement showed, close on five hundred cubic feet, the size of the small room or chapel being about nine feet square and the area left clear within just sufficient for two people to stand in.

It was obvious that any proper examination of the manuscripts would be impossible in this 'black hole', and also that the digging out for this purpose of all its contents would cost time and a good deal of physical labour. It would have been premature and worse than useless at the time to suggest clearing out all the bundles into the *cella* of the temple, where they might have been examined at ease, for Wang Tao-shih was still much oppressed by fears of losing his position and patrons, in fact all the hard-won results of his pious labours at the sacred site, in consequence of the rumours which any casual observers might spread against him in the oasis. Occasional pilgrims were likely to drop in even during this 'slack season' of the site, and it would have been imprudent for the Tao-shih to keep his shrine closed against such. All we could secure for the present was that he would take out a bundle or two at a time and let us look rapidly through their contents in a less cramped and dark part of the temple precincts. It was fortunate that the large antechapel, as restored by him, included a small room on either side provided with a door and paper-covered windows. So here a convenient 'reading-room' was close at hand for the old library, so strangely preserved, where Chiang and I were screened from any inquisitive eyes, even if an occasional worshipper came to 'kotow', ring a bell, and light his stick of incense before the big and ungainly statue of Buddha.

Before proceeding to give an account of the surprising 'finds' which that first rapid examination of 'specimen' bundles from the great deposit yielded, it will be convenient to record here some details about the hiding-place to which they owed their preservation, and also to state what indications could be gathered from it as to the origin and date of the deposit. From what Wang Tao-shih had told us it appeared that, when he first settled at Ch'ien-fo-tung some eight years before, he found the approach to this cave-temple almost completely covered with drift-sand. Judging from the conditions of other caves close by and the relatively low level of this particular shrine, it is probable that the drift-sand which had accumulated behind the fallen rock debris of the antechapel area rose to nine or ten feet at the mouth of the entrance to the *cella*. As only a few labourers could be kept at work from the proceeds of pious donations coming at first driblet-like with lamentable slowness, it had taken two years or more to lay bare the whole of the wide passage, over twenty-four feet deep, and then to clear out the heavy masses of sand which had found their way into the *cella*. When this task had been accomplished, and while work was proceeding on the new statues which the Tao-shih was eager to set up, the labourers noticed a small crack in the frescoed passage wall to the right of the entrance. There appeared to be a brick wall behind the plastered surface instead of the solid conglomerate from which the *cella* and passage are hewn, and on breaking through this the small room, or side chapel, with its hidden deposit was discovered. . . .

Highly gratifying as the variety and interest of these unhoped-for discoveries was, my foremost attention was claimed by a task that was all-important for the time being. It was to keep Wang Tao-shih in a pliable mood and to prevent him from giving way to the nervous flutterings with which the chance of any instrusions and of consequent hostile rumours among his patrons intermittently filled him. Chiang Ssŭ-yeh's genial persuasion and any reassuring display that I could make of my devotion to Buddhist lore and Hsüan-tsang's memory proved helpful for this end. At times the priest's apprehensive and suspicious look would yield to one of placid contentment or even pride at our appreciation of much that was to him value-less lore, even though he grew visibly tired of climbing over manuscript heaps and dragging out heavy bundles. I had taken care in advance to assure him of a generous donation for his shrine in compensation for the trouble and possible risk he was facing over my examination of his treasures.

Late in the evening a big selection of manuscripts and painted fabrics properly packed lay ready on one side of our 'reading-room', awaiting removal for what our diplomatic convention styled 'closer examination'. But there remained the great question whether the Tao-shih would be willing to face the risks of this removal, and subsequently to fall in with the true interpretation of our purpose. It did not seem prudent as yet to approach him with ignoble words about sale and purchase, or to attempt removal except in strictest secrecy. But as we were leaving his shrine, tired with the day's work, I took occasion to engage the priest in another long talk about our common patron saint. I claimed it as an obvious proof of the Arhat's guidance and favour that I should have been privileged to behold such a great hidden store of sacred texts and other relics of piety, in part connected, perhaps, with his Indian pilgrimage, within a cave-temple which so devoted an admirer of T'ang-sêng had restored to its full splendour. As we stood in the loggia, which the Tao-shih had adorned with the frescoes of his saintly hero's adventures, I emphatically called his attention to the panel which showed Hsüan-tsang returning from India as he leads his horse heavily laden with sacred manuscripts. It was the most effective parable in support of my plea to be allowed to render accessible to Western students as much as possible of the relics which Wang Tao-shih had discovered, and yet was keeping from daylight.

Chiang Ssŭ-yeh remained behind and used all the forces of his persuasive reasoning to urge upon the priest that continued confinement in a dark hole was not the purpose for which T'ang-sêng had allowed him to light upon these remains of Buddhist doctrine and worship. Since he himself was quite incompetent to do justice to them by study, it would be an act of real religious merit to allow Buddhist scholars in India and the West to benefit by them. That this pious concession would also be rewarded by an ample donation for the benefit of the shrine was an argument which lost none of its force from being advanced with discretion—and supported by a preceding unconditioned gift of silver. It was impossible to feel sure what impression all such talks produced on the mind of the Tao-shih. He seemed constantly to vacillate between fears about his saintly reputation and a shrewd grasp of the advantages to be attained for his cherished task by accommodating me with regard to useless old things.

In any case it was for Chiang Ssŭ-yeh alone to tackle the question of the best way to secure quietly the manuscripts and paintings selected. As it proved, I had not trusted in vain his zeal and diplomatic ability. It was towards midnight, and I was about to retire to rest, when he came with cautious footsteps to make sure that nobody was stirring near my tent. A little later he returned with a big bundle, and my satisfaction was great when assured that it contained all my 'selections'.

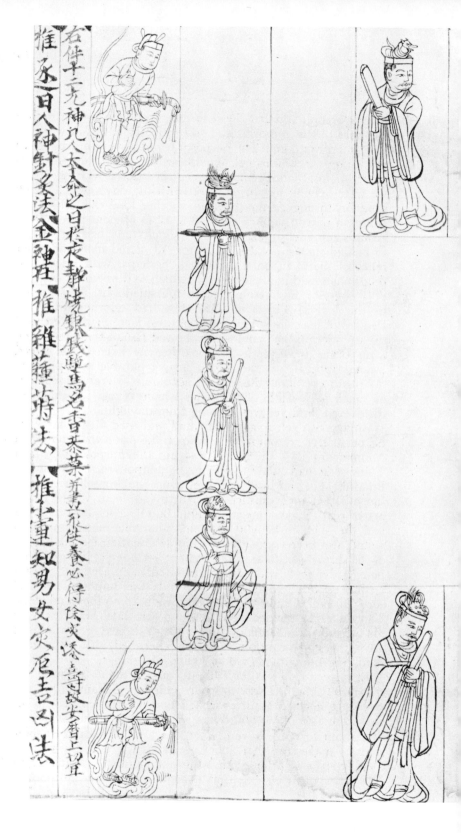

342

Calendar Dated 978 A.D. This piece is decorated with the illustrations of the year-god and the Great Spirits who represent the 12 cyclical animals.

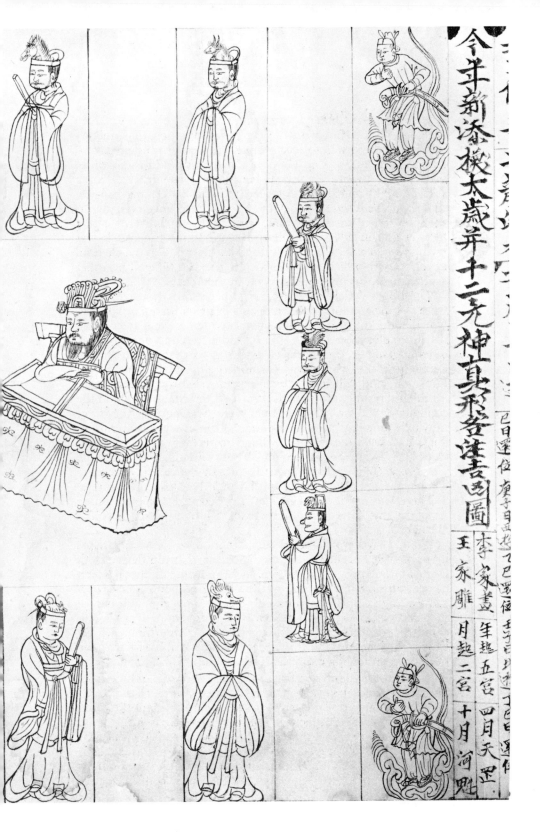

今年新添梭太歲并十二元神真形愛逢書四圖

李家畫

王家雕

年起五宫　四月天罡

月起二宮　十月河魁

The Tao-shih in the end had summoned up courage to fall in with my wishes, but with the explicit stipulation that nobody besides us three was to learn what was being transacted, and that as long as I was on Chinese soil the origin of these 'finds' was to be kept entirely secret. He himself was afraid of being seen at night outside his temple quarters. So Chiang Ssŭ-yeh took it upon himself to be the sole carrier. For seven nights more he thus came to my tent, with loads which grew steadily heavier and in the end needed carriage by instalments. It was trying work for my slightly built scholar friend, and the cheerful devotion with which he performed it remains, like all his other zealous help, deeply impressed on my memory.

The hopes which that first day's successful work had raised were not disappointed by the results of my subsequent labours. Nor did the difficult conditions with which we had to contend in the exploration of the great hidden deposit undergo any essential change. But there is no need to describe in similar detail how the search was continued day after day without remission, and still less to record in quasi-chronological order all the interesting finds which rewarded this 'digging'. That the contents of the walled-up chapel were no longer in the order in which they had been at the time of discovery was apparent, for it had been disarranged when the recess was searched for valuables. Even the assortment of the contents in each bundle was likely often to have been disturbed. Besides, it was mere chance in what order the Tao-shih would hand out the bundles.

There was no time during that hurried search to appreciate properly the antiquarian import of all that passed through my hands. . . .

What, however, attracted my attention to the manuscripts most was the chronological assurance that I could derive from them at the time. A considerable proportion of those which passed through my hands in the course of our eager search proved to be accurately dated. Before long the number of such records, many quasi-official, was large enough to allow a definite conclusion to be drawn as to the time limits within which the contents of this great cache were likely to have been brought together and finally walled up. The large majority belonged to the tenth century of our era, and, while those from its second and third quarter were frequent, none of the dated documents came down later than the second reign of the Sung dynasty, the last recorded *nien-hao* corresponding to A.D. 990–4. So I was led to assume that the walling-up of the chamber was likely to have taken place in the early years of the eleventh century. Here I may at once mention the fact that the examination of the pictures and woodcuts has fully confirmed this conclusion, the latest dates recorded on them being of the years 980 and 983. . . .

The thought naturally suggested itself that it was some destructive invasion, such as that of the Tanguts might have been, which led to the walling-up of the little chapel and the subsequent complete oblivion of the cache. But there were indications also prompting the surmise that the small well-sheltered recess may have served previously as a place of deposit for all kinds of objects held of sacred use, but no longer needed in the various shrines and monastic quarters. Among such I may specially mention numerous small bags carefully packed and sewn up in cloth which contained nothing but tiny scraps of paper bearing Chinese characters, apparently fragments of religious texts. They had evidently been picked up and collected for the same superstitious reason which now causes Chinese people to rescue from floors and streets all bits of inscribed paper for ceremonial burning. In other and much larger bundles, the contents consisted mainly of torn ends of Sūtra rolls stiffened with thin sticks of wood; of wooden rollers once used in manuscript rolls; silk tapes; cloth wrappers and similar library 'waste'. Elsewhere ex-voto rags of fabrics, small broken pieces of silk-paintings, painted wooden 'strainers' once belonging to banners, and the like were found tightly wrapped up in covers, along with block-printed pictures of sacred figures, silk streamers, etc.

It was impossible to doubt that these were relics of worship swept up from different shrines and put aside on account of religious scruples. It seemed very improbable that such insignificant remains could have been collected and sewn up systematically in the commotion of a sudden emergency. . . .

Not knowing how long we might rely on the Tao-shih's indulgence, all I could do during those first days at his cave was to work in great haste through the contents of the 'mixed' bundles. With the constant flow of fresh materials pouring down upon me, there was no chance of closer examination even in the case of art relics and of such manuscripts as were neither Chinese nor Tibetan and of which, consequently, I was able myself to estimate the full interest. All I could do was to assure their being put apart 'for further study', as we styled removal in diplomatic convention. More bitterly than ever did I regret the great hindrance created by my total want of Sinological training. Amidst the smothering mass of Buddhist canonical literature Chiang Ssŭ-yeh's zealous help, too, might not prevent Chinese texts of historical or literary interest from being left behind, even in the bundles that we were able to search. . . .

345

It had cost five days of strenuous work to extract and rapidly search all 'miscellaneous' bundles likely to yield manuscripts of special interest, paintings, and other relics which I was eager to rescue first of all. It was fortunate that these bundles, being less convenient building material than the tightly wrapped uniform packets of Chinese and Tibetan rolls, had been put by Wang Tao-shih mostly on the top or in other more or less accessible positions, when he had last stuffed back his treasures into their original hiding-place. But there still remained, rising against the walls of the chapel, that solid rampart of manuscript bundles. I was naturally anxious to have these, too, cleared out in order to be able to search them rapidly, but felt scarcely surprised when this proved a troublesome undertaking in more than one sense. We had so far succeeded in overcoming the Tao-shih's relapses into timorous contrariness by discreet diplomacy and judiciously administered doses of silver. But now, when faced by the heavy labour of clearing out the whole chamber and by the increased risk of exposure thus involved, the priest became distinctly refractory.

So prolonged efforts and fresh assurances were necessary before, under protest as it were, and after carefully locking the outer gate of the temple, he set to this great toil. Considering how little adapted his slender physique was for it, I felt glad that he now allowed himself to be helped by a priestly famulus whose discretion could be relied upon. By keeping them both steadily to the task in spite of renewed remonstrances, I succeeded in having by nightfall of May 28th the whole of the regular 'library bundles' taken out and transferred to neat rows, mainly in the spacious *cella* of the temple. . . .

I decided to face all risks rather than forego the endeavour to rescue the whole hoard. Though Chiang Ssŭ-yeh did not conceal from me misgivings justified by his knowledge of local conditions, he loyally did his best to persuade the Tao-shih that removal of the collection to a 'temple of learning' in India, or in the land of those who held sway in the ancient home of Buddhism, would be an act which might well be approved as pious. The big sum I had authorized Chiang to offer for the collection, if ceded in bulk (forty 'horseshoes' of silver, about Rs5,000, which I should have been prepared to double if need be), was used by him as a powerful argument. It would enable Wang to retire to his native province and a life of peace, if Tun-huang should become too hot for him. Or else he might spend it all on new structures for religious use near the cave-temple, which by his restoration he could claim to have annexed as his own with all its contents known or unknown, and thus secure much-increased merit and glory.

346

Diamond Sutra   It dates from around 700 A.D. and contains characters designed by the Empress Wu.

Arguments and pleadings proved vain. Having before resignedly closed his eyes to my gathering whatever I thought of special artistic or antiquarian interest, the Tao-shih now manifestly became frightened by the prospect of losing his precious *chings* as a whole. A display of sulky petulance on his part made, for the first time, our relations become somewhat strained, and only by very careful handling did we obviate what threatened to become a breach. The Tao-shih persisted in urging with all signs of sincere anxiety that any deficiency in those piles of sacred texts was bound to be noticed by his patrons, whose publicly recorded subscriptions had helped him to clear and restore the temple; this would lead to the loss of the position which he had built up for himself in the district by the pious labours of eight years and to the destruction of his life's task. Former scruples reasserting themselves, he reproached himself for having given up sacred objects which his

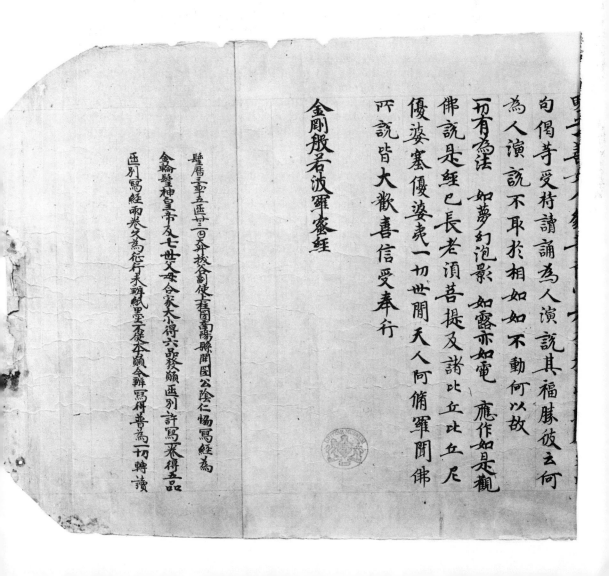

patrons had as much right to control as he had, and doggedly asserted the need of consulting them before taking any further step.

These discussions, carried on intermittently, helped to gain time for the clearing of the newly disclosed mixed bundles, and by the evening of the second day it was completed. But when I returned early next morning in order to start the close search for the regular Chinese bundles for any remnants of Central-Asian texts, or other relics of special interest that might be hidden among their rolls, I found to my dismay that the priest, seized by a fit of perturbation and qualms, had found strength to shift back overnight almost the whole of them to their gloomy hiding-place. The exertion which this *coup* had cost him only added to the sullenness of his temper. But the quantity of valuable paintings, non-Chinese manuscripts and other relics already removed gave us a material advantage. This and the Tao-shih's unmistakable wish to secure a substantial sum of money for new building operations that he contemplated, led at last to what I could well consider a substantial success in our protracted diplomatic struggle. The agreement arrived at assured me fifty compact bundles of Chinese, and five of Tibetan, text rolls, besides all my selections from the 'mixed' bundles which had passed through my hands. The payment made for all these acquisitions amounted to four 'horseshoes' of silver, or about Rs500. When I now survey the wealth of archæological materials alone that I carried away for this sum, the bargain may well seem great beyond credence.

The experience gained of the Tao-shih's pusillanimous frame of mind made me doubly anxious to lose no time in removing the heavy loads of Chinese and Tibetan rolls. So far it had been my devoted Chinese secretary who night by night struggled to my tent with the loads of my daily 'selections'. But the new task being wholly beyond his strength, I sought help on this occasion from Ibrāhim Bēg and Tila Bai, another trusted old follower. Two midnight trips which they made to the temple with Chiang, under the screening shadow of the steep river-bank, allowed the huge sackfuls to be safely removed to my store-room without anyone, even of my own men, having received an inkling. Prolonged absence from his clients in the oasis had caused the nervousness of Wang Tao-shih to increase. So as soon as our transaction was completed he hastened to resume his seasonal begging tour in the district.

In order to assuage his spiritual scruples as well as I could and to give visible proof of grateful attachment to my 'patron saint's' memory, I had previously arranged through the priest to have one of the abandoned smaller shrines in the southern group of grottoes redecorated with a new clay image of Hsüan-tsang. The Tun-huang sculptor's work in due time produced an artistic eyesore, but widely advertised by the Tao-shih it helped to dispel suspicions about my long visit. So when a week later he returned I found him reassured that the secret had not been discovered, and that his spiritual influence, such as it was, had suffered no diminution. Thus it became possible to make him stretch a point further and allow me to acquire some twenty more bundles of Chinese manuscripts, with supplementary selections from the 'mixed' bundles, against an appropriate donation for his temple. When later on I proceeded to the packing, the manuscript acquisitions filled seven cases, such as horses could carry, while five more were required to hold the paintings, decorated textiles, and other miscellaneous relics. The safe packing of the painted silks proved to be a very delicate task needing great care, and I was glad to utilize for it the days when sandstorms made photographic work in the caves impossible. The risk of causing suspicion in Tun-huang by a sudden large order of cases was avoided by the precaution I had taken to bring some 'empties' to the site and by securing the rest by discreet instalments.

The forethought and care bestowed on such necessary safeguards did not remain unrequited. I had the satisfaction of seeing that the shy Tao-shih, honest in his own way, now breathed freely again. It seemed almost as if in a dim way he recognized that it was a pious act on his part to let me rescue for Western scholarship as much as cirumstances would permit of those ancient Buddhist relics which local ignorance would allow to lie here neglected or to be lost in the end. When I finally took my departure from the Caves of the Thousand Buddhas, his quaint sharp-cut face had resumed its customary expression of shy but self-contented serenity. We parted in fullest amity. But the most gratifying proof I received of the peaceful state of his mind was when, on my return to An-hsi four months later, he agreed to give up, for that 'temple of learning' in the distant West of which I had told him so often, another big share of the Chinese and Tibetan manuscripts in the shape of over two hundred and thirty compact bundles. How this was successfully achieved through Chiang Ssŭ-yeh's persuasive diplomacy and in perfect secrecy has been told in my *Personal Narrative*. But it was only when all the twenty-four cases, heavy with manuscripts rescued from the priest's precarious keeping, and the five more filled with paintings and other art remains from the same hoard, had been safely deposited in the British Museum, that I could feel true relief.

THE TREASURE SHIP OF SUTTON HOO

In 1939, just before the outbreak of World War II, a team of archaeologists discovered the greatest treasure ever dug from English soil. The discovery consisted of the possessions of an Anglo-Saxon king, which had been buried in his long ship beneath an earthen mound in about A.D. 650. Precious jewels, silver bowls, coins, shields, and weapons were among the remarkable objects uncovered in the ship.

C. W. Phillips of Cambridge, who directed the excavation, describes the exciting highlights of the discovery. Working quickly, under the shadow of impending war, he and his assistants carefully removed and preserved each item. After their work was finished, a jury awarded the entire treasure to a Mrs. Pretty, on whose land the ship had been found. She, in turn, generously donated the collection to the British Museum —one of the most valuable donations the museum has ever had.

Excerpted from RECENT ARCHAEOLOGICAL EXCAVATIONS IN BRITAIN: *Edited by R. L. S. Bruce-Mitford. (Routledge, Kegan Paul, 1956) written by*

C. W. PHILLIPS

THIS great find came to light during the last few weeks of peace before the outbreak of the Second World War in September, 1939. A sense of imminent danger overshadowed the discovery and spurred on the work of the excavators. In the event, seven years were to pass before its full import could be realized, because all the finds had quickly to be removed to a place of safety. For a few days the discovery was front page news, and then it was swept away by a torrent of history in the making. . . .

Before describing the circumstances which led to the sensational finds of 1939, something must be said about this part of East Anglia in Anglo-Saxon times. The kingdom of East Anglia comprised Norfolk, Suffolk and the eastern parts of Cambridgeshire, though these were debatable grounds with Mercia, and the realm is not likely to have come into full existence much before A.D. 500. Bede in his *Ecclesiastical History*

(A.D. 731) records that its royal family was known as the Uffingas, or kin of Uffa or Wuffa. This man, who was probably related to the royal family of Uppland in Sweden, was the grandfather of the most famous of the East Anglian kings, Rædwald, who held the title of Bretwalda, or Overlord of Britain, for a while and died in A.D. 624-625. In describing the baptism of Swidhelm, King of Essex, by St. Cedd, Bede tells us that the ceremony took place 'in vico regis qui dicitur Rendlesham, id est Mansio Rendili' (in a town of the King's called Rendlesham, that is to say, Rendil's steading). The little village of Rendlesham still survives at a point nearly equidistant between the estuaries of the rivers Deben and Alde, and about four miles from Sutton Hoo. We thus know that there was a royal residence of some importance close to our site, so that the presence of a royal burial ground need occasion no surprise. Further, ships belonging to the royal establishment may well have been kept on these two rivers. Since 1939 intensive research has been directed to identifying the site of the royal hall at Rendlesham. Some interesting facts and possibilities have been established, but nothing conclusive is yet known.

(Attention was now turned to the eleven mounds on the slopes above the River Deben.)

The largest mound was oval in form with its long axis roughly east and west. Mr. Basil Brown began to run a trench through the mound along this axis, beginning at the east end. The important fact is that, almost at the very beginning of opening this trench, and while he was just inside the edge of the barrow at old ground level, Mr. Brown recognized several of the rusted iron clench nails of a boat's hull occurring in the material of the mound in the order, and at the angle, which showed that the decayed end—either bow or stern—of a boat was protruding from the ground under the barrow. It was Mr. Brown's great contribution to the Sutton Hoo excavation that he at once saw the implication of this discovery and took steps accordingly. He rightly assumed that a boat was buried in the ground under the mound, that its length was not likely to be much less than that of the mound's longer axis, and that its keel lay roughly along this. In the event it turned out that the barrow had been considerably reduced in length, so that the other end of the boat surfaced well beyond its existing limit of 1939. No further attempt was made to open up the end of the boat, but all effort was directed towards removing the whole of the upper part of the barrow on a width of some fifteen feet on its long axis.

It was in the middle of May that the present writer got wind of these events through a hint from Mr. Basil Megaw, Curator of the Manx Museum, that he was receiving requests for information about the Viking boat burials of the Isle of Man from Ipswich Museum. An early opportunity was taken to go to Ipswich, and the site was visited in company with Mr. Maynard. When I crossed the short stretch of heath from Mrs. Pretty's house and saw the large dump of sand that had already been moved out of the excavation I had no clear idea of what I was going to see in a few moments. When it came the sight was a shock. There, slightly adumbrated by the removal of the greater part of the middle of the overlying mound, was more than half of a boat which seemed unlikely to be less than 100 feet long overall. In the event its length proved to be 89 feet, but the first impact was staggering. I at once saw that this work ought to go no further without the knowledge and counsel of the Ancient Monuments-Department of the Ministry of Works, and the British Museum, and proposed that they should be telephoned to at once. With Mrs. Pretty's consent this was done within the hour and a standstill was agreed upon. . . .

Before I took over the work it was already committed to the plan of proceeding by opening a great central trench. This was economical in effort but made a proper study of the barrow as such nearly impossible, besides creating the practical difficulty that, as the excavation deepened, two minor cliffs of sand some fifteen feet high began to loom dangerously over the main scene of work, which was at the bottom of the middle part of the boat, all of which was well below the old ground surface. We relieved this threat as far as possible by making a wide walk at old ground level on each side of the trench in which the boat lay under the barrow, and by cutting back the sides of the barrow outside these walks into outward-leaning slopes, well-fronted and retained by planks. Like much else at Sutton Hoo, this was a makeshift arrangement which only succeeded because we were lucky in having much less wind and rain than may normally be expected in an English summer.

We may now discuss the soil conditions of the excavation. It can have been seldom that, in England, work depending for its success on the tracing of decayed wooden structures has been carried out entirely in sand, but this was the case at Sutton Hoo. The heath consisted of post-glacial sand to a depth far below the range of the excavation. Occasionally diversified by a little light gravel and small rafts of clay, it was a bright yellow colour and very compact where it had not been moved at the time of the burial. This was helpful, for it was very easy to find the precise limits of the great trench which had been dug to receive the boat. The mattock strokes of the trench diggers could still be faintly seen here and there on its sides, and the infilled sand fell away from them with ease and precision, enabling us to note that the sides were vertical all round. It followed from this that the boat was lowered and not slid into the grave. An interesting point was that the site chosen for the royal cemetery was also one which had been much camped on during the Neolithic-Bronze Age transition in the first half of the second millennium B.C. Both in 1938 and 1939 pottery of 'beaker' type, which had been scraped up by their builders as part of the surrounding soil, was found in the barrows, and the marks of the fires of those who had used this pottery could be seen in section beneath the old ground surface under the ship-barrow. . . .

It has already been shown that the work of April and May predetermined the general lines which the excavation must follow. On taking over the site on 10th July it was necessary to make a clear decision how to proceed. There were already plain signs that there had been a burial chamber, and so it was determined to concentrate all efforts on studying and clearing the burial area. Only then would it be possible to make a complete examination of the boat. It seemed beyond hope that the burial would be quite intact in view of the way in which most ancient burial mounds have suffered more or less disturbance by seekers after treasure. Doubtless it would be found that the chamber had been pillaged within a few years of its completion and long before it rotted and collapsed. At Sutton Hoo we found evidences of such an attempt which, on the showing of some scraps left behind by its authors, seems to have been made round about A.D. 1600. They had given up when they reached the level of the old ground surface and found nothing, not having noticed signs of the collapsed chamber or having dug down the extra ten feet which would have brought them to the bottom of the boat and their reward. Our hope was that the chamber had collapsed before any robbery had been attempted, in days when there was still knowledge of the presence of treasure, and, most providentially, this proved to be the case.

The shadow of the impending war lowered over all stages of the Sutton Hoo excavation in 1939. There could be no delay, particularly after we became aware that the burial chamber had some contents, even though the first to be recognized were

354

Treasure Ship of Sutton Hoo   The iron clench nails, fastening the oak beams of the hull, are clearly visible.

no more remarkable than some curiously well-preserved wooden wedges and some crushed sheets of thin bronze which later proved to be part of a large cauldron.

It was possible to form only a vague idea of what could be expected. Seen in retrospect it is now tolerably obvious that the best would be of Anglo-Saxon date and so, since the basic ideas behind the burial must be pagan, it could hardly post-date the conversion of the East Angles to Christianity by very long.

Thus some date in the middle of the seventh century A.D. might be expected, but at that time our minds naturally went back to the great ship-burial discoveries at Gokstad and Oseberg in Norway which belong to a period nearly three hundred years later. These burials, though robbed of their best treasures, had still contained a remarkable array of furniture, mostly in wood, but, since our site was in sand, it was clear from the earliest stages that little of this kind could have survived. . . .

By 20th July the burial chamber had been largely cleared of sand and turf infilling. The last stages of this had been a delicate business. We had now reached a point where various vague sand-encrusted forms were beginning to appear on what we knew must be the bottom of the boat, and the problem was how to advance into the area without treading on still hidden items of the funeral deposit which was obviously present. In excavation work there are often occasions on which a light, easily erected and adjusted overhead gantry device with a travelling cradle would be a godsend. Comfortable and close suspension over the scene of work free from all danger of doing damage by one's own weight is required. In the absence of anything of this kind the problem was solved by a patient, step-by-step exploration of the area from the bow end. Once a safe stance had been established inside, careful reconnaissance from this point of vantage and from the sides of the excavation showed that the plan of the burial deposit was in the form of a letter H, with the two uprights inside and parallel with the two ends of the burial chamber and the cross-bar joining them down the middle along the keel of the boat. Thus there were two practically clear areas on each side, from the gunwales down to the middle deposit over the keel.

Before saying anything about the detailed discovery and removal of the deposit, it will be well to give a quick preliminary description of its main features, to clarify what follows.

Put simply, the stern end of the chamber was the area of most importance, with all the symbols and accoutrements of royalty placed close together in a group. The chief objects were: an iron standard and ceremonial whetstone; a splendid helmet, sword and shield, with the jewelled fittings of the sword belt; jewelled epaulettes for a cuirass; a set of seven assorted spears and a dirk; an exotic bronze Coptic bowl from Egypt containing the finest example of a 'hanging bowl' yet known, in which in turn were the remains of a harp; a matched set of ten silver bowls imported from the Byzantine Empire and two silver spoons, one with the name of Saul and the other with the name of Paul on it in Greek letters. Setting off from this group along the keel line of the boat towards the bow was first a group of decayed and crushed drinking-horns with silver mounts, and then a great silver dish which had been placed on the top of a pile of miscellaneous objects containing, among many other things, decayed clothing, shoes, a lesser silver dish, and a coat of mail. Finally, across the bow end of the chamber were disposed in line a great iron-hooped wooden tub and three bronze cauldrons placed in descending order of size. Near these was some complex ornamental iron tackle which is regarded as being used to hang these vessels over a fire. If any wooden furniture had been placed to fill up the spaces along each side of the chamber, it had entirely disappeared and could have had no metal elements in its construction. No sign of a bedstead was present, and the remains of sacrificed animals were entirely wanting, either as bones or teeth or, by implication, through harness or other gear.

The Sutton Hoo funeral chamber was never cleaned up with all its contents in position at one time for a single dramatic photograph. The complexity and fragility of much of the deposit made this impossible, but many record photographs were made at every stage of the work, chiefly by Mr. O. G. S. Crawford, and they are quite adequate when considered in sequence.

Objects had to be cleared and removed as soon as we became properly aware of their presence, and this meant that much of the gold treasure came out first, followed quickly by the Coptic bowl and its associated objects. The work went on swiftly with blunt bodkin, knife blade, and brushes of various calibre. The method of survey consisted of making a well-braced, strictly rectangular, light timber frame which was strung to produce a reticulation of ten centimetre squares. This could be firmly and accurately anchored to datum points so that the relationship of the various objects to each other could be studied and plotted on squared paper by being observed through the overlying string grid.

The body of skilled voluntary helpers and witnesses at

357

crucial times of the excavation was a memorable feature of the work. From an early stage Professor and Mrs. Stuart Piggott were present, and to them, in the chance but most welcome presence of Professor J. B. Ward-Perkins, fell the task of clearing, recording and lifting the main treasure of jewellery on 22nd July. This was a relatively easy task because of the marvellous state of preservation of these gold objects and their concentration in quite a small space. The only major pieces of jewellery not found and removed at this stage were the jewelled epaulettes and the fittings of the sword and scabbard. To Mrs. Piggott fell the thrill of brushing the sand from the first piece of jewellery found, one of the two exquisite terminals of the sword knot. This came on 21st July. Hard after it came the second terminal, and when these appeared our feelings were as much those of apprehension as of elation, for there was then no doubt that we had heavy responsibilities before us. But there was no time to brood over this. If remarkable and valuable finds were present, the conditions of the excavation demanded that they should be removed and secured without delay. Naturally it was the discovery of the jewellery which forced Sutton Hoo on the attention of the world. . . .

I shall not easily forget the day shortly after the discovery of the treasure when Mr. Kendrick first visited the site. I went to meet him at Woodbridge station and took with me one of the best of the small jewelled buckles, carefully wrapped, in a tobacco tin, so that he could have an advance idea of what he was to see when he reached the main treasure at Mrs. Pretty's house. It was a dramatic moment when I drew him into the waiting-room to show the buckle and the scale of the discovery became clear to him.

The Science Museum played its part by sending the late Lt.-Commander J. K. D. Hutchison to study the ship and to carry out a proper survey of its lines with the aid of members of the Museum staff.

It was no longer possible to neglect the general security of the site when it became known that valuables were being discovered. The assistance of the East Suffolk police was sought, and until everything had been cleared from the site it was under a police guard every night.

The limits of this chapter do not permit a detailed description of the uncovering and removal of each item of the burial deposit. The process continued from 21st July, when the first item of the treasure was recognized, till 29th July, when the work was completed by the removal of the remains of the big bronze cauldrons at the bow end of the chamber. It was an arduous experience not made any easier by the number of distinguished visitors who were present from time to time and the need for meeting the requirements of the public press. Further, many of the finds were rich, strange, and difficult of successful removal.

A number of remarkable moments stand out in the memory. The first was on 22nd July, when the main treasure of jewellery was found. This requires no further comment, except that it was here that a find of the greatest scientific importance, vital to the whole excavation, was made in the shape of thirty-eight gold coins in the purse, all of them struck in the kingdom of the Merovingian Franks in France. There has been argument about the precise dating of these, but one thing appears to be certain. On the evidence provided by their presence in the grave it cannot be older than A.D. 650. Another climax was on 26th July, when the big silver dish was lifted. It was clear that this was partly covering at least one other silver vessel, and we could not guess what else might be found. As a precaution a considerable preparation was made of bowls of water, wet moss, cotton wool, and boxes, etc., to deal with any fragile objects which might appear. Arrangements were also made to photograph every phase of the proceedings, and the assorted mass of decayed cloth, pillow-down, shoes, gourd cups, etc., which was revealed justified our care. Another dramatic moment was when the great whetstone began to emerge from the sand. It was projecting upwards, and the sinister-looking bearded human heads carved on the emergent end gave it a daunting look. The first guess was that it was a sceptre. When removed from the ground it proved to be in form a whetstone, but it is interesting to note that the best opinion now considers that it was indeed a symbol of power.

In various ways the remains of the shield, the helmet and the drinking horns were all very difficult to disentangle and remove, the latter being reduced to such a smashed pulp that the only way to get them out was to undercut and remove the whole mass on an iron plate for direct removal to the British Museum Research Laboratory, where, incidentally, two of them have been shown to have had the record capacity of six quarts.

The iron standard which lay across the stern end of the chamber against the foot of its cross-wall was also a very difficult object. All the metal was severely corroded, and, since it was built up of a number of slender rods and bars and was still essentially intact, it also had to be gently undercut and eased on to a plank suitably padded before being lifted out in one swift stroke by the combined movements of four people.

But perhaps the most odd performance was that of a large

purplish lump of material about which nothing could be said except that it must be a badly corroded silver object. This also was lifted out on an iron plate and set aside while our attention was turned elsewhere. It stood quietly in the rays of the setting sun for some time and then suddenly heaved upwards slightly with a metallic click. On examination it proved to have been a set of ten matched silver bowls which had been nested together and placed upside down in the grave. In the course of time the two uppermost bowls had been reduced to little more than silver chloride, hence the purple colour, but of the remaining eight, six were in a perfect state of preservation save for some slight corrosion round the edges. Those underneath had been almost completely protected, and as the mass dried out with the overlying weight of sand removed, it sprang apart like an opening concertina.

Since the great find at Sutton Hoo had all the form and trappings of a royal grave, it was with some surprise that the excavators early became aware that it had never contained a body. The absence of obvious human remains did not of itself provoke comment, because the conditions of this grave set deep in damp sand were most unfavourable to the survival of any organic remains. But no cremated bones were found, and all the other evidence on the way of the disposition and character of the finds pointed in the same direction. There was really no room for the proper laying out of a body at the more honourable end of the grave, nor were there any of those smaller, more personal objects found which would have been on a clothed body. Chemical tests later carried out on the grave goods have gone far to prove that no body was ever placed in any attitude in this part of the grave. Thus the most remarkable burial assemblage in Britain has proved to have been almost certainly a cenotaph, and this fact has posed a nice problem for those whose task it is to interpret the results of the excavation. Theories which have been advanced to account for it include the suggestion that the man commemorated was lost at sea, that his body was lost beyond recovery on a stricken field, or that he was in fact a Christian and was buried elsewhere in consecrated ground, though family custom and public policy still required this expensive and essentially pagan monument to his memory. Here we have no time to probe further into the enigma of these pagan rites in an East Anglia which, by A.D. 650, was substantially Christian. Some of the objects found have certainly had a Christian origin, like the silver spoons, and others are capable of a Christian interpretation, but the whole taken together is still the provision for the passage to Valhalla.

Royal Helmet   This head piece was found in the burial chamber of the Treasure Ship.

When the contents of the burial chamber had been cleared it remained to study the vessel in which it had been placed. The ship has still not received the attention which is its due. This is partly the result of the lamented death of Lt.-Commander Hutchison during the war. It must have been a major vessel of its time even though there was evidence that it was well past its prime at the day of burial, and it is almost the only great example of early Anglo-Saxon skill in woodwork which has come down to us.

The problem which faced the excavators was how to body forth a faithful view of the boat as it had been when it was already known that none but the faintest traces of wood were likely to remain. Here the method of construction of the boat came to our aid. It was clinker-built from oak planks averaging one inch in thickness, and its skin had been fastened throughout by iron clench nails riveted up over diamond-shaped iron roves. Outside the area occupied by the burial chamber every one of these was still in its place relative to its neighbours, because none could move once the ship was tight buried in the grave with close-packed sand both inside and outside the skin. Thus the complete decay of the timbers affected their position not at all. The problem was how to extract all the sand from inside the boat, leaving all the nails in place and visible, and with much care and vital help from the absence of rain and wind this was achieved.

A curious fact is that, had the boat contained no metal in its construction, it would still have been possible to get a fairly accurate idea of its form by studying the pattern of old bracken roots in the sand; for wherever wood had been, there were often traces of these roots, which had followed the more nutritious conditions provided by its decay right down to the keel.

The boat proved to be 89 feet long and 15 feet wide amidships, tapering to a sharp point at each end, though it was impossible to say how these had been finished off at their extremities, or whether there had been any kind of figurehead. There was no proper keel and the boat had no arrangements for sailing, relying entirely on propulsion by oar. All deck-work and seating had been stripped out before the burial, and nothing was left in it but the ribs. . . .

The great find which has been described above raised some very delicate questions. Obviously such precious objects in silver and gold came within the scope of the law of treasure trove. It therefore followed that their legal ownership would have to be established by a coroner's inquest, and this duly took place in the village hall at Sutton on 14th August. The finds, which had for the time being rested in the British Museum, were taken back to Suffolk under armed escort, and placed in the custody of the police; and twelve Suffolk citizens had to decide whether the objects had been lost or hidden in the ground with the intent to recover, or whether the original owners had voluntarily divested themselves of their property in them. If the verdict was in the first sense, then they became the property of the Crown, which would have to compensate the finders with the full value of the collection, not as mere bullion, but as works of art. It would be for the jury to say who the 'finders' were. If in the second sense, then they became the personal property of Mrs. Pretty as the owner of the land on which they were found. On the evidence placed before it the jury had no difficulty in finding a verdict in the second sense. There could be no doubt that the placing of all these treasures in the grave was a public act and that there was no intent to recover them, whatever may have been the private feelings of some of those present at the time.

The value of the Sutton Hoo treasure has been estimated at a very substantial six-figure sum. Since in some sense the objects make up the first English regalia known, they are of great national importance without reference to their scientific and intrinsic value. Could they remain in private hands, and where would the money come from if the owner was prepared to sell them? By an act of great generosity and public spirit Mrs. Pretty solved all these problems when she presented them to the nation. The National Collection has never received a greater gift during the lifetime of a donor.

EASTER ISLAND

On Easter Day in 1722, the Dutch explorer, Roggeveen, discovered a remote island in the South Pacific. He was received by a strange people, many of whom were stark naked
and tattooed; and he noted that the ears of a few were artificially lengthened by means of ornamental discs inserted
through the lobes. They were a wild but friendly people living
in the stone age—and all round them the Island was popu-
lated, too, with great stone statues gazing enigmatically across
the land. Later, other explorers visited this lonely place, and all
agreed that the stone giants belonged to an earlier period.
But who carved the statues, who transported them, and who
erected them?

Thor Heyerdahl, the Norwegian explorer and anthropolo-
gist, had always been interested in the origins of culture in
the Pacific. His Kon Tiki expedition made him world-famous.
Subsequently, in 1955 and 1956 he visited Easter Island in an
attempt to unravel the mystery of the stone statues.

From the Islanders Heyerdahl learned something of their
traditions and their legends, and from the soil he gained evidence to confirm their stories. Long ago, they told him, there
were two groups of peoples who lived on the Island: those
with ornamental disks in their ears, known as the long-ears,
and those with normal ears, known as the short-ears. The
long-ears were the rulers, and for centuries they dominated
the short-ears. They also peopled the Island with the stone
giants.

But a day came when the short-ears revolted, and the
long-ears fled to a peninsula. Their land was defended by a
ditch into which they hurled firewood, so that when the attack
should come they would be protected by a wall of flame.
Eventually they were overcome by treachery, and most of them
perished in the blazing fires of their own defensive ditch. Only
one survived the holocaust. "I," said the 20th-century mayor
of Easter Island to Heyerdahl, "am one of the descendants of
Ororoina, the sole survivor of that massacre."

From that moment of long ago, the short-ears forgot the

statues and the ways of life imposed on them by the long-ears, and they deserted the crater quarry which was the birthplace of the stone giants.

When Heyerdahl's archaeologists cut trenches along the length of the defensive ditch near the peninsula, they discovered, at a certain depth, layer upon layer of ash. This ash can now be dated to approximately 300 years ago. No one can say for sure, but perhaps it represents the remains of the fires that consumed the Easter Island artists.

In the following extract Dr. Heyerdahl describes the quarry, the statues, and the strangeness of Easter Island.

Excerpted from AKU-AKU, *(George Allen & Unwin, 1958) written by*

THOR HEYERDAHL

ANYONE who is dreaming of a trip to the moon can get a little foretaste of it by climbing about on the dead volcanic cones of Easter Island. Not only has he completely forsaken our own hectic world, which seems to be immeasurably far away in the blue, but the landscape can easily give an illusion of being on the moon: a friendly little moon hung between sky and sea, where grass and ferns cover the treeless craters which lie gaping sleepily towards the sky, ancient and moss-covered, lacking the tongues and teeth of their fiery days. There are a number of these peaceful volcanoes here and there in green hummocks all over the island. They are green outside and green within. The time of eruptions is past and so remote that at the bottom of some of the largest craters sky-blue lakes with waving green reeds mirror clouds flying before the trade wind. One of these waterlogged volcanoes is called Rano Raraku, and it is here that the men in the moon seem to have been most busily at work. You do not see them, but you have a feeling that they have only hidden themselves away in sealed-up holes in the ground, while you yourself walk about in the grass at your ease and survey their interrupted tasks. They have fled in haste from what they were doing, and Rano Raraku remains one of the greatest and most curious monuments of mankind, a monument to the great lost unknown behind us, a warning of the transience of man and civilization. The whole mountain massif has been reshaped, the volcano has been greedily cut up as if it were pastry, although sparks fly when a steel axe is driven against the rock to test its strength. Hundreds of thousands of cubic feet of rock have been cut out and tens of thousands of tons of stone carried away. And in the midst of the mountain's gaping wound lie more than a hundred and fifty gigantic stone men, finished and unfinished, in all stages, from the just begun to the just completed. At the foot of the mountain stand finished stone men, side by side like a supernatural army, and one feels miserably small in approaching the place, whether on horseback or driving in a jeep along the ancient roads, which the vanished sculptors laid down, leading to their gigantic workshop.

Dismounting from one's horse in the shadow of a great block of stone, one sees that the block has features on its underside: it is the head of a fallen giant. The whole expedition could creep under it and find shelter in a rainstorm. On going up to the foremost figures, which are buried in the earth up to their chests, one is shocked to find that one cannot even reach up to the colossus' chin. And if you try to climb up on to those which have been flung down flat on their backs, you feel a regular Lilliputian, because often you have the greatest difficulty even in getting up on to their stomachs. And once up on the prostrate Goliath you can walk about freely on his chest and stomach, or stretch yourself out on his nose, which often is as long as an ordinary bed. Thirty feet was no uncommon length for these figures: the largest, which lay unfinished and aslant on the side of the volcano, was sixty-nine feet long, so that, counting a storey as ten feet, this stone man was as tall as a seven-storey house. That was a burly giant, a regular mountain troll.

In Rano Raraku you feel the mystery of Easter Island at close quarters. The air is laden with mystery; bent on you is the silent gaze of a hundred and fifty eyeless faces. The huge standing figures look down at you with an enigmatic stare: your steps are watched from every single ledge and cave in the mountain, where giants unborn and giants dead and broken lie as in mangers and on sick-beds, lifeless and helpless because the intelligent creative force has left them. Nothing moves except for the drifting clouds above you. It was so when the sculptors went, and so it will always be. The oldest figures, those which were completed, stand there proud, arrogant, and tight-lipped; as though defiantly conscious that no chisel, no atomic power will ever open their mouths and make them speak.

But even though the giants' mouths were sealed seven times over, anyone going about in the chaos of uncompleted

Easter Island Statues Some of the gigantic images on the island.

figures up the mountain slope could learn a good deal. Where-
ever we climbed and wherever we halted, we were surrounded,
as in a hall of mirrors, by enormous faces circling about us,
seen from in front, in profile and at every angle. All were
astonishingly alike. All had the same stoical expression and the
most peculiar long ears. We had them above us, beneath us,
and on both sides. We clambered over noses and chins and
trod on mouths and gigantic fists, while huge bodies lay leaning
over us on the ledges higher up. As our eyes gradually became
trained to distinguish art from nature, we perceived that the
whole mountain was one single swarm of bodies and heads,
right from the foot up to the very top of the precipice on the
uppermost edge of the volcano. Even up here, five hundred
feet above the plain, half-finished giants lay side by side staring
up into the firmament, in which only the hawks were sailing.
But the swarm of stone phantoms did not stop even up here on
the topmost edge, they went on side by side and over one
another in one unbroken procession down the side of the crater
into the interior of the volcano. The cavalcades of stiff hard-
bitten stone men, standing and lying, finished and unfinished,
went right down to the lush green reed-bed on the margin of
the lake, like a people of robots petrified by thirst in a blind
search for the water of life.

We were all equally overwhelmed and impressed by the
gigantic enterprise which had once been interrupted in Rano
Raraku. . . .

When we began to dig the impression was no less astonishing.
The famous Easter Island heads were large enough already,
standing on the slope at the foot of the volcano, but when we
dug our way down along the throat the chest appeared, and
under the chest the stomach and arms continued, and the whole
of the huge body right down to the hips, where long thin
fingers with enormous curved nails met under a protruding
belly. Now and then we found both human bones and remains
of fires in the strata of earth down the front of the statue. The
heads looked quite different standing there with bodies and
arms beneath, instead of as head hunters' trophies, as we are
accustomed to see the Easter Island statues in encyclopædias
and travel books. But this uncovering solved none of the problems of Easter Island; it was merely a fascinating sight which
the Routledge expedition once experienced before us. We had
the greatest difficulty in throwing a line over the highest heads,
and only the best climbers attempted to struggle up the rope,
for when these statues were completely excavated some of them
stood as much as forty feet high, or as high as a four-storey

Easter Island Statue   Here is a close-up of one of these gargantuan
images.

house. The last bit, from the eyebrows upwards, was the worst, for here the rope was pressed tight against the giant's forehead and did not afford a decent grip.

It was difficult enough for a rope-climber without encumbrances to ascend the skull of one of these standing giants, but it was more difficult to understand how it was possible to carry up a large hat which was to be placed on the very top of the head, especially considering that the hat too was of stone, and could have a volume of two hundred cubic feet, and weigh as much as two elephants. How can one lift the weight of two elephants to the level of the roof of a four-storey house, when there are no cranes and not even a high point in the neighbourhood? The few men who could find room for themselves up on the figure's skull could not possibly have dragged an enormous stone hat up to the small flat space which was their only foothold. And although a crowd of men could stand on the ground at the foot of the statue they were mere Lilliputians, who could not stretch their arms more than a fraction of the way up the lower part of the giant. How then could they have pushed the weight of the two elephants high in the air, right up past the chest, and on past the towering head up to the very top of the skull? Metal was unknown, and the island was practically treeless.

Even the engineers shook their heads resignedly. We felt like a crowd of schoolboys standing helpless before a practical conundrum. The invisible moon-dwellers down in their holes seemed to be triumphing over us, asking: 'Guess how this engineering work was done! Guess how we moved these gigantic figures down the steep walls of the volcano and carried them over the hills to any place in the island we liked!'

There was little use in guessing. We must first have a really good look round, to see if the mysterious old-time genii had been careless enough to leave behind something which could give us even the smallest hint.

To tackle the problem at its root we first studied the numerous uncompleted figures which lay on the ledges in the quarry itself. It was clear that all the work had been broken off suddenly; thousands of primitive unpolished stone picks still lay in the open-air workshop, and as different groups of sculptors had worked simultaneously on many different statues, all stages of carving were represented. The ancient stone-cutters had first attacked the bare rock itself and made the face and front part of the statue. Then they had cut alley-ways along the sides and made giant ears and arms, always with extremely long and slender fingers, curved over the belly. Next they had cut their way underneath the whole figure from both sides, so that the back took the shape of a boat with a narrow keel attached to the rock.

When the façade of the figure was complete in every minute detail it was scrubbed and thoroughly polished: the only thing they took care not to do was to mark in the eye itself under the overhanging brows. For the present the giant was to be blind. Then the keel was hacked away under the back, while the colossus was wedged up with stones to prevent it from slipping away and sliding down into the abyss. It was a matter of utter indifference to the sculptors whether they carved the figure out of a perpendicular wall or a horizontal slab, and head upwards or downwards, for the half-finished giants lay all over the place and leaning in every direction, as on a battle-field; the only thing that was consistent about them was that the back was the last part to remain attached to the rock.

When the back also had been cut loose the break-neck transportation down the cliff to the foot of the volcano had begun. In some cases colossi weighing many tons had been swung down a perpendicular wall and manœuvred over statues on which work was still proceeding on the ledge below. Many were broken in transport, but the overwhelming majority had come down complete—that is to say complete but for legs, for every single statue ended in a flat foundation just where the abdomen ends and the legs begin. They were sort of lengthened busts with complete torsos.

At the foot of the cliff lay a thick layer of gravel and decomposed rock, often piled up into ridges and regular hillocks. This was the result of thousands of tons of stone splinters which had been carried away from the quarry by the sculptors. Here the giant men had been temporarily raised up into a standing position in holes which had been dug in the rubble. Not till now, with the statues standing thus, did the sculptors set to work on the unfinished back, and the neck and hinder parts take shape, while the waist was decorated with a belt surrounded by rings and symbols. This little belt was the only piece of clothing the naked statues wore, and with one exception they were all men.

But the mysterious progress of the stone colossi did not end here among the rubble. When the back also was finished they were to go on to their wall-less temples. Most of them had gone already: only comparatively few were still on the waiting list for transportation from their holes at the foot of the volcano. All the fully completed giants had moved on, mile by mile over the whole island: some had finished their journey up to ten miles from the quarry where they had first taken human shape, and the very smallest weighed from two to ten tons apiece.

Father Sebastian (a missionary on the Island) acted as an outdoor museum director in this deserted lunar landscape. He had climbed about everywhere and painted a number on all the statues he could find, and there were over six hundred in all. All were of the same greyish-yellow black-grained stone: all had been hewn in the same gigantic workshop in the steep face of Rano Raraku. It was only there that this special colouring of the rock was found, and knowing this one could recognize a statue simply by its colour even if it was lying prostrate among other huge boulders a long way off.

The strangest thing was that the colossi had been carried about not as shapeless lumps which could stand a knock or two, but as perfectly smooth human forms, scrubbed and polished front and back, from the lobes of their ears to the roots of their nails. Only the eye-sockets were still lacking. How had it been possible to move the complete finished article across country without rubbing it to pieces? Nobody knew.

Crater of Rano Kao The stone for the great statues of Easter Island was quarried here.

At their destination the blind stone men were not erected just by dropping them down into a hole: on the contrary, they were lifted up in the air and placed on the top of an *ahu*, or temple platform, where they remained standing with their base a couple of yards above the ground. Now at last holes were chiselled for the eyes; now at last the giants might see where in the world they were. And then came the top of the macaroon cake. Now they were to have 'hats' put on the tops of their heads—'hats' which weighed from two to ten tons and in the latter case could tip the balance against two elephants.

Actually, it is not quite correct to talk about 'hats', even though everyone does so nowadays. The old native name for this gigantic head decoration is *pukao*, which means 'topknot', the usual coiffure worn by male natives on Easter Island at the time of its discovery. Why did the old masters lift this *pukao* up on top of the giant in the form of an extra block? Why could they not simply cut it out of the same stone with the rest of the figure? Because the important detail was the *colour* of the topknot. They went to the opposite end of the island, seven miles from the stone quarry in Rano Raraku, and there they had hewn their way down into a little overgrown crater where the rock was of a very special red colour. It was this special red stone they wanted for the statues' hair. So they had dragged yellowish-grey statues from one side of the island and red topknots from the other, and had placed one upon the other on top of more than fifty raised temple platforms all round the coast. Most of these platforms had a couple of statues side by side, a great many had four, five or six, and one had no fewer than fifteen red-haired giants standing side by side, with their base twelve feet above the ground.

Not one of these red-haired giants stands in his old place on top of the temple platforms to-day. Even Captain Cook, and probably Roggeveen also, arrived too late to see them all standing in their old places. But our first explorers were at any rate able to testify that many of the statues were still standing at their posts with red *pukaos* on their heads. In the middle of the last century the last giant crashed down from his temple, and the red topknot rolled like a blood-stained steam roller over the pavement of the temple square. To-day only the blind hairless statues in the rubble-filled holes at the foot of the volcano still stand with heads raised defiantly. They stand so deep in the earth that no native enemy has succeeded in pulling them down, and a single attempt to cut off one of the heads with an axe was totally unsuccessful because the ancient executioner had not managed to cut his way more than a hand's breadth into the giant neck.

Easter Island Images on the outer slope of Rano Raraku.

The last statue to fall was dragged down from its *ahu* about 1840 on the occasion of a cannibal feast in a cave near by. It had a topknot two hundred cubic feet in size on the top of its thirty-two-foot tall body, which in turn stood on a wall almost the height of a man. We have all the measurements and also the density of this fallen giant; it weighed fifty tons and was transported two and a half miles from the quarry in Rano Raraku. Let us imagine ourselves taking a ten-ton railway truck and turning it upside down, for the wheel was unknown in Polynesia. Next we capsize another railway truck alongside the first one, and tie the two firmly together. Then we drive twelve full-grown horses into the trucks, and after them five large elephants. Now we have got our fifty tons and can begin to pull, and we have not merely to move this weight, but drag it for two and a half miles over stony ground without the slightest injury being done to it. Is this impossible without machinery? If so, the oldest inhabitants of Easter Island mastered the impossible. One thing is certain: this was not the work of a canoe-load of Polynesian wood-carvers, who set to work on the bare rock faces when they landed, merely because they could find no trees to whittle. The red-haired giants with the classical features were made by seafarers who came from a land with generations of experience in manœuvring monoliths.

Now that we have got our fifty-ton load to the right place, the four-storey stone man must be got up on to a wall and made to stand upright, and then the topknot has to be put on: it alone weighs in this case ten tons, and has been carried seven miles as the crow flies from the topknot quarry. Seven miles is a long way in country like this, and thirty-two feet in excess of the stone platform is a good height anywhere when the object to be lifted weighs ten tons, as much as twenty-four full-grown horses. But it was done. And the whole thing was pulled down again in 1840 by cannibals, who undermined the foundation stones in the wall and celebrated their deed by eating thirty of their neighbours in a cave.

I stood on the top of the crater of Rano Raraku and had a magnificent view all round over the grass-clad island. Behind me there was a fairly steep slope down into the overgrown interior of the volcano, where the little sky-blue crater lake lay as clear as a mirror in a broad framework of the greenest reeds I ever saw. Perhaps it seemed a brighter green in contrast with the grass all over the island, which now, in the dry season, was beginning to turn yellow. In front of me there was a steep drop down the terraced wall of the quarry to the flat ground at the foot of the volcano, where the members of the expedition were working like ants, excavating the brown earth around the gigantic figures. Their horses stood tethered here and there, looking pitiably small alongside the burly giants. From here I had a good survey of what had happened in the past: this was the focal point and centre of Easter Island's most conspicuous problem. This was the statues' maternity home: I was standing on a sturdy embryo myself, watching the swarms of others all down the descent both before and behind me. And on the slope at the mountain's foot, both outside and inside the crater, the new-born stood erect, blind and hairless, waiting in vain to be hauled away on their long transport.

From up here I could see the course the transport had taken. Two of the figures which were completed inside the crater had been on their way when all work suddenly ceased. One had just come up on to the edge of the crater on its way out, the other was already on its way down through a gully on the outside, when the transportation had suddenly stopped, and there they lay, not on their backs, but on their stomachs. Along the old stoneless grass tracks over the plain, as far as the eye could see, others lay singly and in irregular groups of two and three. They were blind and hairless, and all the indications were that they had never been set up where they lay, but had been abandoned just anywhere along the route, while being transported from Rano Raraku to the platforms that awaited them. Some had gone right away, beyond the hindmost hills and ridges. And there, beyond the horizon, far away to the west, lay the little volcano Puna Pao with the topknot quarry. I could not see it from where I stood, but I had been down into its blood-red interior and seen half a dozen topknots lying like giant stone cylinders down in the precipitous little crater, while the old master hairdressers had conveyed a number of the largest up over the steel slope. These now lay in a dump outside, waiting to be conveyed further. Others had evidently been abandoned while under way to their future owners, for here and there a solitary topknot lay on the plain. I measured the largest topknot which had been carried up out of the red crater. It was 650 cubic feet in size and weighed roughly thirty tons, or as much as seventy-five well-grown horses.

My own comprehension was insufficient to grasp this far-reaching Easter Island engineering scheme, and I turned resignedly to the native shepherd who stood by me in silence, gazing at the abandoned giants which lay about on the plain.

'Leonardo,' I said, 'you are a practical man, can you tell me how these stone giants could have been carried about in old times?'

'They went of themselves,' Leonardo replied.

BOY FROM THE LEAD MOUNTAIN

Very occasionally, a startling find is made that enables us to see, face to face, the people from another century. Such was the discovery of the frozen boy from El Plomo (the Lead) Mountain in Chile, in 1954. He was a boy of the Inca Empire of the 15th century.

In that century, the Incas entered on a meteoric career of conquest and they established a rich and wonderful capital at Cuzco in the highlands of Peru. The Incas knitted together their empire with a tremendous system of roads, tunnelling through rocks and bridging chasms. For a time, they ruled unchallenged over more than 2,500 miles of South America from Colombia to Chile. But in the 16th century, the Inca Empire fell to Pizarro of Spain.

The frozen boy in the high mountain was an offering to the Inca gods. Like other human sacrifices, he had been dressed in his best clothes and then buried alive.

Excerpted from ANAIS DO XXXI CONGRESSO INTERNACIONAL DE AMERICANISTAS, *(Sao Paulo, 1955) written by*

GRETE MOSTNY

ON 16th February, 1954, two men came to my office in the National Museum of Natural History in Santiago de Chile and told me of an archæological discovery they had made in the mountains. They brought with them a silver statuette dressed in cloth and feathers and described other discoveries, including the 'mummy of a little Indian girl', clothed, according to them, very differently from those in the Museum. With this mummy they found various bags and two toy llamas. I intimated that the Museum would be interested in having this collection, and they told me that the mummy had been found in a tomb at a height of approximately 17,700 feet. As the summer would soon be over, they had thought it wise to keep it at a lower altitude while deciding on its future. So I proposed that they should bring the mummy down to Santiago and report again to the Museum when they had done so. On 15th March, the two men came again with the silver statuette and another made of shell. They informed the Director of the Museum, Don Humberto Fuenzalida, and me that the mummy was in their house at Puente Alto (a village on the outskirts of Santiago). I went to see it next day. The mummy turned out to be the frozen body of a young boy dressed in Inca costume and in such a remarkable state of preservation that he looked as though he were asleep. Realizing the importance of the discovery, I went straight back to the Museum and left a note for the Director urging him to get hold of this collection at once. Consequently Señor Fuenzalida went to Puente Alto the same evening and arranged to buy it for the Museum at a cost of 45,000 Chilean pesos (nearly £100 at that time).

The body was then taken to the Department of Legal Medicine to be kept overnight in their cold-storage room. We thought this would be the best way to treat a frozen body, but after a few hours it became clear that the cold, damp atmosphere could do harm and the doctors decided to keep the body in a dry place at a normal temperature. So the next day we transferred it to the Museum itself where it has remained.

I thought this long introduction necessary, since it is the first official account of this extraordinary discovery. Interest was aroused all over the world and newspapers have published many contradictory reports. . . .

According to the miners who made the discovery, the body was found near the peak of a mountain called 'El Plomo' (meaning the mountain of lead), in the province of Santiago. In this region there are three buildings, called by mountain-climbers the 'Pircas of the Indians'. *Pirca* is a South American word for a dry-stone wall. In one of these, below the level of the ground, was the tomb which contained the boy and his possessions.

A group of mountaineers was near this place on 1st February, 1954, and happened to see two men descending the mountain with a heavy sack on their shoulders. It turned out later that the boy's body was hidden in this sack.

In April, an expedition organized by the National Museum of Natural History and consisting of mountaineers from the Chilean 'Club Andino' under Señor Luis Krahl, together with anthropology students from the university, climbed 'El Plomo' to check the facts given by the miners. Only Señor Krahl and two of his companions reached the place and brought back a report on what they saw.

There are on this mountain two groups of buildings, one at

a height of 17,000 feet forming an elliptical enclosure, called by mountaineers the 'altar'. This was probably a Pre-Colombian temple. The major axis of this building deviates twenty-two degrees to the north-east. The second group, at 17,700 feet and very near the peak, consists of three rectangular buildings, the largest with an annexe in one corner. It is worth noting that the major axis deviates twenty-two degrees to the north-east, as in the temple below. The enclosure is just over seven yards long and three and a half yards wide and the walls are about three feet high. The interior is full of earth and stones. In the centre is the tomb, a three-foot cavity, consisting of one floor in a frozen state, covered by a flat stone lid. This report supports the information given by the miners who discovered the body. The miners said that the body was surrounded by its possessions (of funeral furniture), and that it was soft and flexible when they found it and hardened later. In fact, when it arrived at the Museum it was still fairly soft, even though it had been in contact with the air for six weeks.

From Señor Krahl's report, we can deduce that these were ceremonial buildings belonging to a Pre-Colombian race who, from archæological evidence, were the Incas and their contemporaries, though naturally the place may have been frequented by earlier races.

The body was found in a sitting position with the knees doubled up, the legs crossed, the right forearm resting on the knees, the left hand holding the right. The last two phalanges (the tips) of the three middle fingers of the left hand showed by their characteristic appearance and colour that they were frozen twenty-four to forty-eight hours before death. It was Senor Krahl who noticed this phenomenon, well known among Andean mountaineers.

Medical and radiological examinations proved that the body was that of a boy; the ossification of his skeleton was not yet complete and he still had some of his first teeth. His age could be ascertained as being between eight or nine years. His first metatarsal (the first bone of the arch of the foot) was unusually short and thick as though reverting to an ancestral type. It was possible to identify such organs as the brain, heart, diaphragm and possibly the liver. On the whole the skeleton was normal though the hands and feet were small in relation to the rest of the body. It was not possible to see any more details by X-ray because of the excessive density of his clothes, accentuated by the partially frozen state of the body and its incipient mummification.

The hair was smooth, greasy and black with the hair follicles well preserved. The face was wide and so was the nose though this was harder to tell because of a post-mortem deformity. But the features could be identified as Mongolian in type, which was to be expected. The colour of the skin varied between different shades of brown, being darker where not protected by clothes. It was possible to make an examination of the blood and conclude that it belonged to group 'O' and to take finger prints which did not differ very much from those observed today.

The boy was dressed in a black woollen tunic, woven in one piece, folded in the middle with a hole for the head which was not quite in the middle of the material. The sides were sewn together and the back and front decorated with a fringe of red wool and four stripes of white vicuña fur. Over his shoulders he wore a woollen rug with a texture like hemp, grey with coloured stripes. This showed signs of hard wear and was darned in several places. It was made of two pieces of cloth sewn together and was tied under his chin with a thick knot which may have caused the post-mortem deformity of the nose, as the head was lying on one side and forwards with the nose resting on the knot. Traces of cloth on the forearms and hands show that the boy had tried to cover these bare parts of his body. He was wearing leather, fur-trimmed moccasins, made in one piece with an embroidered strap, which was sewn onto the leather with a welt. The only seam was in the middle of the toe. The moccasins did not show much sign of wear and the sole was perfectly clean.

His head-dress consisted of a band from which hung a long thick fringe of black wool. A crest of black and white condor feathers was joined to the centre fastening of this band and placed on the head in such a way that the feathers stayed erect on the forehead. A woollen cord passing under the chin kept the head-dress in place. He also wore the characteristic *Llautu* (head-band worn by the Incas and their subjects). The head was encircled five times with a well-twisted black cord and the turns fastened together by another cord which passed under the chin.

He had a silver ornament shaped like a double crescent with holes in the top so that it could hang over his chest. When the body was brought to the Museum this ornament had become detached and was found in the folds of the *Llautu*. On his right forearm was a bracelet made of one sheet of silver, trapezoid in form and curved to fit the arm. This was fastened by a thin thread of wool passing through two holes on the inside edge.

His hair reached below his shoulders and was arranged in a great many small fine plaits. His face was painted red with

Preserved in Snow   This is the mummy of an eight or nine year old Inca boy who was buried alive approximately 500 years ago. His perfectly preserved body was found in 1954 by two Chilean miners. The child was seated on the floor of his tomb surrounded by his possessions.

diagonal yellow stripes.

He carried a hanging bag made from a rectangular piece of woven cloth, folded in the middle and sewn up the sides. This contained remnants of cocoa leaves. Apart from his actual clothing, he had with him another bag, made in the same way but entirely covered with red and white feathers. This was packed tightly with cocoa leaves. There were five more bags made of a thin skin which was probably part of the intestine of a mammal of the llama species. The two largest contained little balls of human hair, odds and ends of red wool, and a coarse substance not yet analysed. Another contained nail parings, very irregularly cut, milk teeth, very much worn down, and also a tiny piece of red wool. The other two also contained nail parings and wool.

Also in the collection were two small figures, thought to be llamas or some other animal of that species. One was a male animal made of a gold and silver alloy, the other, carved out of shell, was smaller and less detailed.

Buried separately but in the same enclosure was a figure of a woman standing about four inches high, made in beaten silver and soldered together. The arms were folded with the hands between the breasts, the hair parted in the middle and falling in two plaits over the shoulders. The figure was elaborately dressed in the manner of the Inca women. Five of these clothed figures are known already, three in gold, one silver and one shell. These were also found on 'El Plomo'. Our figure and the one made of shell are the only ones found with a head-dress.

From this discovery various conclusions can be drawn. The body was that of a boy of eight or nine years, a subject of the Incas. But we do not know to which of the many races of the Inca Empire he belonged. His head-dress gives us a clue, since the chroniclers of the time all stress the fact that Indians from different parts of the realm were distinguished by their different head-dresses which they were forbidden to change under the threat of dire punishment. Nobody has yet described a head-dress such as the one worn by this boy. There are, however, some indications that the boy belonged to a people of the Altiplano (the high mountain area of the Andes). It seems that the people of the Altiplano wore moccasins instead of sandals. The chest ornament is identical with one found on the island of Titicaca and with another in a drawing of a chieftain from Collasuyu. This chieftain also wore a bracelet like the boy's and it is known that the rich people of La Paz wore bracelets of gold and silver. The crest of condor feathers is another indication that he came from the Altiplano. In the corner of the drawing of the Collasuyu chieftain a condor is depicted on a shield.

The boy wore a black *Llautu*, one of the privileges conceded by the Inca to a conquered nation—in the ceremonies of *Capac Raymi* the young candidates also wore black *Llautu*. But the boy from 'El Plomo' was too young for this ceremony. On the other hand there were some tribes who always wore the black *Llautu*.

Both tunic and rug were made of rough, ordinary cloth. The tunic was so short that it barely covered the boy's trunk while the general rule was that it should reach the middle of the thigh. But we must not forget that he was a child and we know little of the way children were dressed. We can tell from drawings that his tunic was not identical with that worn by a Royal Prince, but it does seem probable that this boy was the son of a provincial nobleman, or at any rate of a rich man.

The boy was not of an age to wear trousers or to have his ears pierced. According to Inca custom, a youth received his first pair of trousers at the age of fourteen or fifteen at a special ceremony at which all those of noble blood had to pass tests of physical prowess to gain the privilege of pierced ears, trousers, the carrying of arms, and the cutting of their hair. They would then be given their real names too.

In his short life the child from 'El Plomo' would already have passed through one ceremony which would have taken place when he was one or two years old. On this occasion his most senior uncle would cut his hair and his nails and give him the name he would keep until puberty. The hair and nail parings would be kept carefully, and in fact we found them, together with his milk teeth, in the little bags of animal gut.

By the time of his death the boy's hair had grown and reached below his shoulders. It seems to have been arranged for a special occasion just before his death. One of the most interesting features of the 'El Plomo' discovery was the painting of the face. The colour red seems to have been a favourite and was used by warriors to frighten the enemy and also for feasts and dances.

But how did the boy come to be buried on top of the mountain? It is known that the Incas and other Andean races attributed supernatural powers to the mountains. The higher and more imposing the mountain, the greater its power, and they had a special reverence for those covered with eternal snow. 'El Plomo' was one of these, hence the buildings found on or near the peak and the traces of paths leading up to them. The place has long been known by miners and muleteers and they called the buildings, as I have said, the 'Pircas of the Indians'. Many years ago the same miner who discovered the boy's body found gold and silver statues in one of the buildings. But these have long since been sold and nobody has been able to trace their present owners. Mountaineers have said that there is another place among these buildings which may contain the body of yet another sacrificed child. I have no doubt that the body now in the National Museum of Natural History *was* a human sacrifice.

Most of the chroniclers of old Peru agree that human sacrifices existed in the time of the Incas. On special occasions men, women and children were sacrificed as tribute from the provinces of the Empire. These sacrifices were offered when a new Inca came to the throne, in time of victory, when the Inca was ill, or in the case of any calamity. There were four ways of sacrificing the victims: strangulation, pulling out the heart, crushing the neck with a stone, and burying alive. It seems that this last method of sacrificing children was more common among the mountain people. Sometimes they were sacrificed in pairs, a boy and a girl, the children being about ten years old. The victims were dressed in their best clothes. Among the objects that accompanied them to the grave, little figures of llamas in gold and silver have been specially mentioned. Certainly the feather bag containing cocoa leaves was part of this funeral furniture while the hanging bag and the small bags containing wool, nails and teeth were among the personal belongings of the victim.

The boy on 'El Plomo' was certainly buried alive. It has been seen from radiological examination that his body suffered no wound or shock. He would have been given a strong intoxicating beverage called *chicha* to drink and taken to the tomb in an alcoholic stupor and would have been frozen to death before he could recover as we can see from the peaceful expression on his face.

THE LOST ROADS OF THE INCA

The ancient Inca lords ruled over a mighty empire covering more than 2,500 miles of beautiful but difficult country. Their civilization was based on conquest and efficient organization—conquest not only of neighboring peoples but also of terrain. The genius of their engineers built a system of roads that knit the empire together. The Inca highways scored the jungles, were supported on solid causeways across the marshes, were carried aloft along the mountain peaks, and spanned the raging rivers. But in the end this great empire fell to the Spaniards in the first half of the 16th century.

In the following extract Victor von Hagen describes how he and his team traced the old Inca roads, and how the royal road from Cuzco to Lima led them to the site of the Bridge of San Luis Rey.

Excerpted from HIGHWAY OF THE SUN, *(Vistor Gallancz, 1956) written by*

VICTOR VON HAGEN

IT was in 1548. At the side of a road which went on out across the bare Andes, a young soldier was keeping his vow to write down the 'wonderful things of these Indies'. Pedro Cieza de León looked again at the stone-paved highway he had followed for so many leagues and then he wrote:

Accordingly the Inca constructed the grandest road that there is in the world as well as the longest, for it extends from Cuzco to Quito and was connected from Cuzco to Chile—a distance of eight hundred leagues. I believe since the history of man, there has been no other account of such grandeur as is to be seen on this road which passes over deep valleys and lofty mountains, by snowy heights, over falls of water, through the living rock, and along the edges of tortuous torrents. In all these places, the road is well constructed, on the inclining mountains well terraced, through the living rock cut along the river-banks supported by retaining walls, in the snowy heights built with steps and resting places, and along its entire length swept cleanly and cleared of debris—with post stations and storehouses and Temples of the Sun at appointed intervals along its length.

In the four hundred years since the young traveller wrote this, much of this grandeur has been laid waste by the insults of time; much is in ruins, many of the superbly made halting-places of the road reduced to formless mounds. Here and there, during the intervening centuries, explorer-archæologists have wandered over the empty spaces of Peru and have painstakingly pushed away the debris of time to ferret out some of the clues with which to reconstruct an empire. But between what is known and what is not known, between what we have learnt of the ancient cities along the road and what is still hidden, lies a great gap. We know only that the thread which bound the widely separated communities was the Road—that ubiquitous overwhelming Road—which Cieza de León described as the 'grandest and longest in the world'.

What then if this fabulous road were to be found and followed from end to end? What if one were to employ the techniques now available in the scientific fields of archæology and geography, and were to make use of advanced methods of travel such as the double-transmissioned truck and the aeroplane? Would it not then be possible to discover the route taken by its various subsidiary roads, and so make their heights and lowlands accessible to those who would search for the many forgotten cities? And if these were found might they not reveal the secret of how the Incas lived, how by building their amazing roads they were able to communicate with almost telegraphic speed with the most remote sections of their empire?

To travel this ancient route, seeking to find some light on the enigma of the history of Man in the Americas, was my dream. . . .

Once we had made the high pass at La Raya, we were out of the Lake Titicaca region and almost at once had dropped down into the warmer valley of Vilcanota, where the air was almost benign. We could well understand how the people who became the Incas abandoned their origin place around Titicaca to seek out the warmer climate of this valley.

For some days we followed the Inca road through pleasant villages not much changed since the time when their Inca ruled the land, until we came to the great temple of Kontiki Virachoca. The temple was now in ruins but even so the fragments of high stone and adobe walls and rounded stone pillars spoke of the great architectural genius of the Inca. As we drove, the road was at times clearly revealed and then at other times so thoroughly erased that we could find no trace of it. At Chuqui-cahuana, for example, we found a length of well-preserved road, part of the Royal Road, measuring fifteen feet from wall to wall. On we went northward

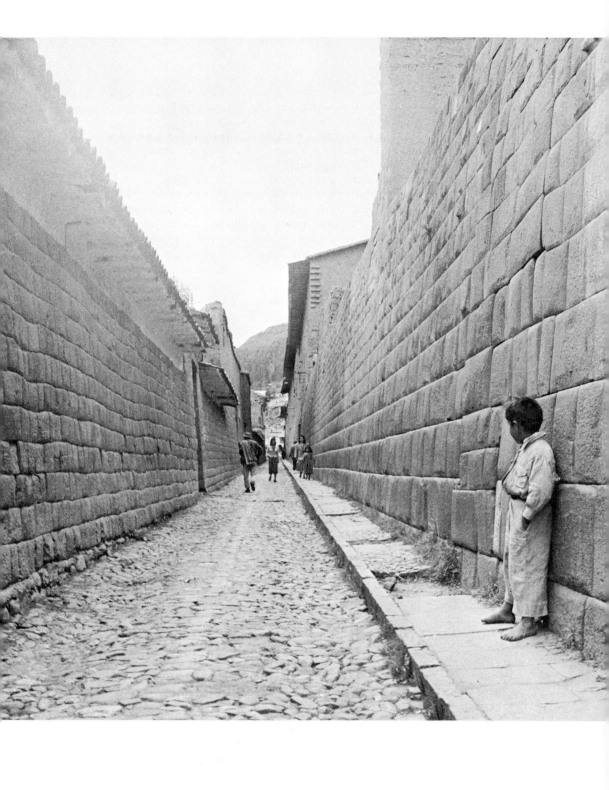

through hills now purple with the blossom of the potato, past the Lake Urcos which lay like an emerald at the bottom of cultivated hills.

Not far from this we came to ancient stone quarries at the gates, so to speak, of Cuzco. Here was an enormous passageway, with one of its sides faced with carefully fitted red stone, the mark of the Inca stone-mason. It was once, so we believed, a control station or sort of toll-gate, and the entrance to the road from the south which led through a large pre-Inca city into the immediate valley of Cuzco. From here northward this old Inca road more or less becomes a modern road.

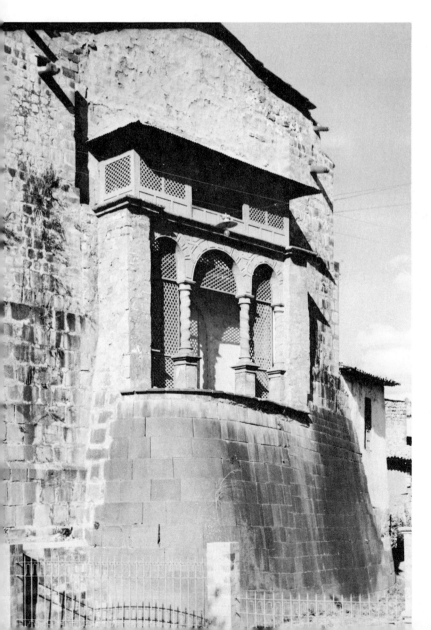

Church of Santo Domingo
This wall of the present Church of Santo Domingo at Cuzco, Peru is an ancient wall of the Inca Temple of the Sun.

On our way along this, which was once the Appian Way of the Incas, we passed multitudes of people in holiday attire, many of them driving gaily decorated llamas ahead of them, all going towards the Sacred City. Many wore their distinctive regional headgear—the women of Ayaviri their large flat hats trimmed with beautiful upending brocade; those from Sicuani woollen wimples which encased the head nunlike and fell across the shoulders. Groups of Indians trotted along hugging musical instruments, as if they would protect them from the dust of the fast-travelling cars. Some carried harps shaped like ancient rebecks, which they stroked as they walked; others had reed pipes on which they softly fluted.

The crowd increased as it converged in Cuzco. We made our way down the road and entered the square called Rimac-Pampa. This was once the exit place of the great road to the south, and was the Speaking Pampa where the people gathered to listen to the harangues of the Inca's officials. It was still *the* gathering-place, crowded now with auto buses and jostling people, noisy with the sound of raucous radios and loudspeakers.

We had arrived over the Royal Road at Cuzco, the capital of the Incas.

Hernando de Soto, so the chronicler said, came first upon Cuzco at sunset.

The sun's great rundle sinking with an enormous burst of reddened glory had lighted up the city so that even the poorer buildings took on a burnished golden look. As the retreating sun's rays touched the beaten gold plates that adorned its walls, the pyramided Sun Temple, towering over the lower buildings around it, gleamed as if it were cased in metal.

Curzo lay in a protected hollow at the northern end of the valley. The hills were bare; no trees except the stunted *molle* grew here. On the northern higher slope of the city stood an enormous stone fortress, a structure so immense that at first sight de Soto and his companion doubted that any army could breach it. Narrow and long 'like a puma's tail', Cuzco was made up of narrow streets, its smaller buildings painted yellow and red, the larger buildings constructed of enormous, beautifully laid stonework. In the centre was a great square, larger than the Plaza of St. Mark's in Venice, which, because of the luminous atmosphere, seemed so near that a bolt from a crossbow could have been shot into the centre.

Captain Hernando de Soto had good reason to study Cuzco intently. For in this fateful year of 1533, he was one of two hundred Spanish soldiers engaged under the command of

Francisco Pizarro, the Spanish Captain General, in the conquest of an empire five times the size of Europe. De Soto was, according to his chronicler, 'a handsome man, dark in complexion, with full beard and dark restless eyes, of cheerful countenance, an endurer of hardships and very valiant'. At thirty-five, as a *conquistador* of Peru, he was in the full tide of his glory. Rather above middle height, graceful on foot and horseback, he rode in the Moorish style and looked well accoutred in buckler and helmet with a straight sword by his side. Now after his 450-mile ride over the Royal Road from Cajamarca to the south where the Inca King Atahualpa was being held for ransom, de Soto looked down on Cuzco in intent contemplation. He had consented to be escorted to the capital of the Incas, by a retinue of Indians with only one other soldier companion, Pedro de Barco, in order to speed the payment of the gold and silver ransom—and also so that he might get to know something of the size of this strange kingdom, of its roads and its defences, for the Spaniards had come not only to siphon off a winnowing of Inca gold but to make conquest of the source of all of it.

Hernando de Soto's first sight of Cuzco filled him with amazement: 'Cuzco, grand and stately, must have been built by people of great intelligence. The city is certainly the richest of which we have any knowledge in all the Indies. . . . Neither gold nor silver, they tell me, can be taken out of here on the pain of death and there are many goldsmiths here and workers in silver.'

De Soto was received as a god. Carried through the city in a gold-plated litter and followed always by a curious throng of women and children, he saw the storehouses for wool tunics and cotton cloth, strange chambers filled with arms and accoutrements of war, such as quilted-cotton armour, sharp-edged swords, star-shaped halberds, while still more rooms were filled with corn and shellfish and seaweed—all in the form of tax tribute. He was careful to note, for he was primarily an officer making an 'esimate of the situation', the fact that out of the great square went 'four roads which led to all parts of the empire'.

Actually, these were the principal highways to the four divisions, the *suyus*, of the empire: the Chinchay-suyu road, over which de Soto had arrived, went north-west to Quito, five hundred leagues distant in what is now Ecuador; the Cuntu-suyl road to the coast stretched off to the south-west; the Collasuyu which, 'so the Indians sayeth', went to a great lake, began at the south-east corner; while the road to the jungles also began from the north-west, at a small plaza called the 'Salt Window', and was called the Anti-suyu road. The sum of these four divisions, the Inca Empire, was known as the Tawantin-suyu, the 'Four Quarters of the World'.

The people, so Hernando de Soto learned, had originated round Lake Titicaca as wanderers and food gatherers. Eventually they migrated northward. By the year 1000—since 'blood and cruelty is the foundation of all good things'—they had disposed of the original inhabitants of this valley and taken possession of the treeless land about Cuzco. Their food, their llama husbandry, their architecture, their ceramics, were Andean in pattern. Yet as these people were exposed to dearth and hunger and seasonal droughts, they began to oppose the titanic force of Nature and to attempt to alter it for their benefit.

The Incas made repeated conquests and organized the peoples they had defeated; they developed the formulæ that made an Andean empire possible, becoming a disciplined people, and, within the frame of their mountain glebe, over the centuries evolved into a unified empire. It expanded at the expense of its neighbours, absorbing the surrounding lands like an amœba. It enveloped them, digested them, and made them part of itself. What the Incas could not absorb, they killed. About A.D. 1200, the chieftains of the Quechua-speaking peoples announced their official descent from the Sun God. They called themselves 'Incas', and as such became the hereditary rulers of the Quechuas.

Under the aggressively active Inca policy of conquest and assimilation, the Inca realm expanded in all the four directions. Roads were built and a *chasqui* or courier system was organized. A caste of record-keepers, trained so that they could read the story of the past, invented the *quipu*—a series of coloured and knotted strings by means of which records could be kept of grazing lands, gold-mines, numbers of people and tribes, tributes and deposits.

Having grown great, the Incas had come to believe that it must always have been thus, and therefore what did not conform to the established idea of the Inca past was eliminated from human memory—and so well that the impression left was that before the Inca there had hovered a void over the Andes.

The Incas ruled their people with an iron, but a just hand. Every detail of their life, from womb to tomb, was prescribed. The state was not for the people nor was equality the ideal. It was rather a blending of tribal communism and theocracy, a perilously balanced fusion of two antagonistic systems.

The common people were manipulated like figures on a chessboard, becoming part of the decimal system of classifi-

Lost City of the Inca Located high in the Andes is the ancient city of Machu Picchu. It was discovered less than 60 years ago by Hiram Bingham of Yale University.

cation with division all along the social line. An elaborate hierarchy of territorial officials was set up. The highest under the Inca was the Tuc-ri-cuo (He-who-sees-all), the ruler of a division of ten thousand people. And so the categories went down the line to the least common multiple; for every ten thousand of the population there were 1,331 officials.

Everything was regulated in this welfare state. No one moved on the roads without permission; there was work-service for taxes; there were contributions to state and religion; and each man was automatically a member of an agrarian militia. If a section of the realm was underpopulated, a whole tribe was moved into it. Loyal subjects were settled in a newly conquered land, while the recently conquered tribes were moved out and transferred to a 'safe' community where they could be absorbed. Under this policy, most of Andean America was conquered. From Chile to Colombia, a distance of 2,320 linear miles, the land was unified, the jungle was invaded, the desert coast pervaded. No tribe, no force, could resist the pressure of this benevolent despotism.

Of this realm Cuzco was the capital. Thoroughly cosmopolitan, the city was inhabited by symbolic groups from the four divisions of empire. Each section of the city was given over to a particular tribal group, each with its own attire, own head-dress. If they were *yuncas* of the coast, they went muffled like gipsies; the *collas* (koyas) wore caps shaped like a wooden pump-box; the *canas* wore another kind of cap of greater width; the *cañaris* had crowns of interwoven thick laths; the *hunancas* had short ropes attached to their hair which hung down to the chin. Cuzco was the microcosm of its empire.

There was only one way by which this community of people could have been held together, and that was by the communicating roads. All Indians were obliged to give one-third of their time to work-service, and while each tribal unit had to build and maintain the Royal Road running through its section, the direction and master plan were laid down by technicians sent out from Cuzco. These master architects charted the direction the roads would take, planned the way-stops and figured out the distances that the *chasqui* couriers would run and where their platforms would be set up. With these communications completed, nothing could occur in any place in the realm without the officials at Cuzco being made immediately aware of it. All this and much more did Hernando de Soto see and learn during his stay in Cuzco.

The summer of the dry season had come before he quit the city. In that time he gathered much gold, wrote his report, and prepared to move out. Cuzco was now gay with arriving Indians, for it was the season of the Sun Festival, the Intiraymi, celebrating the time when, as the Indians believed, the Sun God came down to live with them. From all sides Indians were pouring into the city to prepare for the pageantry of the Sun God. What must have been the thoughts of Hernando de Soto when he turned on the hill of Karmenka and looked back on Cuzco! He, although he knew it not, was the last European to see it in its pagan state. Soon he was to gather his three hundred thousand gold pesos of loot, sail to Spain and eventually return to chase the twin phantoms, Youth and Gold—and lose both, along with his life, in the turgid waters of the Mississippi.

But on that bright June day of 1533, as this man of 'good impulses' rode beside his treasure-laden llamas along the high road back to Cajamarca, he moved out from this golden city through throngs of Indians coming to Cuzco for the festival of the Sun God.

Four hundred and twenty-one years after Hernando de Soto had left it, we, searching for the remains of those roads of an empire which he had so effectively helped to destroy, arrived in Cuzco.

The oldest continuously inhabited city in all the Americas—it dates back to about the time that the Battle of Hastings was fought—Cuzco shows little traces of its various epochs. There are the Inca walls—superbly fashioned of stone, laid with an instinctive feeling for the beauty of pattern in stone—which impart a feeling of the greatest antiquity. There too is the magnificent architecture of colonial Spain and in close proximity adobe houses which are without either dignity or grandeur. Between these contrasts is no evidence of growth. Cuzco is like a woman who when born is already old.

Hernando de Soto would have found little in this present-day observance of the Sun Festival to remind him of the city he saw before its rape, even though much of modern Cuzco is built upon the walls and foundations of the Incaic city. What had once been the Curicancha, the Shrine of the Garden of Gold, a structure whose walls were covered with gold as finely beaten as onion-skin paper, is now the Santo Domingo Convent. The sanctuary of the Sun Virgins, where chosen women were reared to care for the ritual of the Sun, is, ironically enough, the cloistered nunnery of Santa Catalina; and standing on the site of the Snake Temple, the palace of the last great Inca, is the Church of the Jesuits. Time, man, and earthquake have not been kind to Cuzco. Yet the Sun Festival was once again bringing the Indians back into their city, and the streets were enlivened by their gaudy finery.

Cuzco was, naturally, an important point for us. The four roads of the empire had gone off from the centre of the city, and around it were the remains of its most imposing structures. . . .

We began our further journey with a preliminary exploration along the north-western route, that same Chinchay-suyu which Hernando de Soto had taken when he finally left Cuzco and followed his loot-laden llamas.

Here the Inca road is still made daily use of by Indians arriving with their llamas. At the top of the hill, at Karmenka, there once stood Huaca-puncu, the 'Holy Gate', the first shrine an Indian found on his journey northward. 'One made sacrifices here,' wrote Cieza, 'so that the Inca road would not collapse or be destroyed.' We found beautifully cut stones taken from this shrine embedded in the Church of Santa Ana, which now occupies the former site of this sacred place that once guarded the Royal Road.

We leisurely followed the road northward. Tracing its course was a little like putting an anagram together. Located on the west side of the narrow valley, the old road crossed the modern highway at times and lost its identity. Then, where the highway curved to make a gradient, the Inca road would emerge again and could be followed, measured, and studied, until it entered the environs of a village, where it would again disappear. So with varying success we followed it until we came to the swamps.

Fifteen miles north of Cuzco lies a wide-spreading quagmire. The Incas in the fourteenth century built a long causeway across this, which is still used. More than a metre above the flooded lowland plains, twenty-four feet wide and eight miles long, it was one of the triumphs of Inca engineering. Traversed by all who entered or came from Cuzco, it has, through the centuries, often been described as: 'a great swamp which could only be crossed with difficulty, had the Inca not built a wide paved causeway . . . with walls on both sides so firm that they will last a long time'.

At the northern end of all this, we came to Zurite. Here on the sides of the mountain were the long parallel walls of agricultural terraces ascending the sides of the Andes like a gigantic flight of steps, and here we looked for Xaqui-Xahuana, the lost city of which all the *conquistadores* spoke, that place which one of the Inca Kings, referring to his flight from the penetrating cold of Cuzco, had called 'my refuge'.

City Street   A narrow street through the stone homes of the ancient Inca city of Machu Picchu.

The village of Zurite dates only from 1570, the site having been given to one of the Spanish conquerors as his fief, and he had, as was then the practice, torn down the ancient buildings and utilized the stone. The modern market, used now by the Indians who still. in ancient dress, come down from the hills, is located in front of a large mouldering church. Since we could see that the church was constructed of the ancient stone-work, we begged its sacristan to open the place for us. As he fumbled with the enormous lock, we were surrounded by hordes of boys shouting for the Peruvian equivalent of baksheesh. Once inside the church, the light from our torches revealed crumbling mud walls hung with huge canvases of paintings which had come from the eighteenth-century Indian ateliers of Cuzco and were in marked contrast to the moulding walls broken by nature's tremors and man's neglect. Nothing here gave us a clue to the ancient city we sought until we reached the richly wrought altar of chased silver fashioned in eighteenth-century baroque style. The date was 1770. Hanging here among the silver flowers and cherubs we found a likeness of the donor, El Cacique D. Juan Quayna-Sucnu, attired in flowing cape, knee breeches, and silver-buckled shoes. At one side was his younger son, wearing the long surcoat of the period. Facing him on the other side was his wife at prayer. Behind her stood another son. The legend above this read: DOÑA ISABEL ESTRADA CON SU HIJO ANDRES GUANA-SUCNU. The Quayna-Sucnu family, according to the sacristan, had been owners of the Zurite valley but time—and here he spread out his crippled hands to suggest the cupidity of man—had robbed them of it. Learning that their descendants still lived nearby, we crossed his wrinkled palm with a piece of silver and, following him out of the church and across fields planted in corn and wheat, came to a small house of sun-baked adobe. Dogs held us in check until an old man appeared at the door. Shading his eyes from the bright sun, he begged our business in a quavering voice.

Hearing it, he said, 'You stand on it—Xaqui-Xahuana'— and, somewhat puzzled as to why foreigners should come to ask about that which time had entombed, he led us up a hill trail along which we saw those characteristic stone walls, always the first evidence of former Inca occupation. From the top we looked down, and there before us were the ruins of the 'Lost City', built around a plaza where once large buildings fanned out to form a lunette. This former pleasure resort of Inca nobles had been the last stop before the wayfarer on the Royal Road crossed the Anta swamps over the giant stone causeway on the way to Cuzco. 'This valley,' our chroniclers had written, 'once contained sumptuous buildings for recreation to which the lords and many people from Cuzco came for their diversion,' and now we were looking at all that was left of these same 'sumptuous buildings'. While Silvia made a sketch map of the ruin, I found numerous pottery fragments, the finest we had seen in the Cuzco area.

These plains had seen much history. Here, early in their existence as a nation, the Incas were brought to the edge of defeat by the tribe called the Chancas. Finally victorious, the Incas had their enemies' bodies skinned and stuffed in such lifelike attitudes 'that the human form was made to appear in many positions. Some of them,' averred a Spaniard who saw them, 'had stomachs formed like drums on which they appeared to be playing; others were set up with flutes in their mouths.' The Incas had built a houselike tomb in which these horrid battle trophies were kept. There they remained for two hundred years, or until the Spaniards entered Cuzco.

Our old guide led us back to his house and there showed us some 'ancient things', Inca fragments of stone and vases, hand-wrought nails, Spanish coins which dated from the times of Charles V, a beautifully etched silver partisan, a cruel-tipped lance and a sword handle, a rusty, encrusted sword blade; and then, most curious of all, a silver ornament with a unicorn's head crudely stencilled on it, which bore a bit of sixteenth-century Spanish doggerel, ending with: 'And this belongs to Francisco de Carbajal.'

Those who have read the *Conquest of Peru* will recall that witty cut-throat, Francisco de Carbajal, who, when close to eighty years of age, had come to Peru to become Gonzalo Pizarro's Captain General during his bid for the empire of Peru. Our old man had found this memento while ploughing the same battlefield on which, in 1548, Carbajal had met his death. 'Never was Marius or any Roman general Carbajal's equal in cruelty, for in every phase . . . he showed himself a past master; the trees wherefrom he hung his victims, from Quito to Potosí, bear witness to it.'

It was during the civil war which was fought all over the Andes between the Spanish forces that Carbajal peopled the trees with bodies of his enemies and so earned the sobriquet 'Demon of the Andes'. At the end, Carbajal led his men out to Xaqui-Xahuana to do battle with the Viceroy's. Before the battle was joined Carbajal's men began to desert, and before he himself could take to his heels, he was captured by his own troops, who hoped, with such a prize, to make their peace with the victors. He was roundly abused when the party reached the Viceroy's camp; the soldiers would have had his

Agricultural Terraces Ancient agricultural terraces of Machu Picchu, Peru. Note the supporting frames of the stone buildings.

head had another officer not stayed their hands.

'To whom,' said Carbajal in haughty jest, 'am I indebted for this protection?'

'Do you not know me?' asked his would-be protector. 'You have pursued me for five thousand leagues through the Andes all these years.'

'I crave your pardon,' retorted Carbajal. 'It is so long since I have seen anything but your fleeing ass that I have fully forgotten your face.'

On his eighty-fourth birthday Carbajal was led out to be beheaded. His executioner, a tailor, had been instructed to quarter his body. 'Treat me, dear little brother,' Carbajal said, 'as one tailor would to the other.'

Shortly the four pieces of the body that had been Carbajal were hung in chains at the four entrances of the Royal Roads into Cuzco. . . .

The Apurimac had been the Rubicon of the Incas. For centuries it held their northward conquests in check; but once their technology advanced to the point where they could bridge it, they hung a suspension bridge, the greatest in all Peru, across it. Immediately they pushed their empire northward at a fearful pace.

It was known as '*the* Bridge', and in the minds of the early Spaniards, it was co-extensive with Peru itself. For the early Spaniards, the crossing of it filled them with fright and terror. Records and letters are filled with their plaints of how the bridge swung in the heavy wind, how deep was the dark abyss, how terrifying the thunder of the roar of the water as the sounds ricocheted against the vertical rock-walls; how their pulses raced, their eyes grew dim and their hearts faint as they hung on to the rope-cables and made a traverse of it. 'It is,' said one *conquistador*, 'no small terror that is caused by seeing what men must pass through in these indies.'

The longest continuously used bridge in the Americas, millions of people crossed over it during the five hundred years of its existence. Inca armies of conquest flowed over it; gold for the ransom of Atahualpa made its one-way passage across it; Spanish knights fought their civil wars over and around it; and for three centuries colonists used it while moving on the King's business. Even in the days of the South American republics this bridge was the only way of crossing the 'Great Speaker' (the roaring Apurimac). Yet it would have been forever forgotten had it not been for two Americans; in 1864 George Squier stopped long enough in his journey through the region to give it, by means of the only authentic illustration ever made of it, a detailed and accurate description; and in 1927 another American, Thornton Wilder, immortalized it in *The Bridge of San Luis Rey*.

David Samenez had insisted on accompanying us out to the bridge site. He was after all, he reminded us with much jesting, the owner of the Bridge of San Luis Rey. Moreover, he had been born at the hacienda of Bellavista, close to where the ancient road made its descent to the bridge.

This hacienda, which drew its water from the weeping glaciers of Soray thirty miles distant, lay on a flat table-land overlooking the gorge of the river. It had been developed by David's father, a man who did not allow his gentle birth to prevent him from working with his hands, an eccentricity which in the last century in Peru was considered a social crime. He had built up his hacienda, had fought against a dictator, holding off a large contingent of troops near to the site of the old bridge, and in 1935 had served his country briefly as President of Peru. All this we had learned as, mounted on our borrowed horses, we made our way over the highway.

The mountains were beautiful that day—Salcantay, its hoary head unbelievably high in the cobalt blue of the sky, accompanied as it were in the heavens by Mount Huamantay with its five thousand feet of glistening snow. An undulating greensward planted with lucerne lined the ancient highway, whose road bed here had been destroyed by the passing caravans of four centuries.

We moved on beyond to where the earth yawned out widely and there began the ride downward. It took us some hours to get to La Blanca, once a way stop on the descent of the Inca road toward the canyon which led to the great bridge. But from La Blanca we could go no further. The landslides caused by the rampaging Apurimac had destroyed the rock walls of the canyon. The careful stone terracing of the Incas, erected as long ago as 1390, still hung in sections over the abyss, yet there was no longer any way of getting down. Our binoculars, following David's pointing finger, picked out far below the stone steps that led to the bridge ramparts. All else was obscured. To reach the bridge, we should have to cross to the other side of the river and approach it from its northern side.

On our way back we watched the setting sun painting the snow-capped mountains with radiant rainbow colours, and David pointed out to us the snow-covered Yanacocha fifteen miles away. Even as he did so, my powerful binoculars picked up another river plunging down the precipitous slopes to join the Apurimac. About midway between the glacier and the river were the ruins of Choque-quirao, the only extensive Inca

Machu Picchu Stairway   Here in the ruins of Machu Picchu is an
example of the skill with which the Inca built.

ruins known in this part of the Vilcabamba Range. They could be reached, he said, in a two days' walk from the village of Inca-huasi. Did David know, I questioned, if the road led to Vilcabamba? (the last fortress of the Incas, still lost in the mountains).

My great-uncle was one of the first to visit the ruins of Choque-quirao. He kept a journal which I have in the house. He once travelled beyond these ruins and he insisted that those roads led to Vilcabamba, in just the region which you pointed out to me on the map.'

We knew this to be true, for when Hiram Bingham found his way to the ruins in 1912, he had seen written on the walls the name of JOSÉ BENIGNO SAMENEZ 1861. One day, I knew, we should have another try at this fabulous Vilcabamba, but to go now would be to upset our carefully planned schedule. I felt at this moment like an earthy Pangloss, always interrupting our wishful thinking with, 'Let us cultivate our garden.' But if we could not now go to Vilcabamba, we could at least visit and inspect all that was left of the Bridge of San Luis Rey.

We began early in the day, so as to avoid the excessive heat. Before the peaks were lighted by the ascending sun, we gathered our gear and Indians together, and were driven to the left bank on the north-west side of the Apurimac. Here we began the 1,500-foot descent into the gorge. Encumbered as we were with cameras and guide-ropes, our descent between the stands of fiercely spined cactus over loose gravel-sand was a little like the performance of a slow-paced slalom. The heat at the bottom, even in the morning, was furnace-hot, and the cactus and sharp-spined acacia accented the desertlike look of the place. As we walked along, heat waves danced before our eyes like St. Elmo's fire, and to add to our discomfort the flies gave us no rest, flying round us in clouds and biting viciously.

In this September month we found the Apurimac at its dryest, the land slashed with canyons like the wadis of Africa. The dryness was only a temporary state, for the shallow rivulets could rise with callous ease and within a fierce day of rain be raging torrents. The sides of the gorge were a horrible sandstone desolation cloven down in giant cuts, while below was a wide waste landscape. The gorge itself rose abruptly to the *puna* and higher above us, almost as a mirage, were snow-covered mountains.

We were not alone in feeling the heat. Our Indians felt it too. I remembered reading in some history how the 'Inca took the Indians from the coastal desert of Nasca to transfer them to the River Apurimac; because that river, where the royal highway goes from Cuzco to Lima, passes through a region so

409

hot that the upland Indians . . . cannot live in its heat.' So the Inca, bearing this in mind, took Indians from the coastal regions to settle in these hot regions even though the River Apurimac has only a small place to settle, for, passing through high and rugged mountains, it has very little useful land, and yet the Inca would not have this little bit go to waste but wished it to be used for gardens so as to be able to enjoy at least the abundant good fruit which is raised on the banks of that famous river.' But whatever orchards had been there had long since been destroyed by time, and by the high bourne of this river, a headwater of the Amazon, which had its source a hundred miles south-west in the barren mountains of Chumbivilca.

The small biting flies were at their worst when late in the morning we came to the vertical rock walls that once sustained the bridge. At this point the Apurimac cuts into a gorge of solid rock walls which rise straight and sheer to considerable height. Confined to a narrow channel, the river roars its disapproval in such deafening tones that we had to communicate by hand signals.

A tunnel through which the road ran lay above us some thousand feet on the side of the limestone cliff. Henrik notched up his rucksack, played out the rope and started the climb. He found a narrow ledge and secured himself. Dick Lawrence followed, holding fast to his camera. Next went David and Charles, then Silvia and last, myself. The Indians found their own way. I could see Henrik far up edging toward an overhanging rock that jutted out above the river. It was a slow process. Perspiration pouring down my face attracted the insects and the flies which, since my hands were well occupied, I had no option but to endure. By the time I reached a spot where I could rest and wipe my face, blood freely mingled with the sweat.

One of the most dangerous aspects of the operation was the crumbling stone. A projection which we supposed strong enough to use as a belay turned out under the pull of our ropes to be virtually as shifty as beach sand. Dick Lawrence, who had taken the greater punishment since he would not relinquish either his tripod or camera to anyone, was having trouble overhead. There had been a steady rain of sandstone and now and again a sharp curse, but as I could see little, I was unaware until later how dangerous some of those moments had been. Henrik led us very expertly up and over to the section of the precipice from which the bridge once hung suspended.

We were now standing on what had once been one of the most

410

important of the Inca roads. The celebrated tunnels were ahead of us and from this vantage place we could see now, and for the first time, the place of the bridge. The Inca road coming out of Mollepara, the last *tampu* station on the Cuzco side, had been run over the high-placed *pampa* to Bellavista near to the edge of the gorge. From that point it had zigzagged down the artificially terraced canyon to the valley 1,500 feet below. It had then followed the valley to the gorge, where mounting steps had been cut into the walls of an obelisk-shaped pinnacle. This had been reached by a narrow, inclined path, once ingeniously built with retaining walls; and from there the road mounted to a platform cut into rock. The thick suspension cables of the bridge on the Cuzco side had been fastened deep down in the floor of the platform. The cables, suspended from two stone towers, were then carried to the other side where, we were to find later, there was a similar natural platform. From the platform on our side of the river, the road twisted upward until it came to the cliffs which, because they were of extremely friable sandstone, could not be surmounted. Faced with this geological fact, the Inca engineers tunnelled through them. The tunnel near which we were now standing was about two hundred yards long and inclined upward as it turned with the cliff. From here the road climbed to the heights of the naked 'idol mountain' and then, adapting itself to the topography of the land, it went north to the next *tampu* station.

Lawrence, having taken up a position on an edge overhanging the abyss of the river, set up his camera to film us filing into the blackened mouth of the tunnel. As it was impossible to hear over the reverberations of the 'Great Speaker', we waited for his arm signal, then we moved by him and entered the tunnel. Sunlight poured into its darkened throat. I stopped at the first window openings. Then I suddenly realized that Lawrence had not followed us. I turned back in panic, and not seeing him, flung myself on my stomach to look down below into the churning river. He was nowhere to be seen and I was about to rise and go for the others when I saw him struggling just below me within hand-reach in the branches of a tree. He had fallen and had been caught in a tree growing out of the ledge. There he hung, suspended between heaven and hell. Somehow he had managed to hang on to his camera. This he handed to me, then he climbed up, terribly shaken, to the tunnel-ledge. There was not much more camera work for the rest of that afternoon.

The walls of the tunnel, which was 250 yards long by actual measurement, were pierced with openings to allow in the light and air. Through these 'windows', into which I climbed,

I could see the snow-topped peaks of Mount Marcani beyond us. The tunnel had been fashioned by the Incas much as the Romans mined rock. After a fierce fire had been built against it, water was thrown on the hot rock, splitting the friable lime and sandstone. The Incas, with their knowledge of working stone with stone, were presented with no problem. Their daring techniques in engineering were something else. At the end of the tunnel, which had once been connected with a stone stairway cut and built into the rock, we eased across that dangerous cleft and, gaining the circular stairway, went very slowly down the step-road. Cieza de León back in 1543 had had trouble with these same stairways, even when they were in good repair: 'Here the road is so rugged and dangerous, that some horses laden with gold and silver had fallen in and been lost, without any chance of saving them.' Several hundred feet below, we came to what had been the platform, on which we found the remains of the two enormous stone towers or pillars supporting the cables of the bridge. Two hundred feet directly in front of us, across the Stygian gap of the river, we could clearly see the other side of this 'bridge of the . . . Apurimacchaca'. Cieza had written that it 'was the largest bridge encountered from Cajamarca . . . with the road well built along the sides of the mountains. . . . The Indians who built it must have performed herculean labour. . . .'

No precise data can be given for the bridge's construction. After the year 1300 the Incas expanded their realm to the edge of the Apurimac and about this time, according to their chronicles, Inca Roca, then chieftain, finished the bridge. This would have been *circa* A.D. 1350. The detailed description of its structure is given by the Cuzco-born historian Garcilaso de la Vega, surnamed 'The Inca':

> The Apurimac bridge which lies on the royal road from Cuzco to Lima has its pillar support [he called it stirrup] made up of natural rock on the Cuzco side; on the other side [where we were now standing trying to figure it all out] was the stone tower, made of masonry. Under the platform that held this tower, five or six large wooden beams were inserted as thick as oxen—they stretched from one side to another. They were placed one higher than the other like steps. Around each of these beams, each of the suspension cables is twisted once so that the bridge will remain taut and not slacken with its own weight, which is very great.

Until nineteenth-century technology ushered in the use of iron chains for suspension cables, this Bridge of San Luis Rey, hanging by enormous rope-cables across the Apurimac, was one of the largest bridges of its type known. The Incas had no knowledge of the arch, nor, for that matter did any other of the preliterate peoples in America. Depending as it does upon the principles of gravity, pressure, and weight, the arch is yet earthbound and passive, and therefore could not have been used here even had the Incas been familiar with it. Instead, they perfected the principles of the suspension bridge by reversing the arch-curve and giving it wings.

The Bridge of San Luis Rey, like all suspension bridges on the Royal Road, hung from rope cables hand-twisted from the fibres of the maguey plant. Those of this bridge, of 'the thickness of a man's body', were just laid over the high stone towers for their 'suspending' and then buried in the thick masonry on the platform of the towers. From the suspended cables, supports

Military Tower A part of the fortifications of the citadel city of Machu Picchu.

hung down, and to these the bridge platform made of wood planking was attached. Cables attached to the main bridge served as wind bracing.

Although the materials were primitive, the essential nature of the technology of the Inca suspension bridge is, in principle, the same as the best constructed suspension bridges of to-day. Rope bridges have been built since immemorial times, but few other cultures before the advent of recent eras built so well as the Inca. This particular bridge indeed was so well made that it lasted for five hundred years, the cables, of course, being renewed every two years as a part of their work-service by Indians living at the *tampu* of Cura-hausi. This system of maintenance, so efficacious that the Spanish conquerors maintained it throughout the colonial period, disappeared only after the 'wheel' conquered the Andes, and the bridge which had served as a highway for foot and mule traffic for a period of five hundred years was allowed to fall into slow decay.

The Incas built for eternity: permanence was to them, as it was with the Romans, the base of all their construction. If the Inca road system is here occasionally compared with the Roman road system, it is because, until very recent times, there have been no other communication systems that can be compared with either. Other civilizations had, of course, their highways, but until the advent of the Romans none maintained a road system.

However, structurally an Inca road differed greatly from a Roman road. The Romans employed heavy-wheeled carts with rigid front axles which necessitated a deep road-bed. The Incas, since their roads were travelled only by those on foot and by llama herds, had no need for the road-bed. But apart from this the two civilizations, Inca and Roman, were amazingly similar in their concept of road engineering. While there is no denying Rome's place in civilization's sun, the Incas, living on a neolithic cultural horizon tied to stone tools, still conceived a communication system that stands extremely high in comparison with the Roman.

The Romans had three thousand years of experience to draw on. The facets of Old World thought and techniques regarding the building of roads are a vast web stretching from the first wagon ruts of ancient India to the stoneways of the Persians. Remote as certain of these areas were, and removed from each other by time and space, the Romans had all these centuries of cultural heritage on which to draw. The Inca had none of these, yet an Inca road is in many aspects superior to a Roman road. Every feature of a Roman road is paralleled in an Inca road except that, for the most part, the Incas built—literally—in

Silver Image   A small metal sculpture of the Incas.

the clouds. The Apurimac Bridge, for example, was part of a highway which came from heights the like of which no Roman had ever seen. The passes the Romans conquered were as nothing compared to these in the Andes; Mont Blanc, the highest peak in Europe, is 15,800 feet high; yet here in Peru we have walked over Inca roads *built* at this height. The old Roman roads which crossed the spine of the Italian promontory of the Apennines were no higher than the city of Cuzco, which is 10,200 feet above the sea. Again we turn to our Cieza. As a boy in Spain, he knew the Roman Road. He had walked between Tarragona and Cadiz over the Via Augusta, built in the first century B.C. and rebuilt every quarter of the century by the Caesars. He drove his mules over the Via Argenta, which ran between Mérida and Salamanca—a road which was started by Tiberius, continued by Nero, and fully repaired by Caracalla in A.D. 214—so he and others like him knew what they were saying when they wrote as a general rule that there is 'nothing in Christendom that equals the magnificence of the Inca roads'.

The remarkable thing is the similarity in approach to the 'idea' of roads between the Inca and the Roman. Both civilizations were of the land. Both had land armies, and land armies need roads; and since a road is only a road if one can go back over it, both believed that the road must be well built and well maintained. The Romans, it is true, ruled the straight line into civilization's thinking, whereas the Inca's road surmounted obstacles rather than avoided them, and as a general rule their engineers employed what I will call 'directional straightness' —that is, between two given points their road ran unerringly straight. Caius Caesar personally laid down vast stretches of road, and the Claudian family, when public funds were not available, defrayed expenses for road-building out of its own privy purse. In Peru the road-building programme was also identified with the rulers and the roads were called after the Inca who built them. For example, one 2,500-mile-long road that ran to Chile was known as Huayna Capac Nan, or the 'Road of Huayna Capac'. Often an Inca would order a road to be built for himself grander than that of his predecessors. The Romans put up milestones as markers, while the Incas built their *topus* 'with the distance between them a Castilian league and a half'. Along their road, the Romans placed night quarters or *mansiones*; in Peru, the Incas erected and maintained *tampus* every four to eight or twelve miles (according to the difficulty and arduousness of the terrain) along the entire route of their roads. Roman couriers had a change of horse-mounts at *mutationes* to hurry up messages along the Imperial Way; the

Incas, depending on foot, had their *chasqui* stations every two and a half miles as way-stations for the trained runners who carried messages over the most terrifying terrain in the world.

The bridge, 'the little brother of the road', was ever an important link in the great Inca road system. How many of them there were along the length and breadth of the Andes, we cannot be sure. But of them all, the Apurimac-chaca, the Bridge of San Luis Rey, was the greatest. Few who passed over it did so without pausing to wonder at this miracle of engineering. As to its length, the Inca historian, Garcilaso de la Vega, guessed it to be two hundred paces long—'Although I have not measured it, I have asked many in Spain who did.' Cieza, that most accurate of observers, thought it was 'fifty *estados*' or about eighty-five metres (250 feet) in length. Sir Clements Markham, who crossed it in 1855, estimated the Apurimac-chaca at ninety feet and its elevation above the river's surface at three hundred feet, while Lieutenant Lardner Gibbon, who made a survey of the Amazon for the United States Government in 1817, estimated its length at 324 feet.

Inca Wall   Detail of a retaining wall such as was built on either side of many of the Inca roads.

When Squier came to the bridge in the summer of 1864, he and his companions lost no time extracting the measuring tapes and sounding lines. They found that the bridge was 148 feet long from end to end and that it was suspended 118 feet above the surging river. That was the first and last time this famous bridge was exactly measured, for although it was still hanging in 1890 it was no longer used and the cables, unreplaced, curved dangerously downward into the gorge and were slowly decaying with time. . . .

The afternoon wind came up loud and shrill, as we were standing on the platform that once held the great suspension cables of the bridge, to set the foliage that clung to the rock walls rustling. We knew now that an old adage about the wind and the bridge was true, and that when the afternoon winds blew even the wind-braced cables could not hold the bridge steady and it would swing like a hammock.

It was late afternoon by the time we regained the boulder-strewn shores of the river. The sun was lighting the snow-peaks while the shadows of the mountains fell across the canyon. A long shadow falling across the vertical cliffs gave a curious illusion of a hanging bridge. At that moment I must have been very close to the spot where Fra Juniper had stood looking upward at the bridge when a 'twanging noise filled the air . . . and he saw the bridge divide and fling the five people into the river below'.

' "Why did this happen to *those* five?" the Fra asked himself. "If there were any plan in the universe at all, if there were any pattern in a human life, surely it could be discovered mysteriously latent in those lives so suddenly cut out. *Either we live by accident and die by accident* or we live by plan and die by plan." ' With that soliloquy Wilder began his story. It is an ironic truth that if this tragic story had not been written, this wondrous bridge built in 1350 by the Inca Roca, which was to endure for five centuries as one of the greatest tributes to man's domination of wild nature, would have been lost to memory.

With the dying sun now playing fully on the glaciers, the river canyon became as bright as if it were full day. The shadows were gone and, with them, the illusion of the hanging bridge. When I next looked back, there was again only emptiness between the two vertical walls.

INDEX